CW01668102

BEDFORDSHIRE POLICE 1840–1990

CHIEF CONSTABLES OF BEDFORDSHIRE

1840–1871
CAPTAIN EDWARD MOORE BOULTBEE

1871–1879
MAJOR ASHTON CROMWELL WARNER

1880–1910
LIEUTENANT-COLONEL FREDERICK JOHN JOSSELYN

1910–1939
LIEUTENANT-COLONEL
SIR FRANK AUGUSTUS DOUGLAS STEVENS

1940–1953
COMMANDER WILLIAM JOHN ADLAM WILLIS RN, CBE, MVO, CGM

1953–1971
HENRY RICHARD PRATT OBE, QPM

1971–1979
ANTHONY ARMSTRONG OBE, QPM

1979–1983
SIR WILLIAM GEORGE MACKENZIE SUTHERLAND QPM

1983–1985
ANDREW KIRKPATRICK SLOAN QPM, BA

1985–Present
ALAN DYER O ST. J., QPM

BEDFORDSHIRE POLICE
1840–1990

ANDREW FRANCIS RICHER, M.A.

Published by
Paul Hooley and Associates
29-33 Elstow Road · Kempston · Bedford MK42 8HD

Acknowledgements

The author would like to thank the following people who assisted in the production of this book.

Special thanks to:

The Chief Constable, Mr Alan Dyer, for commissioning the project.

Inspector Robert Darts for his help and encouragement.

Mr Paul Hooley for his expertise, enthusiasm and patience.

Mrs D. E. Richer who typed the manuscript.

Superintendent M. McGrath who visited Colonel Stevens' widow in Ireland shortly before her death in 1989.

Many thanks also to the following:

Chief Superintendent A. Marlowe & Pc D. Hawkey.
Chief Superintendent B. Prickett & Ps R. Child.
Chief Superintendent R. Wood & Mr M. Madigan.
Ex Chief Superintendent J. Kirk, Superintendent P. Phillips, Superintendent R. Miller, Special Chief Commandant P. A. South, Ps J. N. Marshall, Pc R. Knight.

The staff at the County Record Office, Bedford Central Library, and the Police Staff College Library, Bramshill.

Mr R. Hasdell, Mr A. Kelsey, Mr J. Willis, Mr G. South.
Mr R. Whitmore, Mr P. Keens, Mr C. Emsley.
The late Mr R. Coppin, Mr J. Ireland, Mr J. Thorburn, Mrs M. Burke, Mr J. Barnett, Mr E. Meadows.

The National Motor Museum – Beaulieu, *The Luton News*, *The Illustrated London News*, *The Bedfordshire Times*, *South Beds News Agency*.

Barclays Bank plc, Luton International Airport,
Newnorth Print Limited, Vauxhall Motors Ltd., Charles Wells Ltd.,
Whitbread & Co plc, Woburn Abbey.

ISBN No 0 905095 27 8

© 1990 Andrew Francis Richer

Published by Paul Hooley & Associates, 29-33 Elstow Road, Kempston, Bedford.

Printed by Newnorth Print Limited, College Street, Kempston, Bedford.

TO THE MEN AND WOMEN OF
THE BEDFORDSHIRE POLICE

LIEUTENANT-COLONEL HANBURY
The Lord-Lieutenant is the Queen's representative in the county

FOREWORD

by

Lieutenant-Colonel H. C. Hanbury, L.V.O., M.C., J.P.

Her Majesty's Lord-Lieutenant of Bedfordshire

THE Police Force in Bedfordshire was formed in March 1840 as the result of a motion to Quarter Sessions proposed by Samuel Charles Whitbread and supported by other magistrates, including William Bartholomew Higgins, great, great uncle of my wife.

In the first 150 years the Force has experienced and responded to immense social changes and events. Two world wars, a general strike, the after effects of the industrial revolution and, more recently, an equally far reaching technological revolution. Whilst there have been instances of civil unrest throughout the Force history, violence, in the last twenty years, has appeared to be more organised; industrial disputes, demonstrations by political and pressure groups and inner city riots have all affected Bedfordshire.

As well as external pressures there have been equally significant internal changes. In the field of transport the police have moved from foot, horse and cycle to high performance motor vehicles and consideration of the use of aircraft. The emancipation of women, widespread computerisation and advances in communications have also significantly changed the nature of policing.

This book is more than the history of an individual organisation, it is an insight into the social evolution of the last 150 years and, as such, must be of importance and interest to everyone.

After more than 30 years of close association with the Bedfordshire Police, both as a magistrate and as a short time member of the Police Committee, and for the last ten years as Custos Rotulorum, I have gained great respect and admiration for our County Force; for its leadership under the last five Chief Constables whom I have known, and for the very high standard of efficiency and good conduct which all ranks have maintained under increasingly difficult pressures of crime and violence. Bedfordshire has been well served indeed and is rightly proud of its good reputation.

I have great pleasure in commending this book to all who have the interest and well-being of the County and its Police Force at heart.

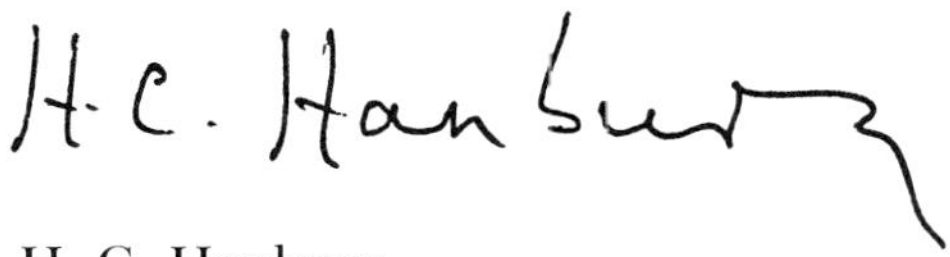

H. C. Hanbury,
Turvey House, Turvey, Bedfordshire.
21st March 1990

CONTENTS

150 Years of Barclays

SOME THINGS NEVER CHANGE . . .

Take Barclays Leighton Buzzard Branch, for example.

There was a Bank on this site as early as 1812; when a pint of beer cost 1d, America was five weeks away, and the latest news was all about a guy called Napoleon.

Of course, it wasn't called Barclays then, but 'Bassett, Son & Harris Bank', and is a relative newcomer to Barclays (it joined us in 1898!)

Messrs Bassett, Son & Harris's New Bank, Leighton Buzzard.

To look at it now, not much has changed; although it is probably a lot more comfortable inside than it was nearly 150 years ago, when the engraving (left) was made.

Oh, and you wouldn't have found our friendly PERSONAL BANKERS there to help you like you will today.

BUT IT IS STILL GIVING THE BEST SERVICE IN THE AREA 150 YEARS ON.

Mind you – a lot *has* changed.

America is only hours away, and as for a pint of beer, well . . .
And Napoleon? Just another name in the history books.

BUT SOME THINGS NEVER CHANGE,
AND AT LEIGHTON BUZZARD,
JUST LIKE EVERYWHERE ELSE, STILL . . .

+++ YOU'RE
BETTER OFF
TALKING TO
BARCLAYS

THE "BEANO" ARRIVES
CHAMBERLAIN PROCLAIMS "PEACE IN OUR TIME"
MALCOLM CAMPBELL
ESTAELISHES A NEW WORLD SPEED-BOAT RECORD – 131 M.P.H.
DAVID STEEL BORN
CONSCRIPTION STARTS
O.H.M.S.
FIRST TELEVISED F.A. CUP FINAL BY THE BBC – HUDDERSFIELD V. PRESTON N.E.
DON BRADMAN BEATS BATTING RECORD: AVERAGING 99.7 RUNS IN 80 TEST INNINGS
1938
QUEEN ELIZABETH
S.S. QUEEN ELIZABETH LAUNCHED
UK FILMGOERS HEAR CHAPLIN FOR THE FIRST TIME
"SMARTIES" GO ON SALE
G-ADHK
THE INNOVATIVE
HAS OPENING DAY PREVIEW
"THE MALLARD" SETS NEW WORLD STEAM TRACTION RECORD – 126 M.P.H.
MALLARD
No 4468
WORKERS ENJOY FIRST PAID HOLIDAY
AMY JOHNSON
VISITS LUTON AIRPORT OPENING
LUTON AIRPORT HAS MADE WORLD NEWS EVER SINCE
LUTON INTERNATIONAL AIRPORT
50
1988

READ THIS, AND YOU'RE ALREADY CLOSER TO LUTON AIRPORT

Brussels will be the latest addition to our rapidly growing Scheduled Services timetable that currently includes Amsterdam, Belfast (Aldergrove & Harbour), Dublin, Cork, Galway, Isle of Man, Mahon, Malta, Malaga, Tenerife, Waterford, Jersey, Guernsey, Knock, Shannon, Kerry and Leeds/Bradford, with more to be added soon.

All aimed at providing your business customers with a range of key destinations and level of service worth a closer look.

LUTON
international
AIRPORT
Close to you.

LUTON INTERNATIONAL AIRPORT, LUTON LU2 9LY.
TELEPHONE: (0582) 405100. TELEX 826409. PRESTEL 34470.

Over 125 years o

In 1863 Mr Henry Burt founded H. Burt & Son, Printers of Bedford. During the following 30 years, Burt's gained an excellent reputation for high quality poster setting and printing and lived up to their promise of "always on time". Expansion of client base and equipment took place from 1932 until 1939 with Incorporation in that year.

Following the end of the War in 1946, the next 20 years saw major changes, culminating in a move to a 25,000 sq. ft. custom-built factory in 1966.

In 1983 Henry Burt & Son Ltd was acquired by Newnorth Artwork, a local graphic design and artwork company and Newnorth-Burt was born.

ine quality print

Today, as Newnorth Print, we still support Henry Burt's original promise of "always on time". With over 100 dedicated staff, and a sales network covering the East Midlands, Home Counties and London, Newnorth can meet most needs in today's print and communications environment.

Newnorth

NEWNORTH PRINT LIMITED

Newnorth House, College Street
Kempston, Bedford MK42 8NA
England

Tel: (0234) 41111/50121
Fax: (0234) 271112

THIS SET OF KEYS CAN
THEY CAN'T O

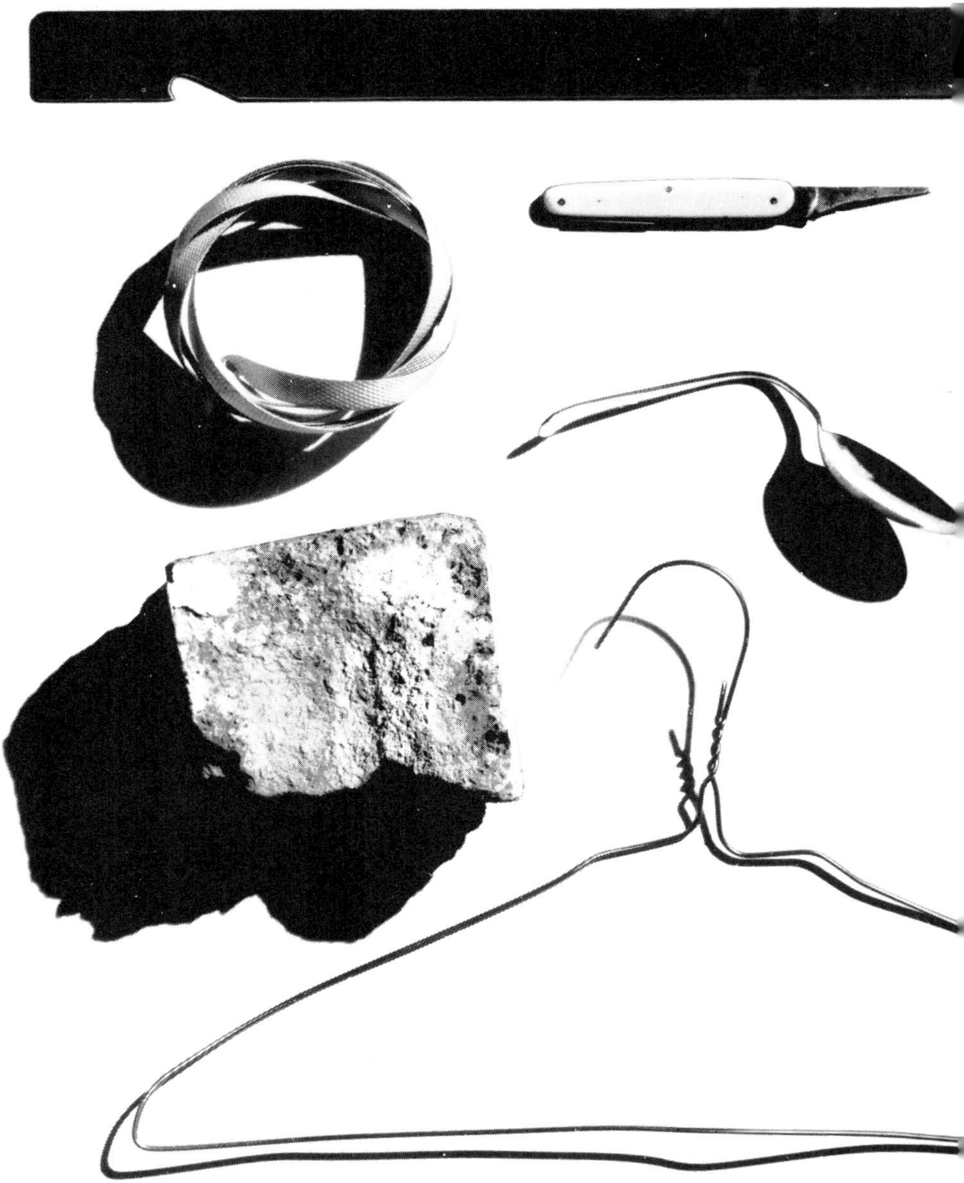

PEN ALMOST ANY CAR.
N A CAVALIER.

4 seconds. That's all it takes to break into most cars.

Any of the objects shown would do the trick, no trouble.

All you have to do is ... well, the less said the better.

(We don't want to add to the 500,000 cars broken into every year.)

However, were a car thief to try and break into a Cavalier, he'd find himself with a major problem on his hands.

For a start, every Vauxhall from the Cavalier L upwards is fitted with our ingenious 'Deadlock' central locking system.

Just lock the door as normal, then turn the door key a little further over to the left.

A steel bolt then drops into the lock housing on each of the four doors, thus freezing the mechanism completely.

Sounds basic, works a treat.

Because even if the thief resorted to chucking a brick through the window he'd discover the door lock buttons are impossible to lift.

Now, say you've locked the door but forgotten to activate the 'deadlock'.

(Let's face it, it's bound to happen sometime.)

No problem. Every door frame is designed with such cunning, that any attempt to break in using the more professional methods would immediately be thwarted.

Leaving our car thief no option but to vent his frustration on another car.

That's a point. What sort of security system has yours got?

VAUXHALL. ONCE DRIVEN, FOREVER SMITTEN.

GM VAUXHALL IS BACKED BY THE WORLDWIDE RESOURCES OF GENERAL MOTORS.

The Brewery in Horne Lane, Bedford, c. 1870.

Mr Charles Wells acquired the Brewery in 1876 and the business remained on this site for a further 100 years.

CHARLE

THE BREWERY

The Brewery in Havelock Street, Queen's Park, Bedford in 1989.

Charles Wells Limited moved to this custom built Brewery in their centenary year, 1976.

WELLS LIMITED

EDFORD · TEL: 0234 272766

WHEN THEY'RE N
THEY'RE DRA

Standing as much as 18 hands high and weighing anything up to a ton, a Shire horse is an impressive sight.

And for many people, it's a very nostalgic one, too.

Seventy years ago, heavy horses were two-a-penny.

Today, they are rarer on our roads than a Lamborghini.

Except, surprising as it might seem, in the busy City of London.

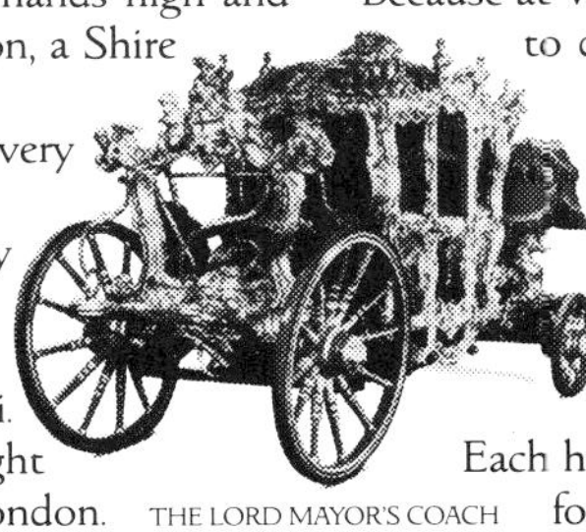

THE LORD MAYOR'S COACH

Because at Whitbread, we still use Shire h to deliver our draught beers.

Not in the same numbe we used to, admittedly: bac 1918, we had some 300 of gentle giants doing the roun

These days, we stable 16 of them at our 235 yea Chiswell Street brewery.

Each horse consumes 50 lbs of chaf fodder and 5 lbs of carrots per

...T PULLING PINTS ...ING CROWDS.

...But the sight of a pair of dapple greys still ...ıg their trade more than justifies the outlay.

Their lives are never routine, either.

...y are frequently asked to appear at horse ...vs, fetes and carnivals.

Once a year, they also enjoy the prestige ...ulling the two-and-a-half ton ceremonial ...h in the Lord Mayor's Show.

Yet no matter how busy they are, there's ...thing our horses never go without.

A summer holiday down on the hop farm.

So come the good weather, they spend a fortnight in the meadows at Beltring in Kent.

And on retirement, they are put out to grass there permanently.

Which seems only fair, when you think how many pints they've pulled for us over the years.

WHITBREAD

Our reputation has been brewing since 1742.

Woburn Abbey thanks the Bedfordshire Police for the care and protection it has extended to the Abbey for the past 150 years

Extract from Queen Victoria's Journal,
July 26-29 1841:

July 26. We reached Woburn Abbey at a little before 6 . . . All the tenants were drawn up on either side of the house. The Duke & D.S.S. of Bedford received us at the door.

July 29. We left Woburn with great regret having spent a very pleasant time there . . . We drove along a very fine, extensive evergreen drive, between firs, pines & laurels . . .

Woburn Abbey
Bedfordshire

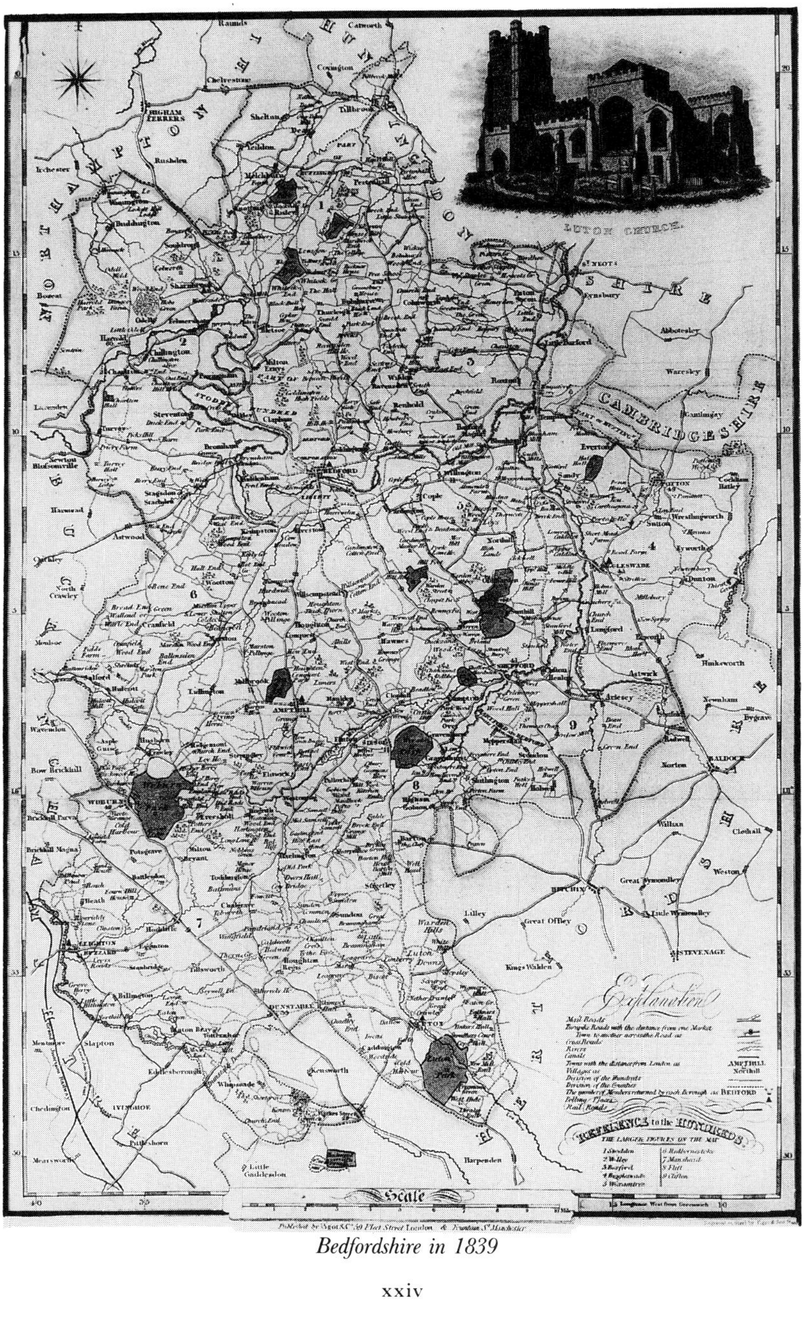

Bedfordshire in 1839

CHAPTER ONE

EVENTS LEADING TO THE FOUNDATION OF THE BEDFORDSHIRE CONSTABULARY IN 1840

THE idea of establishing an organised professional police force is a relatively modern one in the history of this country, originating in the first half of the nineteenth century. Between 1829, when the London Metropolitan Force was formed, and 1856 when each county was compelled to maintain a regular force, the whole police system of England and Wales underwent radical change on an unprecedented scale.

Prior to the advent of the professional police the work of maintaining order and apprehending criminals had fallen on the parish constable system. This system had evolved over centuries, continually adapting to the pressures of social and economic change experienced by successive generations. Responsible citizens were expected to undertake public service to administer the law through the two offices of magistrate and constable.

The office of magistrate can be traced back to the reign of Richard the Lionheart when in 1195 the Knights of the Shires were exhorted to maintain the peace in each county. Then in 1324 a Royal Statute provided that "in every county there shall be assigned a good and lawful man to keep the peace." The powers and responsibilities of magistrates were progressively increased and in the Justice of the Peace Act 1361 their powers were codified by Parliament. The importance of magistrates continued to grow and gradually they assumed responsibility for local administration in general. Inevitably they came to be elected solely from the ranks of the aristocracy, landed gentry or clergy. The court of administration used by the magistrates evolved into the Court of Quarter Sessions which, as the name suggests, sat every three months. The sittings in each year were known as the Epiphany, Easter, Midsummer and Michaelmas sessions respectively.

The office of constable was originally a high state office dating back to Norman times, the word perhaps deriving from the Latin 'comes stabuli' or Master of the Horse. The Norman constable was the foremost of the locally elected officials with special responsibility for maintaining the King's Peace and drawing part of his authority direct from the Crown. However, as time progressed the status of the constable was diminished. As the office of magistrate became established the constable became a subordinate officer – an agent carrying out the executive function of the magistrate in maintaining the peace.

Ultimately election to the office of constable in the annual parish ballot became an onerous burden. The post was unsalaried and the proper exercise of its duties had become incompatible with the full time employment necessary to earn a living. The result was that the more respectable parishioners, usually merchants, tradesmen and farmers, became increasingly reluctant to take on the duties of the constable preferring instead to pay deputies to act in their place. As the wages offered to deputies became more meagre only men of the lowest calibre were employed to act as the constable and the office itself fell into disrepute.

The final collapse of the old parish constable system was precipitated by the tremendous social and economic upheaval experienced in the course of the nineteenth century. England's population doubled to twelve million and widespread industrialisation permanently altered the old rural way of life. The effects of these changes were felt first and most severely in London where standards of living for ordinary people rapidly deteriorated beyond even the rudimentary levels reasonably expected in a civilized society. The corresponding upsurge in crime and disorder prompted a process of constabulary reform which culminated in the founding of the Metropolitan Police Force.

Police reform in the boroughs followed as part and parcel of more widespread local government reforms contained in the Municipal Corporations Act of 1835. This legislation affected the one hundred and seventy-eight boroughs in England and Wales possessing Royal Charters of self government and, as such, applied to the borough of Bedford. The Act provided for the election of town councils, and councillors were elected every three years by the ratepayers. The councillors subsequently elected the mayor annually and aldermen every six years. One of the functions of the council was to establish a watch committee charged with responsibility for appointing sufficient numbers of police to maintain the peace and empowered to draw up regulations for the governance of the constables.

The watch committee of Bedford came into being on the 1st January 1836 and consisted of the mayor, Charles Short, fourteen councillors and four aldermen. The committee decided that "nine fit men will be a sufficient number to act as constables for this borough" and the first seven employed commenced their duties on the 16th January 1836. Six constables were employed to watch by night and were organised into two sections of three, each section performing patrol duty on alternate nights. The day watch was conducted separately and was the responsibility of those employed as day constables. Each constable received 10/6d a week in pay and was supplied with a rattle, staff, glazed hat, waterproof cape and a dark blue coat bearing the constable's number stamped in white on the collar. The post of chief constable was given to the mayor's sergeant at mace, William Coombes, who initially received just the same 10/6d paid weekly to his men but in addition to "his endorsements as mayor's sergeant."

Although the Municipal Corporations Act included provision for the grant of charters to further boroughs, it remained for the Government to consider the position of the counties with regard to the reform of the rural police. The Home Office was already being pressed on this matter by Edwin Chadwick, the secretary of the Poor Law Commissioners and an influential figure in the events surrounding the formation of the Metropolitan Police Force. Chadwick urged that measures be taken to improve the rural police, not least to secure "the suppression of tumults connected with the administration of relief to the poor."

In 1836 the Home Secretary, Lord John Russell, the son of the sixth Duke of Bedford, established a Royal Commission to enquire into the best means of providing "an efficient constabulary force in the counties of England and Wales." The report of the commissioners was not published until the end of March 1839, some three years later. Its findings quoted extensive evidence of incompetence and inefficiency amongst parish constables but its recommendations for reforming the rural police were controversial. The commissioners advocated the creation of a single

Lord John Russell the son of the sixth Duke of Bedford, was the Home Secretary who introduced the County Police Act of 1839 into Parliament. He later became Prime Minister between 1846-1852 and 1865-1866

professional police force, for all rural areas, regulated by the Metropolitan Police Commissioners under a code approved by the Home Secretary. The ancient ties linking the magistracy and the police were to be severed.

The report of the Royal Commission was considered by the Bedfordshire Court of Quarter Sessions in May 1839. Recent experiences in the county had typically reflected the national dissatisfaction with the parish constable system. This dissatisfaction had led to the formation of numerous private 'catch criminal' associations and in Bedfordshire the Olney, Turvey and Harrold association had been founded as far back as 1796.

In 1821, John Hopkins Warden, a respected Bedford constable, had submitted a memorial to the Court of Quarter Sessions outlining the deficiencies of the local policing. "The extent of crime regularly committed in this county, and the organised bands which perpetrate robbery of almost every description, require an active police for many reasons. First, that a general knowledge may be obtained of loose and desperate characters in this county. Second, it can only be by practice that the officer becomes acquainted with the artful devices of experienced robbers, their system of plunder, and the disposal of their booty. The inexperienced constable, who is perhaps new to his office every year, cannot be aware of their manoeuvres; in short he has other objects in view. His business of all things must be attended and knowing that his term of service will soon expire, he cannot, he does not, give it the attention his office and country require. If the magistracy of this county wish to see an active police who will do their duty, it must be made a business of the officer."

Bedfordshire had also seen public disorder connected with the administration of relief to the poor, the type of incident which had caused Edwin Chadwick so much concern. A number of disturbances in 1830 later became known as the Swing Riots and had been fuelled in part by unpopular poor laws. The Poor Law of 1834 attempted radical reform but the discontent of militant unemployed labourers surfaced violently once more.

On May 11th 1835 a newly appointed relieving officer from Ampthill was met by a mob demanding "blood or money" as he entered Lidlington. The following day saw a similar incident at Millbrook. The local justices had ninety-six special constables sworn in and ordered the arrest of the ringleaders at Lidlington. As the arrested men were being transported back to Ampthill a large and menacing crowd gathered and secured their release. Subsequently there was rioting at Ampthill resulting in damage to the workhouse. The reading of the Riot Act had no effect and constables, poor law officials, and local justices were all attacked. The assistant poor law commissioner hurried to London to seek Government assistance and the Metropolitan Police were ordered to intervene. An inspector and twenty constables were immediately despatched and they proved to be very effective. A number of arrests were made and order was quickly restored.

The Bedfordshire magistrates had every reason to concur with those findings of the 1836 Royal Commission which testified to the inadequacy of the parish constable system. While they agreed with the findings they could not be expected to endorse the recommendations. Justices throughout the country regarded the proposal to form a rural police administered by the Metropolitan Police Commissioners as a direct attack on their local authority. It is hardly surprising, therefore, that the Bedfordshire Court of Quarter Sessions rejected the report of the Royal Commission, ostensibly on grounds of expense. The court, however, did accept the need to improve the policing of the county, noting in particular the inadequate remuneration offered to parish constables, the indifferent quality of persons attracted to the office, the undefined nature of the duties of the parish constable, the total lack of co-operation between constables of different parishes and the absence of any effective supervision of their activities. A plan to employ a force of fifteen paid constables was considered briefly but never implemented.

The Government, after considering the report of the commissioners and having canvassed the opinions of the local magistrates, set about drawing up legislation to effect change in the policing of the counties. There can be little doubt that the attitude of the Government was significantly influenced by the growing strength of the Chartists. Founded in support of a people's charter demanding electoral and economic reform, Chartism was a popular working class movement which had quickly been identified as a direct challenge to constitutional authority. By 1839 the idealism of Chartism was being supplanted by dangerous extremism and serious outbreaks of disorder were frequent, particularly in the North and Midlands. The resources which the Government had at its disposal to contain the disorder were stretched dangerously thin and the establishment of a strong rural police appeared to be a necessity.

In initiating the passage of the County Police Bill through Parliament in July 1839, Lord Russell, the Home Secretary stated that "the meetings which have lately taken place and the riots and alarm consequent upon them have made it incumbent on the Government not to lose any time in introducing some Bill on the subject." The legislation ignored the Royal Commission's recommendations concerning a centrally administered police force. Rather the Courts of Quarter Sessions were to be empowered, but not required, to establish police forces in their respective counties. The forces could operate county wide or within a defined district. The cost of running the force was to be met locally, but the Bill authorised the Home Secretary to issue regulations with respect to the pay and governance of police officers and to approve the appointments of chief constables. In this way the Home Office secured for itself significantly greater influence over county forces than it had obtained over the borough forces in the legislation of 1835.

The urgent need to establish rural police forces ensured that the County Police Bill of 1839 was shrewdly designed with practical politics in mind. Any attempt to establish a centrally administered force would certainly have encountered implacable opposition from county magistrates leading to lengthy parliamentary debate. Indeed, it is doubtful if such a controversial measure would have succeeded even in a less troubled political climate; that the proposals gave county magistrates a choice in whether to establish a force, diluted opposition to the legislation even further. The County Police Act of 1839 gained the Royal Assent in August of that year and appears to have been looked on favourably in Bedfordshire. Local opinion may have been partly predisposed towards the legislation because of the county's close association with the Russell family. In any event, in November 1839 six magistrates, led by Samuel Charles Whitbread, gave notice to the clerk of the peace for the county of Bedford "that the subject of the appointment of county and district constables will be brought under consideration of the next Court of General Quarter Sessions at two o'clock in the afternoon on Tuesday, the thirty-first day of December 1839."

In the subsequent debate at the court Whitbread vigorously argued the case for establishing a police force and a committee was formed to consider the matter. The committee consisted of magistrates drawn from each of the petty sessional divisions of Bedfordshire. Minor administrative duties and less serious crimes were regularly dealt with by each district separately in local petty sessions.

The committee's findings were discussed at three adjourned hearings of the Epiphany quarter sessions with the result that on

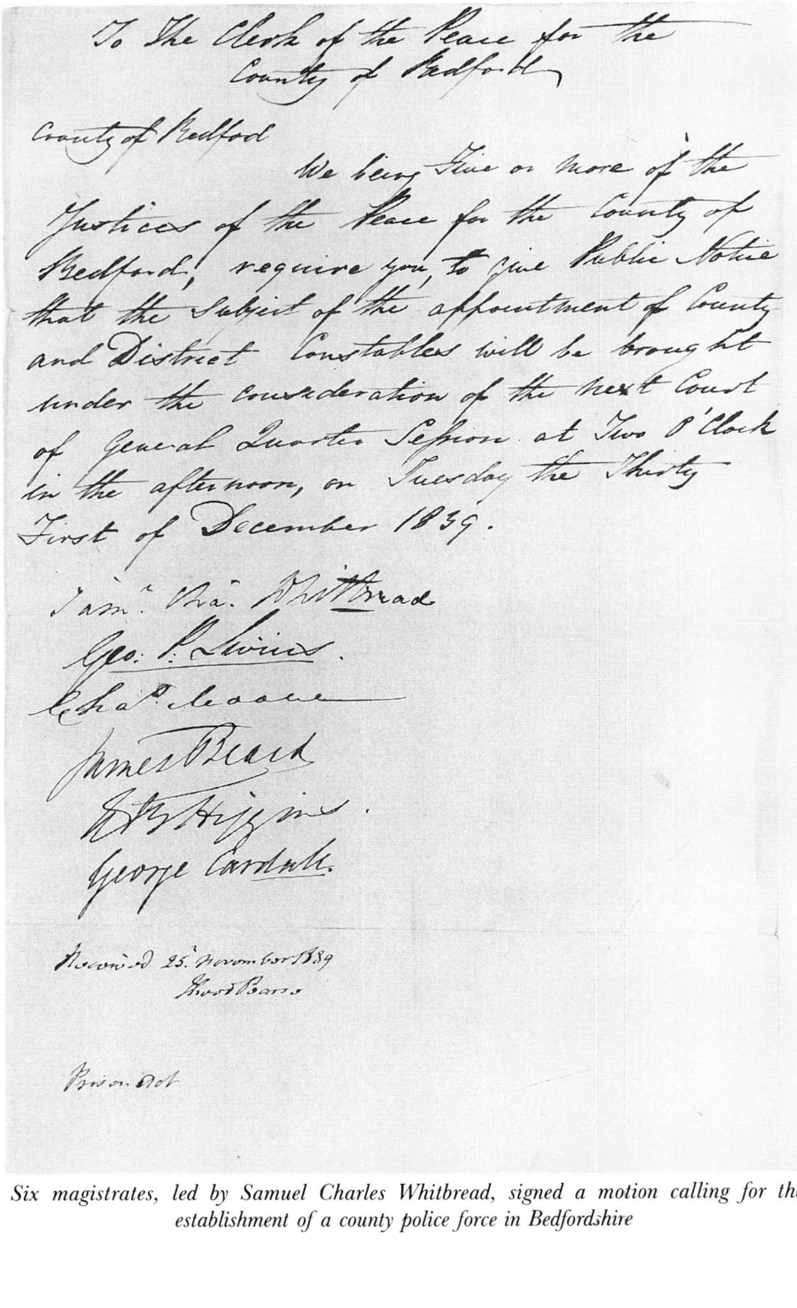

To The Clerk of the Peace for the County of Bedford

County of Bedford

We being Five or more of the Justices of the Peace for the County of Bedford, require you to give Public Notice that the Subject of the appointment of County and District Constables will be brought under the consideration of the next Court of General Quarter Session at Two O'Clock in the afternoon, on Tuesday the Thirty First of December 1839.

Saml. Chas. Whitbread
Geo. P. Livius.
Chas. Moore
James Beard
H. Higgins.
George Cardall.

Received 25. November 1839
Thos Barrs

Prison Act

Six magistrates, led by Samuel Charles Whitbread, signed a motion calling for the establishment of a county police force in Bedfordshire

28th January 1840 a motion to establish a constabulary force was carried by a majority of justices of the county. The minutes from the adjourned sessions show: "Resolved that the ordinary officers appointed for preserving the peace are not sufficient for the preservation of the peace and for the protection of the inhabitants and for the security of property within the county of Bedford. In our opinion it is needed that there be appointed within this county one chief constable at a yearly salary of £250 to include a horse; six superintendents, viz: one for each of the six divisions for petty sessions at a yearly salary of £75 each; forty constables at a weekly sum of 19/-."

When the post of chief constable was advertised there were six applicants and on 18th February 1840 Captain Boultbee gained sufficient votes in a ballot of the justices at the quarter sessions to secure the appointment, subject to the approval of the Home Secretary. That approval was swiftly given and the new chief constable's first task was to recruit the superintendents and constables to serve under him.

In retrospect the actions of the Bedfordshire magistrates in forming a professional police force under the 1839 County Police Act came to be seen as a creditable and forward thinking decision. Of fifty-six counties in England and Wales only twenty had adopted the Act by the end of 1840. Sixteen years later the necessity of maintaining regular police forces in all the counties was recognised by the Government when legislation made the provision of police forces in the counties mandatory. By that time the Bedfordshire Constabulary was well established as an effective and efficiently run police organisation.

CAPTAIN EDWARD M. BOULTBEE

CHAPTER TWO

1840 – 1871
CAPTAIN BOULTBEE

CAPTAIN Edward Moore Boultbee was born near Temple Balsall in Warwickshire in 1797. His early career was spent as a seaman with the East India Company working the shipping lanes between Britain and the Indian ports of Calcutta, Bombay and Madras. In 1818 he was shipwrecked and cast adrift when the 'Cabalva' sank in a violent storm at sea. In later life Captain Boultbee occasionally entertained his dinner guests with a vivid account of the sailors' ordeal and their eventual rescue.

Boultbee's service with the East India Company proved valuable in securing his appointment as the first Chief Constable of the Bedfordshire Constabulary. The formal qualifications required of prospective chief constables under Home Office regulations in 1840 were not particularly demanding – their age was not to exceed forty-five years, they were to be physically fit to perform their duties, be of good character and not have been certified bankrupt. Boultbee's prime attributes for the post were his wide experience of life and his proven ability to manage men in the disciplined environment found on board ship. His organisational ability was tested to the full as he set about the task of finding six men to become superintendents in the Bedfordshire force and a further forty men to be employed as constables.

The First Recruits.

Boultbee began his recruiting drive by travelling to London and Birmingham where police forces had already been established. He hoped to attract men with significant police experience to the Bedfordshire Constabulary and in both cities his enquiries met with considerable interest. However, the salary of £75 he was able to offer prospective superintendents proved to be a stumbling block. £75 was the minimum superintendents' wage permitted by the Home Office regulations issued to county forces, whereas the maximum wage allowed was twice that amount. Consequently, at the Bedfordshire quarter sessions held in March 1840, Captain Boultbee reported the difficulties he had encountered and gave his considered opinion that no respectable person, properly qualified, would take his offer of a post of superintendent for less than £100 per annum. The court agreed to the proposed increase in pay and Boultbee was subsequently able to engage officers from both London and Birmingham as superintendents. Two were employed on 16th March 1840 and two more a week later on 23rd March.

The Bedfordshire Constabulary officially came into being on 21st March 1840 with the employment of the first six constables. They commenced their duties four days later and their progress was recorded in a hand written register of all the constables employed by Boultbee. Their force numbers were allocated according to their respective divisions and not in numerical sequence. Pc 1, Frederick Porter, was suspended from duty on 18th July 1840 for being found drunk on patrol. He was reinstated with a warning that a further disciplinary offence would result in his dismissal and on 7th October 1840 he was dismissed for unsatisfactory conduct. Pc 2, Charles Price and Pc 7, Daniel Herbert, both resigned from the force before completing three years' service. Pc 8, Daniel Hazzard, Pc 9, Edward Scott and Pc 40, William Clough, all remained with the force for substantial periods. Pc Hazzard was promoted to sergeant in 1850 and Pc Scott served for twenty-six years before retiring in 1866. Pc Clough was reprimanded in April 1840 for absenting himself from duty without leave but this minor offence proved no obstacle to his eventual success in gaining promotion. He attained the rank of sergeant in 1850, of inspector in 1856 and on 25th December 1857 he was promoted to superintendent. Boultbee took a keen interest in the welfare of his men and it was typical of him to announce the promotion on Christmas Day.

Boultbee employed fourteen more constables on 25th March to add to the original six but it was not until the 16th June 1840 that he succeeded in bringing the force up to its authorised establishment of six superintendents and forty constables. The records of the first six Bedfordshire recruits reflect the disappointingly high turnover of men employed as constables in the county. In 1840 fourteen men left the Bedfordshire Constabulary, amounting to nearly one third of its total strength. The following year thirteen men resigned or were dismissed from the force. The chief constable was compelled to devote much time to finding new recruits to fill the succession of vacancies. Virtually every other constabulary, including the Metropolitan and borough police forces, experienced similar manpower wastage.

Despite his recruiting problems, Captain Boultbee insisted on the highest standards of discipline. In April 1840 three of his newly appointed constables were each fined 10/- "for playing cricket and drinking in a public house when ordered on duty at Potton Fair." Dismissals from the police service were frequent. Constable 16, Davies, was dismissed on 6th May 1840 for being drunk on duty and the services of Constable 11, Lacey, were dispensed with on 19th August the same year for "general bad conduct." Constable 6, Owen, was "ordered to be discharged" on 5th August 1840 "he being unfit for the situation of police constable."

Although gross misconduct resulted in instant dismissal, Boultbee gave his constables a second chance whenever possible. On 12th October 1858 Constable 11, Champkins, was "reported for tossing for beer with Constable 87, Barret (a Buckinghamshire constable), in a public house at Leighton, afterwards quarrelling in the street with him and coming to blows." Champkins was suspended by Boultbee but later reinstated with a severe warning and a fine of one week's wages.

In April 1843 Boultbee attempted to reduce the number of resignations from the force by dividing the constables into three classes and introducing an incremental pay structure. New recruits became third class constables paid just 17/- a week. Promotion through the higher classes was dependent on length of service and satisfactory progress. Second class constables received a weekly wage of 20/- whilst first class constables were paid up to 23/- a week. Gradually the number of resignations and dismissals fell, allowing the composition of the force to become more stable.

Subsequently the prospects for constables were further improved. The pay structure was enhanced by the introduction of a 'merit' scheme. Recipients of a merit badge for outstanding police work were rewarded with an extra 1/- a week in wages. The career structure was transformed with the advent of the ranks of sergeant and inspector and as a result the differentials in pay between the different classes of constable became less pronounced.

The new force was divided into six operational divisions associated with the petty sessional districts of Bedford, Ampthill, Biggleswade, Bletsoe, Luton and Woburn. Boultbee stipulated that a superintendent was to be placed in charge of each division "visiting the men and seeing as much of them as possible." Eight constables were assigned to the Woburn and Biggleswade divisions, the other four divisions each being allotted six constables.

The officers were widely spread throughout the county. In the Biggleswade division for example, the superintendent and one constable were based in Biggleswade itself whilst the other constables were stationed at Shefford, Girtford, Henlow, Arlesey, Potton, Blunham and Northill.

The Bedford division included the villages of Eaton Socon, Kempston, Turvey and Wilden but not Bedford itself which was policed by the borough force employed by the watch committee of the town council. The county magistrates had approached the council concerning the expediency of uniting the borough and county forces but these overtures had been rejected when the town mayor loftily dismissed the county police as "totally inadequate to perform the various and important services incumbent upon it." Relations between the two forces started badly and remained strained for many years to come.

Patrol Work.

At Captain Boultbee's instigation the first incidents dealt with by the Bedfordshire Constabulary were recorded in three registers which listed serious crimes, known as felonies, lesser offences, known as misdemeanours, and occurrences of a general nature, called informations. The initial entries in each register offer a valuable insight into the nature of the earliest work of the county constabulary.

The first arrest made by the new force reflected the social problems of the Victorian era. "On Saturday, March 28th 1840 Pc 24, Cullen, attended before the justices with John Williams, a vagrant, charged by the officer with disorderly conduct. Reprimanded and discharged." The justices were anxious not to provide board and lodging for vagrants who committed minor offences.

On Sunday, 29th March 1840 the Bedfordshire Constabulary received its first report of a crime. It concerned the theft of two cocks and four hens from the White Horse Inn at Woburn during the early hours of that morning. "The thieves entered by taking off the thatch of the outhouse, the heads of the birds were cut off and left behind." Enquiries were made but without result.

The first major success for Boultbee's men came on Thursday, April 2nd 1840 when they apprehended a horse thief. "Superintendent Ashton and Pc 30, Tutte, attended before the magistrates with Joseph Archer, aged 20, of Roxton, charged with stealing a horse, the property of Richard Scott of Totternhoe. Committed for trial to the quarter sessions on April 3rd. Found guilty and transported for ten years." The practice of transportation continued until 1857.

The severity of the sentences imposed on offenders in the mid nineteenth century is a striking feature of many entries in the registers. "Friday, April 10th 1840. Constable 26, Green, attended before the justices with Luke Golding, aged fifteen years, a native of Cambridge, charged with stealing one silk handkerchief, value 2/6d from James Broach of Castle Lane, Bedford, at Bedford races. Sentenced to six months' hard labour at the house of correction." The Bedford races were held outside the town and the responsibility for policing the event fell on the county force not the borough police. "Thursday, April 16th 1840. Superintendent Bates and Constable 10, Roberts, attended before the justices with John O'Dell charged by a Maulden farmer with stealing a quantity of potatoes at Maulden on the 13th April. Sentenced to three months' hard labour."

The new police force was not solely concerned with the prevention and detection of crime. The maintenance of public order was another of its major responsibilities. "A meeting of three to four hundred persons took place on Monday, April 20th on some disputed land between Bedfordshire and Buckinghamshire. A similar meeting occurred last year in which some persons were severely wounded and several sheep killed. Superintendent Hampton attended with six constables of his division and two from the Ampthill division in plain clothes, in consequence of which the meeting went off without any disturbances."

The constables also dealt with disorder on a less serious scale. On Saturday, 18th April 1840 "Constable 7, Herbert, attended before the justices with James Taylor, 28, of Silsoe, and Henry Belcher, 26, also of Silsoe, for fighting and otherwise creating a disturbance at Clophill." Both were fined 6/6d.

Assaults on the police were frequent in public order situations but the constables received the full backing of the magistrates provided they had exercised their powers lawfully. On Saturday, 18th April 1840 Constable 12, Vear, "apprehended William O'Dell,

29, of Cranfield, on a warrant for assaulting Constable 11, Lacey, whilst in the execution of his duty." O'Dell received three months' hard labour for the assault. "Monday, April 27th 1840. Constable 29, Swain, attended before the justices with Solomon King, a resident of Houghton Regis, charged with assaulting Constable Crouchley whilst in the execution of his duty. Sentenced to six months' hard labour."

The new police were no doubt unpopular in their role of enforcing licensing regulations governing the conduct of inns and ale houses. "Tuesday, 28th April 1840. Pc 23, Dale, attended at the Bletsoe petty sessions with Joseph Gostick, landlord of The Fox public house, Carlton, charged with serving beer during the hours of Divine Service on Sunday morning the 19th of April. Dismissed with a caution on paying costs." This offence was the subject of numerous prosecutions by the police and the sentencing became less lenient after persistent warnings failed to secure observance of the licensing law.

The role of the police force in the event of a fire varied with local circumstances. The constables usually formed part of the local volunteer fire brigade but even when the police had no direct fire fighting role they still attended large fires to perform crowd control duty and investigate possible offences of arson. "Thursday, April 23rd 1840. At 5 a.m. a large fire broke out at Market Street in the premises of Thomas Walter, Esquire." Market Street was situated on the border between Bedfordshire and Hertfordshire and later became the responsibility of the Hertfordshire police. "Superintendent Ashton and two constables attended taking with them the Luton engine, arriving at 6 a.m. Already at the scene of the fire were Constable 32, Priestly, and Constable 30, Tutte, with the Market Street engine. Much property was destroyed. The Luton constables returned to their station at 6 p.m. leaving Constable Priestly in charge of the burnt out property."

The last of the major duties that routinely featured in the earliest activities of the Bedfordshire Constabulary was the investigation of sudden deaths on behalf of the coroner. "Sunday, April 26th 1840. Mr Mansell, a travelling performer, drowned in the river at Biggleswade whilst bathing. A watch and some other property was retrieved from his clothes by Constable 13, Gamble, and delivered to the relief officer to go towards burial expenses."

The role of the police was to be progressively expanded in the years to come but the primary duties of the service reflected in the work of the Bedfordshire Constabulary in the spring of 1840 have remained largely intact to the present day.

Conditions of Service.

The conditions of service applicable to the first constables of the Bedfordshire police were determined partly by the Home Office regulations issued to county forces and partly by the orders drawn up by Captain Boultbee.

Under the Home Office regulations each constable was to receive sufficient uniform for the performance of his duty in all weathers. Uniform was issued to the men each year. Upon joining the force and thereafter in alternate years constables received a greatcoat, coat and cape for outer wear. They also received two pairs of trousers, a pair of boots, a pair of shoes, a hat and a stock. Two badges were supplied, to be fixed on to the outer garments in use on patrol. In the intervening years the men received a smaller issue of uniform consisting of a further coat, badge, pair of trousers, pair of boots, shoes and hat. In Bedfordshire the practice of supplying boots ceased when Captain Boultbee applied to the quarter sessions for the payment of a boot allowance instead. An allowance of 1/6d a month was granted and the men were able to purchase the boots they found the most comfortable. The quarter sessions also ordered the purchase of fifty pairs of handcuffs and a similar number of belts and lanterns for the further equipment of the force.

Under the terms of the County Police Act 1839 the magistrates were obliged to make some provision for the superannuation of the constables and in the Michaelmas quarter sessions, held in October 1840 a pension fund was established to receive contributions, set at the rate of 1/- per month for the constables and 2/- per month for the superintendents. Fines imposed on officers as a result of disciplinary proceedings were also paid into the fund. The mere fact of having contributed to the fund every month did not guarantee the payment of a pension on an officer's retirement. The award of a pension was entirely at the discretion of the magistrates at quarter sessions.

The first pension awards made by the magistrates reflected the absence of any definite rules to govern the administration of the superannuation fund. At the Epiphany quarter sessions in 1861 a pension of £35 per annum was granted to Sergeant Hayward after completing more than twenty years' service with the force. The pension was not guaranteed for life but was "to continue during the pleasure of Her Majesty's Justices of the Peace of this county." At the following Easter sessions Hayward applied for a review of the award, as a result of which his annual pension was increased to over £43.

Such reviews were relatively common. In 1859 Sergeant Cheney, who had been injured on duty and superannuated on a sum of £30 a year, applied for a review of the award and had his pension increased to £50 a year. Captain Boultbee's recommendations were influential in such matters and he was concerned to obtain the best possible treatment for his long serving officers.

The dependants of police officers had no claim on the superannuation fund. In 1858 Constable Charles Flint died after more than sixteen years' service with the constabulary, leaving his widow and family with little means of support. His widow applied to the quarter sessions for assistance but was awarded a gratuity of only £15 from the pension fund.

Dissatisfaction with the administration of police pensions, particularly with regard to dependants, eventually led to the foundation of the Police Mutual Assurance Society in 1867. The society was "open to the whole police force of England, Wales and Scotland" and its aim was to support the widow or named beneficiary of a member upon his death. If the deceased member was a constable, each member of the society contributed 1d towards the benefit fund. If the deceased was a sergeant or inspector, members holding those ranks contributed 6d each and every other member paid 1d. When the deceased member was a superintendent or chief constable, members who held such senior ranks paid 2/6d to the fund and all other members contributed 1d. Superintendent Clough was one of the first Bedfordshire officers to join the scheme and many years later the Police Review magazine recorded the payment of £108.18.9d to his beneficiary.

A similar situation existed with regard to sick pay. The magistrates, in conjunction with the chief constable, were at liberty to stop the wages of an officer unable to perform his duties through sickness. However, they usually allowed payment of a reduced wage to the sick, believing that such a measure would save officers and their families from genuine poverty whilst discouraging potential malingerers.

Captain Boultbee's rules for the conduct of his officers set uncompromising standards of professional behaviour. The rules provided that: "Each man shall devote his whole time and attention to the service. He shall serve wherever appointed and reside where ordered by the chief constable. He shall promptly obey all orders from the persons placed in authority over him. He shall not quit the service without giving a month's notice but shall be liable to immediate dismissal for unfitness, negligence or misconduct."

The first of these regulations was intended quite literally. The working week lasted seven days and an average day's duty lasted ten to twelve hours. The constables patrolled on foot and must frequently have walked upwards of twenty miles during a day. When not on patrol, officers were expected to remain at home, readily available for duty, in case they were required at short notice.

Captain Boultbee further ordered that every constable was to make himself "perfectly acquainted with all villages and places in his beat" and develop a first hand knowledge of the local people likely to commit offences. The men were also to be "consistently sober and fit for duty" and "pay special attention to public houses." Each constable was "to always carry his instructions and memorandum books, in which he will enter occurrences and his whereabouts at all times." The instructions contained information concerning a constable's powers of arrest and the proper conduct of criminal investigations. The constables were expected to rendezvous with their colleagues from neighbouring beat areas at regular intervals. This provided for a free exchange of information within the constabulary through a network of conference points.

The superintendents travelled to many of these meeting points and at the Midsummer quarter sessions of 1840 Captain Boultbee asked the magistrates to consider "the expediency of mounting superintendents and providing a light cart in each division, to be drawn by the superintendent's horse when required, to convey prisoners to Bedford." Subsequently superintendents were paid an annual allowance of £37 to meet the cost of providing their own horse. The carts were purchased from central funds and were specially equipped with candle lamps for nocturnal use.

Superintendents were subject to a different set of rules drawn up by Boultbee. They were expected to enforce discipline and to train new recruits. "On the appointment of a constable" a superintendent "must carefully read the whole book of instructions to him." A superintendent was also to "attend the petty sessions of his division with one constable to keep order."

The superintendents had some discretion in the deployment of officers attached to their division but they were "not to employ the petty constables during the day unless absolutely necessary." The majority of patrols were carried out at night when criminals were at their most active. Constables deployed during the day usually worked a split shift and still patrolled for part of the night.

A further duty of the superintendents was to "send in a weekly report detailing all occurrences within their divisions." The weekly report was a three page document. The top half of the front page contained a daily account of the number of officers on duty, whilst the bottom half of the page formed a pay record sheet. Each constable signed to acknowledge receipt of his week's pay. The second page contained a table of the arrests made during the week, a record of any disciplinary offences which had come to light and a weekly inspection report concerning the clothing and appointments of the constables. Every week each constable had to account for his issue of uniform and to produce a full set of appointments, a truncheon, lanthorn, instruction book, a pair of handcuffs and a button stick and brush. The third page detailed the dates and times of the visits made by the superintendents to supervise the constables. It also contained an account of any incidents that had been dealt with during the week.

The reports relating to the week ending December 28th 1841 have survived to the present day. Each constable received £1.0.6d in wages that week, including the monthly boot allowance. There were eleven incidents dealt with by the force as a whole. In the Bletsoe division a labourer from Harrold had been arrested for trespassing in pursuit of game and a summons had been served on a Sharnbrook butcher for defrauding the toll collector at Bromham bridge. A case of sheep slaughtering at Bolnhurst had been investigated and found to be the result of a bitter internal family dispute. No charges were brought. In the Bedford division, Constable 2, Charles Price, had dealt with both of the incidents contained in the week's divisional report. In the first incident he had arrested a Londoner for attempting to pickpocket on St. Neots bridge and in the second he had taken a local man into custody for being drunk and disorderly. In the Biggleswade division a Potton labourer had been prosecuted for the unlawful snaring of game on a Sunday. However, the most spectacular success of the week occurred in the Woburn division where four inmates of the Leighton Buzzard Workhouse had been detained after breaking into the Duke's Head public house at Heath and Reach and stealing 15 lbs of bacon, 5 lbs of pork, 4 bottles of beer and a hare. In the Ampthill division a disorderly drunk had been taken into custody and a labourer had been arrested for stealing a faggot of wood from a farmer at Houghton Conquest. At Luton one man had been detained after obstructing a constable in the execution of his duty and another arrested for sheep stealing at Houghton Regis.

This was a typical week for the Bedfordshire Constabulary and the evidence suggests that Captain Boultbee had achieved a great deal in a relatively short period of time, establishing a police force able to cope with a variety of incidents with apparent ease. It is impossible to measure the effectiveness of the force in preventing crime but the detection rates were good.

The force had also acquitted itself well in dealing with a royal visit to the county. Between Monday, July 26th and Thursday, July 29th 1841 the young Queen Victoria and Prince Albert stayed with the Russell family at Woburn Abbey. The visit naturally attracted large crowds. Anticipating the need to control the crowds the chief steward of the Russell estate had applied to the Metropolitan Police for assistance, doubting whether the county police were legally obliged to police the event. However, Captain Boultbee and Robert Turle, the superintendent of the Woburn division, attended throughout the royal visit together with a small detachment of constables. The Bedfordshire officers worked closely with the four members of the Metropolitan Police employed to supervise men from the Duke of Bedford's estate sworn in as special constables. The royal visit passed off smoothly, the most serious incident of the four days being the theft of a cash box from the Bedford Arms public house at Woburn.

Public Reaction to the Constabulary.

The achievement of the Bedfordshire Constabulary in the early 1840s produced a mixed reaction in the communities it served. Whilst some citizens saw value in an organised police force others objected to the expense of maintaining the constabulary.

In August 1840 the quarter sessions were petitioned by some of the citizens of Leighton Buzzard: "That sheep stealing and depredations in gardens and in houses has increased to an alarming extent. That the present police, two in number, are utterly insufficient to protect property or maintain good order in the streets. That your memorialists are of the opinion that the police force ought to be increased as soon as possible."

However, three months later a further petition to the quarter sessions from Leighton Buzzard reflected the views of those residents of a different persuasion. "The peace and good order of our locality render the vast expense of a rural police an useless expense of our money."

Opinion was similarly divided in Luton where one petition from the inhabitants related that "the present force is far from adequate to the protection of the vast property contained in warehouses and other buildings in the town," whilst another stated "that your petitioners do not believe they receive a benefit at all corresponding with the enormous expense incurred."

Overall the petitions objecting to the police force outnumbered those requesting increases in the police establishment. Some of the petitions expressed reservations other than those of cost. "We the undersigned being owners and occupiers of lands and houses in the parish of Houghton Regis do hereby respectfully represent to your worshipful bench our utter disappointment arising from the inefficiency of the rural police in this parish for the prevention of theft and the detection of crime, the amount of crime being in no way diminished and the enormous cost being totally disproportionate to the benefit therefrom." The petition was dated 5th April 1841 and was endorsed mainly by farmers but also by the vicar and local publican.

A further petition sent to the quarter sessions reflected resentment at the power of the new police. "That your humble petitioners, the ratepayers of the parish of Toddington have been for upwards of two years under the inspection and surveillance of the rural police without any beneficial results but on the contrary the county rates or charges have been considerably increased. Felonies have been but little or not materially lessened nor has there been any detection of robbery solely by their means and their conduct is generally harsh and overbearing."

Resistance to the idea of the rural police was not unique to Bedfordshire. Rather it was the general experience in those counties where police forces had been established. This national dimension is reflected in an editorial of The Times newspaper dating from early in 1842. "We perceive with great satisfaction that a strong feeling is gaining ground in different parts of the country, and in most respectable quarters, against the continuance of the rural police system."

The Bedfordshire Mercury had considered the question of the rural police in its edition dated Saturday, December 11th 1841. It reported the decision of the Nottinghamshire magistrates to reduce the number of constables employed in that county. It then addressed the achievements of the Bedfordshire Constabulary and it appears that Captain Boultbee and his force had done sufficient to win some approval. "The amount of service to the county derived from the police institution we cannot accurately estimate but we believe it to be very great and highly valuable in promoting the morality of society as well as the protection of property in the county."

The Mercury was, however, very concerned at the cost of the police which over the past year had amounted to "three thousand one hundred pounds, exclusive of extra expense." The paper advocated a reduction in the number of officers employed by the county constabulary and an increase in the number of horses to be employed, arguing that "mounted, one constable could do the duty of three."

On another page the newspaper reported the latest success of the Bedfordshire Constabulary under the headline, "Admirable Conduct of Rural Police." The article related how a burglary at Newport Pagnell in which £30 worth of goods had been stolen was detected by a quick thinking police officer. "The thieves have all been taken and the greatest part of the property recovered through the vigilance, intrepidity and admirable tact of J. McHugh, the policeman stationed in Aspley. On Thursday, 9th December 1841 about four-thirty in the afternoon the officer happened to see from his window where he lodged, three suspicious characters with bulging pockets go into a public house opposite. In a few minutes they were joined by a notorious local fellow named Smith." All four "then went into a wood at a short distance from Aspley. McHugh followed them and very daringly approached to within a few yards of where they stood."

The constable heard the conversation of the men and saw Smith make a purchase of stolen goods. When the four separated, McHugh followed Smith and arrested him for receiving stolen property. When the constable arrived back in Aspley with his prisoner the three men who had sold the stolen goods were seen by Smith returning to the village. "McHugh then charged Smith to aid and assist him when they succeeded in capturing two of the parties, the third one escaping." Subsequently, however, Superintendent Turle apprehended this third man at Fenny Stratford where he recovered further stolen goods.

All four prisoners were dealt with by the Buckinghamshire magistrates, the original offence of burglary having occurred in their county. Thomas Williamson, aged 19 years, a labourer from Newport Pagnell, was found guilty of house breaking and transported for fifteen years. Samuel Garret, aged 18 years, also of Newport Pagnell, was sentenced to one year's imprisonment with hard labour whilst Thomas Burton, aged 24, a labourer from Fenny Stratford, received two years' hard labour. As a result of the assistance he had rendered the police Thomas Smith was acquitted on a charge of receiving. The incident shows how observation and local knowledge were the principal weapons of the constabulary in combatting crime.

Those in favour of the continued operation of the police force argued that any reduction in the numbers would necessarily render it less effective. They believed that the constables would be unable to develop a detailed knowledge of too large a beat area and that a small police force would be unable to deal with any large scale public disorder.

Over the years the vexed question of the utility and expense of the police was to be debated several times at the Bedfordshire Court of Quarter Sessions. The court considered different motions calling for the abolition of the force, for a reduction in its establishment, or for its discontinuance in certain districts. All the motions were comprehensively defeated. The variety of changes proposed reflected the dissent within the ranks of those disappointed with the new police. Some magistrates wanted a cheaper system of policing whilst others saw no benefit in retaining any kind of professional force. The majority of magistrates stood by their original decision to establish a county constabulary. They did not believe that circumstances in Bedfordshire had materially altered to invalidate that decision. They remained convinced that a professional police force was a necessity and they were prepared to bear the expense.

A Case of Murder.

Whilst the justices debated the future policing of the county, the Bedfordshire Constabulary continued working in the normal way. In April 1843 Captain Boultbee reported to the quarter sessions on "a serious case of poisoning at Wrestlingworth which took place in October but which has only lately been brought to light." The case concerned a young widow named Sarah Dazley who had apparently been very unfortunate in two marriages. Her first husband, Simeon Mead, had died suddenly, leaving her with a baby to bring up alone. She had married again but both the child and her second husband had also passed away. The coroner had investigated the death of William Dazley on the 30th October 1842 but had found nothing suspicious. Sarah subsequently left Bedfordshire to work in London.

In March 1843 fresh evidence concerning the death of William Dazley came to light and the coroner ordered the exhumation of his body and a post mortem was carried out. On Monday, March 20th 1843 the inquest held at Wrestlingworth found that William Dazley's death had been caused by arsenic poisoning. Superintendent Blunden of the Biggleswade division travelled to London with a warrant for Sarah Dazley's arrest. By Thursday, March 23rd, she had been taken into custody and committed to Bedford gaol to stand trial for murder at the assizes. The evidence against her was overwhelming. Post mortems were conducted on her first husband and child. The husband's cause of death could not be established but there was conclusive evidence that her child had "died from the effect of arsenic, administered to him with a guilty knowledge by his mother, Sarah Dazley."

At the trial in July 1843 the prosecution concerned itself solely with William Dazley's death. Two chemists testified that they had sold arsenic to Sarah just before her second husband's demise. Other witnesses stated that Sarah had been observed making pills containing arsenic and that she had thrown away the medicine prescribed for William Dazley by his physician. The couple had quarrelled violently on the 13th October 1842, just over a fortnight before the husband's death, and a further witness stated that Sarah had remarked "he struck me, and I'll be damned if I don't do for any man that ever hits me."

The jury convicted Sarah Dazley of murder and the judge passed sentence of death on her. The public execution was the first at Bedford gaol since 1833 and it drew large crowds. Given a final chance to confess, Sarah refused, stating "I did not do it. He (meaning William Dazley) poisoned the child and afterwards poisoned himself."

The hanging took place on the 5th August 1843 at twelve noon. A commemorative broadsheet sold in Bedford at the time described how the executioner retired "leaving her standing alone on the drop, when the signal being given, the bolt was drawn and the unfortunate woman was launched into eternity."

Expansion of Duties and Building Programme.

By 1843 the routine work of the police had come to include the regulation of the highways through the enforcement of the 1835 Highways Act. On 11th August 1843, Constable 3, Smalley, attended before the justices with "John Middleton, 18, from Henley, charged with unlawfully riding and driving a wagon drawn by three horses on 27th July at the parish of Eaton Socon and not having reins to guide the same, according to the statute. Fined 40/-." On Thursday, 27th July 1843, Constable 27, Millard, testified against "Benjamin Hill, 35, of Luton, charged with furiously driving his horse on a public highway on 19th July between Barton and Luton. Fined 5/-."

The constabulary had also started to enforce poaching legislation. By 1846, partly as a result of the Night Poaching Act 1844, poaching offences had become such a prevalent feature of police work in Bedfordshire that Captain Boultbee ordered all such

Harrold lock-up

incidents be recorded in a separate register. "Friday, June 5th 1846. Superintendent Young attended the Woburn petty sessions with James Panter, 27, and William Panter, 23, labourers of Cranfield, charged by James Perry, gamekeeper to the Reverend Smith, with night poaching at Holcut on 29th May. Committed to the house of correction for three months' hard labour."

On the same day, also at Woburn "Constable 38, Edwards, attended with David Taylor, 18, Eversholt labourer, charged on summons by William Woodcroft, gamekeeper to His Grace, the Duke of Bedford, with unlawfully using a snare for the purpose of taking game at Eversholt on the 17th May. Fined 21/6d including costs."

The increasing workload of the police and growing number of arrests put a considerable strain on the resources available to the force for the detention of prisoners. On its inception the constabulary made use of the existing system of parish cages and lock-ups for detaining offenders. These iron and stone buildings had been constructed for the use of the old parish constables and for the administration of relief to vagrants. In March 1840 there were cages in many Bedfordshire parishes including Great Barford, Dunstable, Luton, Cardington, Cranfield and Harrold. The quarter sessions improved the network of lock-ups through a programme of minor repairs and the construction of new cages in Sandy, Shillington and Shefford. However, eventually the pressure of work on the new constabulary exposed the deficiencies of these primitive buildings. Prisoners in police custody were frequently placed in the same cells as vagrants detained by the parish. The constables complained that prisoners rightly objected to the risk to their health and that the practice reflected poorly on the police.

Many cages were inconveniently located, one at Dunstable being situated half a mile outside the town. The title to most of the cages was in dispute between the parish authorities and the quarter sessions whilst other cages stood on the freehold land of private citizens. The magistrates refused to authorise major work on any site where they had no security of tenure, and many cages had been allowed to fall into a poor and damp condition. This generally confused state of affairs was reflected in an incident of 1852 when the parish authorities at Cardington pulled down the lock-up there without reference to either the police force or the county magistrates. The quarter sessions investigated the matter but found it had no means of redress against the parish.

In 1846 the Government had circulated a book containing plans of construction for purpose built police stations. These plans attracted the attention of the Bedfordshire magistrates and the following year the tradesmen and merchants of Luton, dissatisfied with the poor state of the existing lock-up, petitioned the quarter sessions "of the necessity of erecting a commodious station for the police and lock-up house for prisoners." The magistrates considered that the rapid expansion of the town justified the provision of a police station. At the Epiphany quarter sessions of 1848 they ordered that a loan of £800 be secured to fund the proposed building.

Luton's first police station was built on a plot of land at the corner of Dunstable Place and Peel Street, close to the site of the modern telephone exchange. The building provided living accommodation for a superintendent and a constable. The superintendent's residence was situated at one end of the property and comprised a small entrance hall, parlour, kitchen and scullery, and three bedrooms. At the other end of the property was the constable's cottage with just two rooms downstairs and a further two upstairs. The two residences were connected by a long passage which gave access to five cells. Behind the buildings lay a yard with outhouses, stable and chaise house.

Whilst the construction work at Luton went ahead, similar plans were being put into operation at Woburn. The Russell family owned all the land in the parish of Woburn but had initially agreed to sell a small freehold to facilitate the construction of a police station. Subsequently, however, the Duke of Bedford decided not to sell any land but agreed instead to construct the police station at his own expense and lease it to the county for a term of fifty years. The rent was set at just £32 per annum. The county had anticipated raising a loan of £525 to pay for the station and the quarter sessions unanimously passed a motion that "the thanks of the bench be offered to His Grace."

By 1854 the magistrates at Ampthill, Biggleswade and Leighton Buzzard, were all pressing for the provision of police stations in their respective divisions. The existing stations at Luton and Woburn had both experienced troubled histories. As a result, in 1855, the quarter sessions instructed the county architect to conduct a survey of the whole county with regard to the facilities for the detention of prisoners. His report could hardly have been worse. "Leighton; no provision. Ampthill; however temporary the confinement nothing can be worse than the present provision. Biggleswade; the present lock-up here is but little better than that at Ampthill. Sharnbrook; no provision. Bedford; no provision. Woburn and Luton; I have inspected the buildings and do not consider either of them suited for the purpose for which they are required." Luton in particular was "badly constructed."

The quarter sessions responded with a major building programme costing approximately £5,000. Ampthill, Biggleswade and Leighton Buzzard were all to have new police stations at an estimated cost of £850 each. At Leighton Buzzard a parcel of land on Flitch of Bacon common on the Turnpike Road was the proposed site. The early station house at Luton was to be sold and a new one built just a few yards away on the other side of Dunstable Place on the corner with Stuart Street. The new building included a court house as well as a police station at a total cost of nearly £2,400. At Woburn the Duke of Bedford undertook major alterations in return for a substantially increased rent. This arrangement remained in force until 1864 when the quarter sessions obtained the freehold of the site of Woburn police station for the sum of £900.

The provision of a series of purpose built station houses enhanced the professional reputation of the Bedfordshire Constabulary and ensured greater uniformity in the treatment of prisoners across the county. The benefit of providing secure accommodation for the detention of significant numbers of offenders was evident in November 1854 during two days of rioting at Luton. The industry of the town had been in a depressed state for a period of some eighteen months prior to the disturbances and many workers in the hat manufacturing trade had been laid off. Towards the end of 1854 business revived slightly and some of the jobless regained their old positions. The competition for the small number of vacancies was fierce and wage levels were forced down. The workers believed their employers were exploiting the economic situation and an atmosphere of bitterness prevailed.

On Tuesday, 21st November 1854 the town crier at Luton announced that "a meeting of the bonnet sellers" was to take place at five o'clock in the evening outside the town hall to discuss the workers' grievances. A crowd of five or six hundred persons assembled in the town centre but when the hat manufacturers tried to address the crowd they were shouted down and pelted with mud. The mood subsequently became very ugly and a mob rampaged through the streets stoning the manufacturers' warehouses and homes. Damage to property was widespread and the rioting continued until 10 p.m. when the crowd began to disperse.

The following morning, Wednesday, 22nd November, an even larger crowd began to assemble in the centre of Luton. A

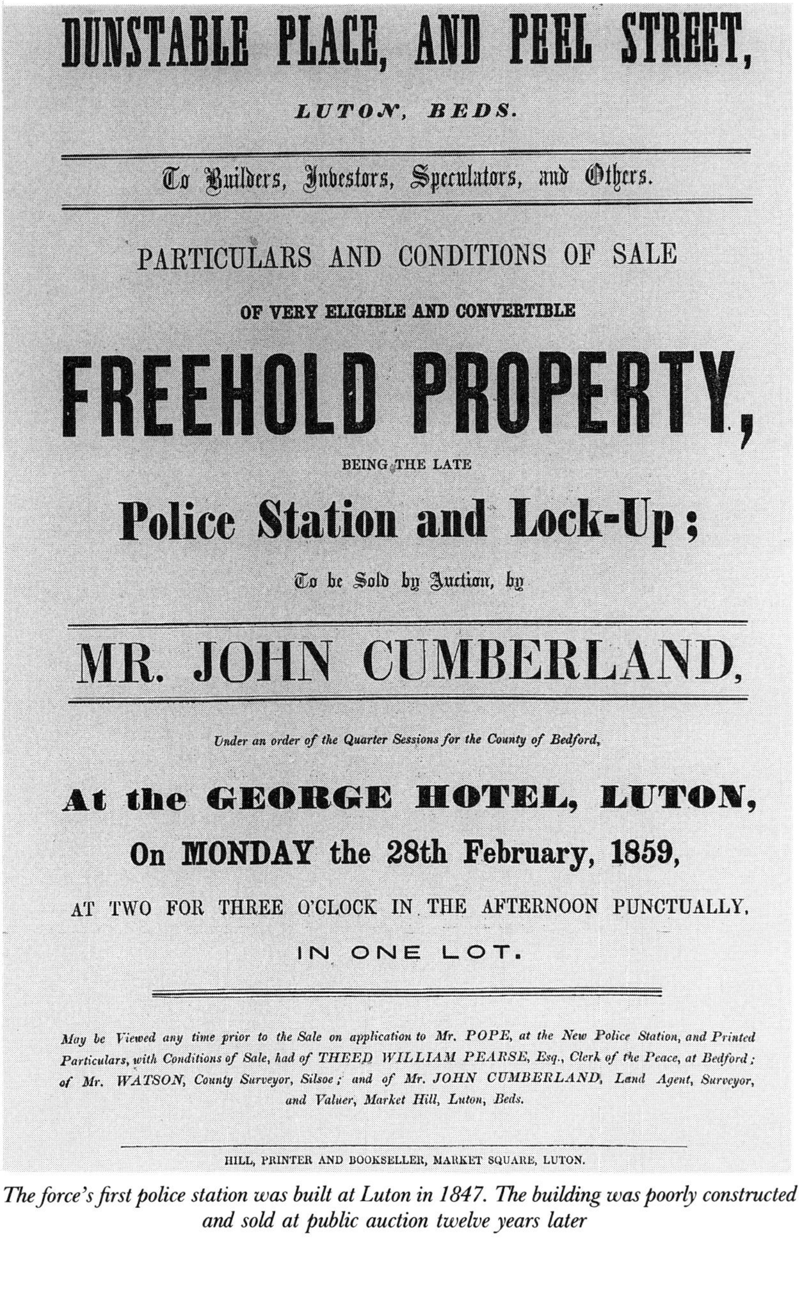

DUNSTABLE PLACE, AND PEEL STREET,

LUTON, BEDS.

To Builders, Investors, Speculators, and Others.

PARTICULARS AND CONDITIONS OF SALE

OF VERY ELIGIBLE AND CONVERTIBLE

FREEHOLD PROPERTY,

BEING THE LATE

Police Station and Lock-Up;

To be Sold by Auction, by

MR. JOHN CUMBERLAND,

Under an order of the Quarter Sessions for the County of Bedford,

At the GEORGE HOTEL, LUTON,

On MONDAY the 28th February, 1859,

AT TWO FOR THREE O'CLOCK IN THE AFTERNOON PUNCTUALLY,

IN ONE LOT.

May be Viewed any time prior to the Sale on application to Mr. POPE, at the New Police Station, and Printed Particulars, with Conditions of Sale, had of THEED WILLIAM PEARSE, Esq., Clerk of the Peace, at Bedford; of Mr. WATSON, County Surveyor, Silsoe; and of Mr. JOHN CUMBERLAND, Land Agent, Surveyor, and Valuer, Market Hill, Luton, Beds.

HILL, PRINTER AND BOOKSELLER, MARKET SQUARE, LUTON.

The force's first police station was built at Luton in 1847. The building was poorly constructed and sold at public auction twelve years later

PARTICULARS.

THE PROPERTY CONSISTS OF

A BRICK-BUILT and SLATED RESIDENCE,

AT THE CORNER OF PEEL STREET,

And formerly occupied by the Superintendent of Police, containing small Entrance Hall, Parlour, Kitchen and Scullery, large Cellar in the basement, and three Bed Rooms.

At the other end of the Property is A

COMFORTABLE COTTAGE

Having Two Rooms below and Two Bed Rooms above,
And adjoining is a Stable and Chaise House, opening into a right of way at the West End of the Premises, in the rear is a Yard, Two Closets, Pump of Water, &c.

THE CENTRE PORTION OF THE PROPERTY CONSISTS OF

FIVE STRONGLY-BUILT CELLS,

A long Passage communicating with the Cells and both Residences, Closet, &c.;
Built with Walls of considerable thickness, and containing a large quantity of Building Materials.

The Premises are BRICK-BUILT and SLATED, and have been erected twelve years, and are situated only a very short distance from the best parts of the town, and may, with a very little outlay, be converted into Manufacturing Premises. It has a Frontage to Dunstable Place of Eighty-one Feet, and to Peel Street of Thirty-one Feet.

Full Possession may be had on Completion of the Purchase. The Fixtures (of which a List will be produced at the Sale) to be taken at a Valuation.

detachment of county constables and two superintendents arrived to reinforce the officers stationed at Luton. A number of special constables were sworn in and the Bedfordshire Times later reported that "Superintendent Godfrey and other officers of the Bedfordshire rural force succeeded for the time in preventing further outrage on property."

Disturbances broke out again on Wednesday evening and two bakers shops were looted. The police intervened once more. The rioting subsided and a number of the ringleaders were arrested. The prisoners were lodged in the Peel Street station house and the majority were successfully prosecuted on charges of assault or riotous behaviour.

The expenditure incurred through the extensive building programme led the county magistrates to divide the force area into seven administrative districts. The cost of certain items in each district was calculated separately and the police rate levied accordingly. The resulting quarterly rate in the Bedford district was a halfpenny whilst in Luton and Leighton Buzzard the rate was more than double that amount at one and a quarter pence. The growth of Leighton Buzzard had caused the town to be separated from Woburn and designated as a seventh police division. The administrative changes had little operational effect however. One superintendent remained in overall charge of the combined Woburn and Leighton Buzzard area, although an inspector was stationed in the new division.

Inspectors of Constabulary.

A further change in the funding of the constabulary was effected by the 1856 County and Borough Police Act. The Act provided for the appointment of Inspectors of Constabulary to enquire into the efficiency of all police forces. Those counties which had not established a force were now required to do so. An exchequer grant, amounting to one quarter of the cost of police pay and clothing was to be paid to all forces which served populations of at least five thousand people and which were certified as efficient by the inspectorate. The Act applied both to the Bedfordshire Constabulary and to the Bedford borough police.

The first reports of Her Majesty's Inspectors of Constabulary were completed in September 1857. The entry relating to the Bedfordshire Constabulary was favourable and on 14th December of that year the county magistrates received a letter from Whitehall. "The Home Secretary has considered the inspector's report upon the state of the police in your county during the year ended 29th September last. He has the satisfaction of certifying that your police has been maintained in a state of efficiency." The Bedford borough police were also certified efficient but the Inspector of Constabulary objected to the separate conduct of day and night watches by two different classes of constable. As a result the borough watch committee ordered that "all constables should be equal and each officer should take their share of day and night work."

The county force received favourable reports in the succeeding years. In 1859 the inspector found "during the year one hundred and eight indictable offences were reported to the police for which ninety-seven persons were apprehended and seventy-seven committed. A good average." The figures included one case of local notoriety concerning the murder of a young Luton woman.

In August 1857 Jane Whitcroft had married Joseph Castle, a native of Ware in Hertfordshire. The marriage proved unhappy and the couple frequently quarrelled. On Monday, 8th August 1859, Jane left her husband and returned to her parents' home at York Street, Luton. The following day Castle visited her there and at length persuaded her to return to Ware with him. Jane's body was later found on the road leading from Luton to Summeries Hill. Her throat had been cut and she had been stabbed several times round the base of the neck. Superintendent Pope attended from Luton and took possession of the murder weapon, a knife, which was subsequently identified as the property of the victim's husband. Castle had fled after the murder but eventually gave himself up to the Hertfordshire police, saying "I've had a row with my wife but I'll not tell you the consequence."

At the trial Castle pleaded not guilty to a charge of murder but the jury, having heard the evidence, took less than fifteen minutes to convict him. The judge then passed sentence, "That you, Joseph Castle, be taken back to the place from whence you came; from thence to the place of execution, there to be hung by the neck till you are dead. And the Lord have mercy on your soul."

The sentence was carried out at twelve noon on Saturday, March 31st 1860 when Castle became the first to die on the gallows at Bedford since the execution of Sarah Dazley in 1843.

Another comment in the inspector's report of 1859 precipitated a lengthy debate between the Bedfordshire quarter sessions and the Home Office on the extent of the inspectorate's powers. "The station houses are all in order but one is required for the Bletsoe division." The county magistrates disagreed, "taking into account the smallness of the division itself, the short distance of its

THE LIFE, TRIAL, CONFESSION, AND EXECUTION OF

JOSEPH CASTLE,

FOR THE MURDER OF HIS WIFE,

At LUTON, on TUESDAY the 9th of AUGUST, 1859,

Tried and condemned at the BEDFORD ASSIZES, March 14, 1860.

O awful sight! a fellow-man,
Hung by the neck to public gaze,
For others to example take,
And check them in their dangerous ways,
And may his fate their warning prove,
'Gainst harbouring malicious thought,
Lead them to pray for heavenly grace,
That to such end they ne'er be brought.

Public executions were the subject of commemorative posters

The treadwheel was a common form of hard labour, as was the crank. Both were banned by Act of Parliament in 1898. The mechanism could be tightened with a screw, making the work more arduous – hence the slang term 'screws' given to prison warders

headquarters from Bedford, the great diminution of crime and the consequent extreme paucity of persons detained in custody within the division." Despite the arguments the Inspector of Constabulary maintained that he would not certify the efficiency of the county force in the future unless a new station house was built at Bletsoe.

The quarter sessions were not prepared to countenance such interference in their local affairs and despatched a delegation direct to the Home Office. It was forcefully argued that there "must be some mistake as regarded the duties of inspectors." They were empowered only to report on the efficiency of police forces with regards to their numbers and discipline. "Inspectors had nothing to do with new lock-ups," but were only authorised to report on the condition of those already in existence. The Home Office replied that other counties had built new station houses at the request of the inspectorate but that Bedfordshire would not be required to do so. The exchequer grant was to be paid whether or not a new Bletsoe station house was erected.

The following year the Inspector of Constabulary certified the Bedfordshire county police force efficient but he noted in his report "although the magistrates consider a new station at Bletsoe not to be required I still think that a small second class station would add to the efficiency of that district as I find that eleven prisoners were kept during the year at constables' residences, five at public houses, and three were remanded to Bedford." The quarter sessions remained adamant that it was "impossible for a stranger to know what was requisite to render the police efficient so well as the magistrates."

The inspector's report of 1863 details the extra work which had been assigned to the county police over a period of time. "The police undertake the duties of weights and measures, assistant relieving officers for vagrants, and inspectors of common lodging houses and nuisances." The superintendents appointed as inspectors of weights and measures were supplied with official and accurate measures of weight and capacity known as "the local standards." During the course of a year the inspectors were expected to travel round the whole of their respective districts examining and adjusting weights and measures used in shops, inns and warehouses. If necessary, they could obtain a magistrate's warrant to force entry to premises where they believed false weights and measures were being used.

The police officers appointed as assistant relieving officers for vagrants were called on to exercise discretion in deciding whether to grant relief to those seeking food and shelter. A minute from the poor law board reads: "He will take care that women and children are supplied with necessary food and shelter. As a general rule he would be right in refusing relief to able bodied and healthy men, though in inclement weather he might afford them shelter. Habitual vagrants should be refused relief." Workhouses were situated in most major population centres in Bedfordshire.

Inspectors of common lodging houses and nuisances protected the public health. A nuisance included "any premises in such a state as to be injurious to health. Any pool, ditch, gutter, waterhouse, privy, urinal, cesspool, drain, or ashpit, so foul as to be injurious to health" was to be reported to the sanitary authorities.

1864 saw a further administrative reorganisation of the county force when the Luton area was split into two new divisions, known as Luton and Luton rural. The police rate in the Luton rural district in the first quarter of 1864 was just one and one quarter pence compared to the two and a quarter pence paid in the town of Luton. The aim of the administrative change was to secure a fairer collection of the police rate and again had little operational effect.

The town of Dunstable still felt a legitimate grievance over the funding of the force. It contributed over £200 a year to the police rates yet enjoyed the services of just two constables in return. The residents had pressed for the provision of a new station house but their requests had been turned down. In 1864 Dunstable was granted a Royal Charter and became a municipal corporation. The new town council decided that Dunstable would be better served if it possessed its own borough police force.

The following year the Bedfordshire Court of Quarter Sessions received notice that a superintendent of police and one constable had been appointed in the borough of Dunstable to enter upon their duties on the 16th September 1865. As of that date Dunstable would cease to contribute towards the county police rate.

The first two police officers employed by the Dunstable borough force were both recruited from the ranks of the county constabulary on promises of better wages. This initially soured relations between the two forces but subsequently they appear to have co-operated in most matters.

The report of Her Majesty's Inspector of Constabulary for the year ending September 1866 included the Dunstable borough police for the first time and so gave a complete picture of the state of policing in Bedfordshire with its three separate forces. The establishment of the county constabulary had by this time risen to ninety officers. Captain Boultbee's salary had been increased to

£350, whilst the superintendents were paid between £105 and £166 yearly, dependent on service and the extra duties they performed. Inspectors received £80 a year, sergeants between 25/- and 27/- a week, and the different classes of constable between 17/- and 22/- weekly.

The rates of pay in the borough forces were roughly equivalent. The Bedford borough police strength had risen to thirteen men. The head constable received £140 per annum, sergeants between 22/- and 24/- per week and constables either 21/- or 22/- weekly. The force had just two ranks, under the head constable. At Dunstable the senior or head constable received £78 per year whilst the junior constable was paid 22/- a week.

The Inspectors of Constabulary were opposed to very small borough forces in principle. The preamble to their report in 1866 stated that "it is a serious drawback to the general efficiency and well being of the police system that small boroughs continue separate." The payment of the exchequer grant to police forces which served populations of at least five thousand people had been intended as an inducement to the smallest borough forces to consolidate with their larger county neighbours. Dunstable's population was well below five thousand in 1866 and the Inspectors of Constabulary naturally regarded the establishment of a two man force there as a step in the wrong direction. However, as Dunstable did not qualify for an exchequer grant on point of size the question of being certified efficient was an academic one. Each year the inspectorate pronounced the force as "too weak to be efficient" in terms of numbers. Despite the misgivings of the inspectors the town councillors were determined to maintain an independent borough police force in Dunstable. The council authorised the construction of a station house with three cells and living accommodation for the head constable. The station opened on 1st December 1867 and was situated in Icknield Road, opposite the junction with South Place.

The Bedford borough police had established a police office in rented premises in Silver Street as far back as 1856. Relations with the county force had remained generally poor and in 1859 the Inspector of Constabulary commented that he found co-operation between the two forces "in a very unsatisfactory state." The inspectorate worked to promote higher levels of co-operation between the county and borough police forces and relations eventually became more cordial. By 1870 the county constables in the north of Bedfordshire were allowed the use of the borough police cells in Bedford for the safe custody of prisoners.

Detection and Prevention of Crime.

Towards the end of Captain Boultbee's term of office the county force achieved some notable successes in dealing with serious crime in Bedfordshire.

On the morning of Wednesday, 30th November 1870, a fifty-two year old woman, Sarah Marshall, was found dead in her cottage at Little Staughton. Marshall was described by the newspapers of the time as an "imbecile woman, who for twenty years had been under medical supervision as an outdoor lunatic." She had been subjected to a violent assault and strangled. Police enquiries revealed that the victim had last been seen alive at 11 p.m. on 29th November, and a medical examination of the corpse fixed the time of death between midnight on the 29th and 2 a.m. on the 30th. Further enquiries led to a 21 year old local labourer, named William Bull, becoming the prime suspect in the case.

On the night of the murder Bull had left Wildman's beerhouse in Little Staughton at 10.15 p.m. Instead of turning for home he had headed in the opposite direction with a fellow labourer. The two men had been met by two further acquaintances travelling on the same road and the four spent some fifteen minutes in conversation together. During this conversation Bull had allegedly said "he was a good mind to go and call old Sally (Sarah Marshall) up that evening as she would call out and make a to do." At least one of Bull's companions tried to dissuade him from goading the old lady but when the four men separated Bull was seen to go in the direction of Sarah Marshall's cottage. At 11 p.m. Bull was seen standing outside the cottage by another local traveller. One further piece of evidence pointed to Bull. Damage to the hedgerow running behind the cottage indicated the route taken by the murderer in making his escape. Bull's house lay directly across the fields from the broken hedge.

The police began to search for Bull but found that he had gone missing from home. In the early hours of Friday, 2nd December Constable Sturges from Keysoe, found Bull at his mother's cottage in Little Staughton. Bull resisted arrest and ran from the house. The newspapers later related that "with a prominent energy and no slight degree of personal courage Sturges gave chase to the fugitive whom he overtook and captured after a severe struggle and conveyed him to Sharnbrook where he lodged him in the custody of Superintendent Carruthers."

Bull's clothing at the time of the arrest was positively identified as being that which he had been wearing on the night of the murder. Blood found on the right sleeve of Bull's jacket and on the right leg of his trousers was believed to have come from a deep wound inflicted on the victim's buttocks.

Bull pleaded not guilty at his trial but on hearing the evidence the jury took just twenty minutes to return a guilty verdict. The prisoner was sentenced to death and subsequently confessed to the crime whilst awaiting his execution. "I pelted her door with stones. She undone the door and stood in the doorway swearing at me and called me a bloody hen roost robber. She struck at me with a long sweeping broom and struck me on the shoulder when the broom head fell off. She picked it up and went into the house and I followed her. When she hit me a second time, I hit her with my right hand on the head and she fell to the ground. I at once got on top of her. I got hold of her throat with my left hand to prevent her shouting and screaming. I tried to have connexion with her, she kicked about but could not holler as I had tight hold of her throat and that killed her." The more unsavoury details of the attack were omitted from the published confession.

It was recorded that "at eight o'clock on Monday morning, April 3rd 1871 the convict William Bull expiated his atrocious crime upon the scaffold within the precincts of Bedford prison." Executions no longer took place in public. Instead "immediately upon the execution being completed a black flag was hoisted in front of the prison as an indication to the assembled crowd outside."

The county constabulary gained widespread recognition for its effective use of the 1869 Beerhouse Act in reducing crime. The Government was keen to investigate any possible link between some forms of criminal activity and the consumption of alcohol. The Beerhouse Act gave police forces extended powers to supervise licensed premises and tightened licensing regulations. Its implementation produced spectacular results in Luton and the policing of the division was singled out for special praise by the Inspectors of Constabulary in their overall report for 1870.

On 30th April 1869 there were forty-nine beerhouses in Luton and there had been sixty-two felonies recorded in the previous six months. Such figures had been typical for some time. Enforcement of the Beerhouse Act resulted in the closure of ten poorly conducted licensed premises in the town and between October 1869 and April 1870 the number of reported felonies fell to just eighteen.

The good work continued on into 1871 when the Inspectors of Constabulary commented on a further year of excellent achievement. "In consequence of the withdrawal of nearly thirteen per cent of the whole number of public and beerhouses in the town of Luton, for misconduct and other causes, crime has diminished in a most remarkable way. With a known criminal population of three hundred persons, one hundred have gone to honest employment, and some fifty have left the neighbourhood." As for the remaining one hundred and fifty the inspector quoted the chairman of the Luton petty sessions: "They are not living on the proceeds of crime for none of any consequence is reported." The inspectorate congratulated the Bedfordshire Constabulary on "the intelligence, zeal and thoughtful nature of Superintendent Pope at the Luton division."

Captain Boultbee's Retirement.

Captain Boultbee retired from the post of Chief Constable of Bedfordshire early in 1871. The Court of Quarter Sessions unanimously thanked him for his "eminent and distinguished service" and granted him a pension of just over £233 a year which represented two-thirds of his annual salary. The constabulary presented the Captain with a gilt and ormolu clock, set on a gilt and velvet stand, bearing a silver plate engraved with an inscription conveying the esteem and regard of all the officers and men. The force also presented an elegant luncheon service to Mrs Boultbee at the couple's home in Goldington Road, Bedford.

In considering Captain Boultbee's achievement as the first Chief Constable of Bedfordshire it is necessary to appreciate the nature of his position. As a county chief constable his authority was far greater than that enjoyed by his counterpart in the borough forces. In the boroughs the watch committee exercised the power to appoint constables, to issue regulations for their governance, to promote, punish or dismiss them. In county forces all these functions were performed by the chief constable and he was not answerable to any higher authority.

A Home Office memorandum on this subject stated, "the head constable of a borough police force holds an inferior position as compared with the chief constable of a county. In fact, in a borough the watch committee discharges several of the functions which with respect to a county police belong to the chief constable."

The Courts of the Quarter Sessions had power to dismiss the chief constable of their county but this was their only sanction. The Bedfordshire Court of Quarter Sessions realised the necessity of appointing a chief constable able to independently organise the new county constabulary and to effectively supervise the subsequent operation of the force.

Captain Boultbee proved more than equal to the responsibility and gained a high reputation as a capable administrator. His judgement was widely respected and he came to enjoy the complete confidence of the quarter sessions. Boultbee was undoubtedly one of the more successful chief constables of the early Victorian era.

In private life Captain Boultbee became a popular figure in Bedfordshire society. He was a happily married family man, relatively wealthy and able to maintain four servants in his household. His professional achievements, quiet authority, and integrity were widely admired. He gave generous support to many local charities as well as personally organising an annual treat for the inmates of Bedford Workhouse and regular charity bazaars at his own house.

On Tuesday, 10th December 1889 at the age of 92 years, after having enjoyed a long retirement, Captain Boultbee died at his Bedford home. In accordance with his wishes the funeral service at St. Cuthbert's Church, Bedford, was kept plain and simple and he was buried in Bedford cemetery.

A few days before his death, sensing that he was nearing the end of his life, Boultbee summoned his old deputy chief constable to say goodbye and asked him to visit all the old officers and men to assure them he had not forgotten them and that they were often in his thoughts.

At Boultbee's death the Bedfordshire Constabulary was already approaching its fiftieth anniversary and was under the command of its third chief constable, Colonel Josselyn. The second chief constable, Major Warner, had enjoyed a comparatively short tenure of office, lasting just nine years.

MAJOR ASHTON C. WARNER

CHAPTER THREE

1871 – 1879
MAJOR WARNER

ASHTON Cromwell Warner was born on 11th August 1835 in Brighton. His forebears were directly descended from the line of Oliver Cromwell and his father, a captain in the Fifth Regiment of Fusiliers, had close connections with Bedfordshire. Warner was sent to Bedford Grammar School to receive his education before he continued the family military tradition, joining the Army at eighteen years of age.

His military career was an illustrious one. During the Indian Mutiny he formed part of the besieged garrison at Lucknow. The siege began in May 1857 and his commanding officer recalled "whenever a volunteer was wanted for a dangerous sortie young Warner was always ready." Warner's younger brother formed part of the column which fought its way through to Lucknow in September 1857 to reinforce the garrison and the siege was finally lifted on the 15th November of that year.

Warner fought in numerous other actions on the Indian subcontinent, was twice mentioned in despatches and received a medal with two clasps for gallantry. At the time of his appointment to major he was the youngest officer to hold that rank in the British Army.

Major Warner retired from military service in 1870 and spent several months studying the duties of a chief police officer under

Admiral McHardy, the Chief Constable of Essex. When the Bedfordshire Court of Quarter Sessions advertised for a chief constable to succeed Captain Boultbee, Major Warner was one of seven candidates who applied for the position. At the Epiphany quarter sessions held in Bedford in January 1871, forty-one magistrates of the county were balloted on the new appointment. In the second round of the voting Warner received the support of twenty-four of the magistrates and was duly elected Chief Constable of Bedfordshire.

At the following Easter quarter sessions held in April 1871 Major Warner presented his first quarterly report to the assembled justices. "I assumed command of the force on the 16th January and since joining I have inspected the whole of the force frequently, and I trust it will not be deemed presumptuous of me to say that I have found everything connected with the force in good working order. The Inspector of Constabulary recently completed his inspection of this force and appeared to be well satisfied with the efficiency of the men."

The early years of Warner's tenure of office saw the construction of new county police stations in both Bedford and Sharnbrook. In 1871 the magistrates decided it was "desirable that provision should be made for a lock-up house and a proper place for holding petty sessions in the Bletsoe division." Subsequently a parcel of land in Sharnbrook was purchased from Richard Orlebar of Hinwick House and in June 1871 an advertisement was placed in the trade publication 'The Builder'. "Persons willing to contract with the justices of the court of Bedford for the erection of a police station at Sharnbrook may see the plans and specifications at the office of the county surveyor."

Two local builders were awarded the contract and the construction work began immediately at a cost of £1,189. In his report dated 29th September 1872 the Inspector of Constabulary remarked, "the station house at Sharnbrook has been completed and is now regularly used, with a good residence for the superintendent, three cells and a court house attached."

That same year the county had purchased a substantial piece of land "with a frontage of sixty feet to Gadsby Street, in the borough of Bedford." The Gadsby Street station house was completed in late 1872 and served a dual purpose as the Bedford divisional station and as the force headquarters. The building comprised "three cells, a superintendent's residence and offices for the chief constable." The county force no longer needed to house prisoners in the Bedford borough police cells.

The Gadsby Street station house built in 1872 is still in existence and is now used by the county Trading Standards Office

The Bedfordshire Constabulary now possessed a network of police stations covering the entire county and the Inspector of Constabulary considered that the force was "very well provided with station houses of an excellent class."

Cattle Plague and Extra Duties.

Whilst the new police stations were being built in the north of Bedfordshire, the constabulary was dealing with a major cattle plague. At the Michaelmas quarter sessions of 1871 Warner outlined the extent of the problem. "I am sorry to say that foot and mouth disease is very prevalent in the county and during the quarter ending 29th September, one thousand, one hundred and fifty-one animals have been attacked with the disease."

The superintendents acted as inspectors of contagious diseases in animals, exercising powers to regulate the movement of cattle, to impose quarantine areas and to order the slaughter of infected livestock. They had received training in how to identify the symptoms of dangerous cattle diseases and worked in conjunction with local veterinarians. The drain on police resources was great but the cattle plague was eventually contained and then eliminated, although some routine police duties were necessarily neglected.

Despite the strains imposed on police resources by the performance of additional duties, the responsibilities of the constabulary were increased still further. Under legislation governing the contamination of food, local authorities were to appoint officers to procure samples of food for testing by public analysts. The officer purchasing any article for analysis was to "notify to the seller his intention to have the article analysed and offer to divide it into three parts, each part to be marked and sealed." One part was retained by the officer and one part given to the seller. The third part was sent for analysis. At the Epiphany quarter sessions held on January 3rd 1874 Major Warner described the implementation of these measures in Bedfordshire.

"The Adulteration of Food Act has been in force in the county for the past six months. During this period two hundred and sixty-two samples of food and drink have been procured by the inspectors of weights and measures. Twenty-four samples have been found adulterated. Nine persons have been proceeded against, seven of them have been convicted and two cases dismissed. The inspectors have made twenty-three journeys to London to the analyst. I find that the carrying out of this Act occupies a very great deal of the inspectors' time and it takes them very much away from their first and original duty as police officers."

The success of the constabulary in relation to contagious diseases in animals, weights and measures, food and nuisances served to enhance the reputation of the police as an efficient, adaptable organisation and ensured that the force remained responsible for enforcing the relevant legislation. Subsequently the Explosives Act of 1875 resulted in the police certifying the safety of sites used for the storage of gunpowder.

The routine work of the constabulary remained much as it had been in Captain Boultbee's day. Major Warner introduced new registers for recording the arrests made by his officers. Each division maintained its own register containing the details of each person apprehended, the date and time of arrest, the charge, the result of the case and finally a full description of the prisoner. The register kept in the Woburn division in 1874 reflects the predominance of Vagrancy Act offences in the regular work of the police during Major Warner's nine years in office. "July 8th, twelve noon. John Vincent, aged 37 years of Taunton, a tramp, arrested for begging from door to door at Hockliffe. Committed for fourteen days' hard labour." "July 15th, one a.m. William Moore, aged 55 years, a tramp, arrested by Constable 36, Whinnett, for sleeping in the open air at Woburn, not having any visible means of subsistence and not giving a good account of himself. Sentenced to fourteen days' imprisonment with hard labour."

The master of the Woburn Workhouse frequently called in the police to deal with belligerent inmates. "August 27th, eleven a.m. Charles Taylor, aged 25 years of Kendal, Westmorland, a labourer, arrested by Constable 36, Whinnett, for wilfully tearing up his own clothes while a casual pauper in the Woburn Workhouse." This was a common form of protest against the strict regime imposed on the residents. "Sentenced to two months' imprisonment with hard labour."

The harsh treatment afforded to vagrants in the courts was viewed as an exercise in crime prevention. Many of the petty thefts dealt with by the constabulary involved tramps. "May 21st, two p.m. Francis Park, aged 21 years, a tramp, arrested for stealing a 2 lb loaf of bread, value three and three-quarter pence, the property of Henry Osborne, at Hockliffe. Committed for one calendar month with hard labour."

The police were also much occupied in tracing men who had abandoned their wives and families, leaving them without means of support. "August 26th, eleven-fifteen p.m. Daniel Fleet, aged 40 years of Husborne Crawley, a bricklayer, arrested by Inspector Tydeman for deserting his two children, leaving them charge to the Woburn Relief Union on 9th May 1874. Sentenced to two months' imprisonment with hard labour."

One of the most important events of Major Warner's term of office as chief constable was the Royal Agricultural Show held at Bedford between Saturday, 11th July and Friday, 17th July 1874. The showground occupied a fifty-five acre site close to Elstow and the Bedford racecourse. As the showground lay entirely outside the Bedford borough boundary the responsibility for policing the event fell to the county constabulary. Major Warner drew up his plans for policing the Royal Show early in 1874. Forty constables from his own force were to be deployed at the showground, supported by sixty special constables sworn in to act for the duration of the event. Warner also obtained the services of a number of detective officers from both London and the Midlands.

Temporary railway stations were erected at the showground and seventy-two thousand visitors from outside the county attended the exhibition, including the Crown Prince and Princess of Prussia.

Warner's arrangements worked well and on Saturday, 1st August 1874 the Bedfordshire Mercury reported a successful arrest made by the detective officers employed during the show. At the Bedford divisional petty sessions "Richard Taylor, a respectably dressed young man was charged with stealing from the person of Elizabeth Willshire at the Midland railway station, the showyard, Elstow." A detective officer from the City of London Police described how Taylor had "walked down the platform to where a young woman was getting into a carriage. He put his hand into her dress pocket and took out two silver coins. He immediately ran down the platform and I followed him and caught him." Taylor had struggled but the City of London officer was assisted by a detective inspector from Leicester, also on duty at the show. The pickpocket was sentenced to six months' imprisonment with hard labour.

Pay and Pensions.

1874 also saw the introduction of the Police (Expenses) Act into Parliament which increased the government grant payable to police forces to one half of the total cost of constabulary pay and clothing. Through the increase the Home Office sought "to secure for the Secretary of State a greater amount of supervision and control over the police forces of Great Britain than he now possesses."

Between 1874 and 1876 Major Warner reported that he had "experienced considerable difficulty in obtaining good men for the force. I believe that the settlement of the superannuation question is one of the chief causes which prevents eligible men from coming forward." There was growing national discontent within the ranks of the police service concerning their pension arrangements. The Inspector of Constabulary also commented on the low level of recruitment. "There is great difficulty in getting suitable men, attributed partly to the general high rate of wages paid for other employ."

Government concern at the rising number of experienced men leaving the police service resulted in the creation of a House of Commons select committee to investigate the administration of police pensions. The committee began its lengthy enquiries in 1875 and in the meantime the rates of pay for the police were improved across the country. In Bedfordshire the increase in wages was substantial. Warner's salary rose to £400 per annum, including an allowance of £100 for housing and travelling expenses. Superintendents received £135 a year on appointment, rising by £5 every five years to a maximum of £180. Inspectors received £95 per annum, again rising by £5 every five years to a maximum of £110. Sergeants received a starting wage of 28/- a week rising to a maximum of 32/8d, whilst constables started on 22/2d and could eventually expect to earn as much as 27/5d a week. The award of merit pay could add 1/2d a week to the wages of constables and sergeants. These new rates of pay were implemented early in 1876 and later that year the Inspector of Constabulary reported that "there is not much difficulty now in getting men."

The select committee published its report on police pensions in 1877 and some of its conclusions proved to be controversial. The committee recommended that police officers should receive a pension as of right after completing twenty-five years' service and that superannuation expenses should be financed directly from the local rates. There was considerable opposition to the adoption of such measures and as the pressure on police recruitment had now eased there was no attempt to introduce new legislation on police pensions.

In Bedfordshire steps were taken locally to augment the constabulary superannuation fund. The county increased the fees charged for the execution of warrants and service of summonses on behalf of other agencies and neighbouring forces. The proceeds were channelled towards police pensions. The magistrates conducted a detailed examination of the general finances of the county constabulary and subsequently the Woburn and Leighton Buzzard divisions were amalgamated at a saving of £80 per annum in administration costs. Such economies allowed for shortfalls in the superannuation fund to be met from the general police rate, although some magistrates resisted this expense on pensions.

The conflict between the magistrates is reflected in the Bedfordshire Mercury's report of the Epiphany quarter sessions of 1879 when the court debated Major Warner's recommendations that a constable of twenty-eight years' exemplary service should receive a pension of £47.13.0d per annum. The constable in question had been certified "incapable through infirmity of body of performing the duties of his office." A magistrate from the constable's own division spoke first in the debate. "I know him very well. He has lived in my parish many years and always conducted himself exceedingly well but he has no family dependent on him at all and it seems a rather large amount to give to a man who is certainly not incapacitated from general work. He is able to get about very well, even in winter, with the aid of a stick. (Laughter from other members of the court)."

Fortunately those magistrates of a more generous disposition were in the ascendant and the first speaker was rebuked in subsequent speeches. "Might I remind my friend that this constable, as all others, has had, during his long period of service, a certain amount of his pay deducted weekly for the superannuation fund. I think therefore my friend's suggestions come in bad grace at this time. (Hear Hear)." At the conclusion of the debate a vote was taken and the pension was unanimously granted.

Whilst the Bedfordshire magistrates genuinely tried to reward loyal, long serving constables with adequate pensions, the financing of the superannuation scheme was fundamentally unsound and the treatment ultimately afforded to Constable John Crick cannot have inspired much confidence among his colleagues. In January 1871 Major Warner reported that "an aggravated assault was committed in the Ampthill division upon Police Constable Crick by some men belonging to Maulden. The constable was so severely injured that his life was in danger for more than a week. Six of the men have been committed for trial at the assizes. The seventh was discharged and admitted as a witness."

Crick's drunken assailants included a bricklayer, a blacksmith and some local labourers. They were tried at the spring assizes held on Tuesday, 14th March 1871 when they received custodial sentences of between four and six months. These sentences were to be served in addition to any time served on remand. Crick was awarded a year's salary from the superannuation fund whilst he recovered from his injuries. Major Warner later reported that

Crick "finding his health, as he thought, recovered, voluntarily resigned one quarter's pension and returned to his duty."

The recovery was short lived and in 1876 Warner informed the magistrates at the Easter quarter sessions that "for the last eighteen months John Crick has frequently been so ill as to be quite unable to perform any duty at all. He is now totally incapacitated from injuries received in the actual execution of his duty and I beg to recommend that he be superannuated on full pay."

Crick was subsequently awarded a pension of £62.8.0d per year, to remain in force for a period of three years. In April 1879, when Crick's case came before the magistrates again, the superannuation fund was dangerously close to insolvency. Crick was awarded a pension for a further three years but he was to receive just 10/- a week. Six months later in September 1879 the Inspector of Constabulary published his annual report. "A very strong feeling exists that the superannuation allowances on retirement after certain periods of service should be on a more defined and secure footing." In fact more than a decade was to pass before police pensions were granted as a right.

Although there was general discontent at the provisions made for police pensions the wage rise enjoyed by the officers of the Bedfordshire Constabulary in 1876 did much to maintain their morale.

The Stagsden Child Murder.

In the spring of that year the force began its investigation of a case which became known as 'The Stagsden Child Murder'. At twenty minutes to six in the evening on Monday, 20th March 1876 a gamekeeper, shooting in Stagsden side gate plantation, discovered a black parcel concealed in the undergrowth. On further examination the parcel proved to be a black skirt wrapped round the body of a dead child. The police were called to the scene and Police Sergeant Mardlin attended from Turvey with Doctor Swinson. The doctor concluded that the child had died of asphyxia and this was confirmed by the post mortem.

Extensive enquiries were made throughout the north of Bedfordshire and on Tuesday, 4th April Sergeant Mardlin travelled to Hampstead in North London to arrest a maidservant by the name of Lucy Lowe. Her employer, the Reverend Joshua Kirkham, believing that a warrant was required, tried to prevent the arrest. The clergyman summoned the Metropolitan Police to his assistance only to be informed by them that the sergeant was acting with proper authority. Sergeant Mardlin later testified: "I caught hold

One of the earliest examples of prison photography. Lucy Lowe who murdered her child at Stagsden

of her arm and said I should not let her go, for no one."

The Bedfordshire newspapers described the prisoner as "about thirty-five years of age and a native of Stagsden, where her parents still reside. Her first husband died some few months after marriage and her second husband deserted her, leaving in her hands three children, all of whom are in the Bedford Workhouse."

Lucy Lowe was tried for murder at the summer assizes held in Bedford on the 3rd July 1876. The evidence against her had been pieced together from enquiries in Hampstead, Bedford and Stagsden which revealed a complete picture of her movements in the first months of 1876. Lowe had left the Kirkhams' employ on January 3rd that year stating that she had obtained a position working for her uncle. Apparently neither of the Kirkhams were aware that Lowe was pregnant.

On the 26th February she was confined at 66, Greyfriars Walk, Bedford, where she gave birth to a baby girl. She subsequently told her landlady at Bedford, Mrs Priscilla Hull, that the baby was to be brought up by relatives, a childless married couple living in Derby. Mrs Hull saw Lucy Lowe leave Bedford with her baby on a train bound for Turvey at 11.15 a.m. on the 11th March. At 1.30 p.m. the same day Lowe arrived at her parents home in Stagsden but without her baby. Her parents knew nothing of her pregnancy and believed their daughter was simply visiting. On the 22nd March Lowe called on Mrs Hull in Bedford, stating that the baby had been taken to Derbyshire. The following day she returned to London and managed to secure her old position with the Kirkhams.

Several additional pieces of evidence sealed the case against Lucy Lowe. It transpired that the clothes found on the dead child had been taken from Mrs Kirkham's wardrobe by the accused. Indeed, one piece of ticking found on the baby matched a second piece found in Lowe's possession at the time of her arrest. Sergeant Mardlin testified: "Both must have formed one piece for they correspond exactly where the piece was cut." Mrs Hull gave evidence that Lowe left Bedford with her baby but did not take any of the baby's clothes or its bottle. In retrospect this was seen as proof that the accused had intended to murder the child, as it appeared she knew the baby would not need further food or clothing.

The defence argued that the child had been unwell and had died of natural causes. Lowe did not take the stand but a prepared statement was submitted to the court. "On the 14th day of March when I left Turvey station the weather was very cold. I wrapped the child in three shawls and carried it along until I got through Stagsden side gate when the child had a fit and died almost immediately. I was very frightened and I left it where it was afterwards found."

The jury took twelve minutes to return a verdict of guilty against Lucy Lowe. "The learned judge, assuming the black cap, proceeded to pass sentence of death." The jury's recommendation of mercy was forwarded to the appropriate authorities and on Saturday, 22nd July 1876 the Bedfordshire Times reported that "by an act of Royal Clemency the woman convicted of the wilful murder of her infant is suffered to escape the gallows for the dreary experience of lifelong immurement, a worse penalty to a sensitive mind." Lowe's reprieve received little coverage in the newspaper which featured a sensational account of the massacre of General Custer's troops at the battle of Little Bighorn.

Events in the South of the County.

In the autumn of 1876 the Inspector of Constabulary reported on the formation of the Luton borough police force. "On the 30th September, this year, the town of Luton in Bedfordshire, having a short time previously become a borough under the Municipal Corporations Act, commenced with a police establishment of its own, separate and distinct from that of the county, of which, to that date, it had formed part."

The new Luton borough force consisted of twenty-two officers – a head constable, inspector, two sergeants and eighteen constables. David Jaquest, an inspector with the county constabulary was appointed as the first head constable and most of the borough officers were recruited from the county force. The authorised strength of the Bedfordshire Constabulary was reduced by fifteen following the inauguration of the Luton borough police. Relations between the two forces appear to have been cordial and members of the watch committee at Luton expressed their appreciation of the assistance offered to them by Major Warner.

The county force was still responsible for policing the villages outside Luton, such as Hyde, Leagrave, Limbury and Stopsley. These villages which had previously formed part of the Luton rural area were now combined with the little that remained of the Luton division to form a new police district, reducing the number of police divisions in the county to six.

The station house at Luton was retained by the county constabulary as the headquarters of its Luton division. Under an agreement in force from the 1st January 1877 the town council was permitted the use of the court house for two days each week in return for the payment of a quarterly rent. The prisoners of the borough force were lodged in the county cells at a charge of "4/- for every day and part day."

In April 1877 the Easter Review was held in Bedfordshire. The review was a huge military spectacle involving large scale troop manoeuvres and a mock battle fought between two army divisions, each comprising three brigades. The scenario of the battle was described in the Bedfordshire Times. "An army concentrated at Cambridge marches on Bedford to sever the direct lines of railway connecting London and the North, detaching a division to the neighbourhood of Dunstable for the protection of its left flank." The division despatched to Dunstable was subsequently to encounter the advance guard of the opposing force at Totternhoe Castle.

The event occupied the whole of Easter Monday, April 2nd 1877 and drew vast crowds of spectators to Dunstable Downs. Major Warner deployed forty of his own officers to police the crowds together with twelve constables from the Buckinghamshire police. The Bedfordshire Times reported the excellent order maintained amongst the spectators. "By the admirable foresight of Major Ashton Warner, Chief Constable of Bedfordshire, a strong force of county police had been detailed to patrol the battleground and keep civilians back from the different positions where the stress of fighting was likely to be most felt."

The review received national press coverage and at the Easter quarter sessions held in Bedford on the following day Major Warner was congratulated by members of the court, who were "glad to see in the London newspapers that our county police and chief constable got great praise for the order kept on the occasion of the review."

Standing Orders and Instructions.

Warner's thorough planning for the policing of major events such as the Royal Agricultural Show and the Easter Review was matched by his methodical administration of constabulary affairs in general. He sought to achieve greater uniformity in the Bedfordshire force by introducing standard operating procedures throughout the whole of the county.

In 1878 the chief constable directed his officers to discontinue the use of parish cages and lock-ups for the detention of prisoners. All persons arrested were to be transported to the divisional station house for the purpose of confinement. In the same year Warner

The Easter Review of April 1877 involved a mock battle fought on Dunstable Downs

distributed the "Bedfordshire Constabulary guide to official letter writing." This guide set out various formats which were to be followed in submitting offence and arrest reports. The constable had only to copy out the format, filling in the appropriate blank spaces to record the particular circumstances he wished to report. Each report was to be signed "I have the honour to be sir, your obedient servant." Bad language was not to be included in statements. "It is unnecessary for a constable to use the full words if he has at any time to report obscene language but give the first letters of the word, thus, B ----- or D --- ."

The guide to official letter writing also contained a catechism for the instruction of the constables.

"Q: What is a constable?
A: A keeper of the peace.
Q: How are you armed by law to preserve peace and to prevent crime?
A: With power of arrest or apprehension.
Q: How would you arrest without a warrant?
A: I would say 'I am a constable'. I would also say 'I arrest in the Queen's name'. I should state the cause of arrest and show my staff.
Q: Do mere words constitute an arrest?
A: No, I must actually touch the person when I say 'I arrest you'."

In another part of the catechism the constable is questioned about his power of arrest in cases of serious crime.

"A: In cases of treason or felony I may arrest anyone on a reasonable suspicion or on a charge being made although I did not see any part of the transaction.
Q: What should be the grounds for such suspicion?
A: 1. The rational statement of a person worthy of credit.
2. Being found in circumstances of a suspicious character such as being near a murdered body or having blood on the clothes or person.
3. Being in company with persons known to be felons or offenders.
4. Leading a vagrant and disorderly life without apparent means of support.
5. The common fame of the country."

The questioner proceeds to ask about a case in which the victim of a serious assault may die.

"Q: Supposing the suspected person absconds. What would you do?
A: I would raise a hue and cry after him.

Q: What do you mean by 'hue and cry'?
A: The old common law process of pursuing by horn and voice all felons and such as had dangerously wounded another."

The guide to official letter writing supplemented the book of instructions each constable carried with him whilst on patrol. Although Captain Boultbee had issued instructions to the force, the earliest surviving copy of full "Orders and Instructions for the guidance of the Bedfordshire Constabulary" dates from Major Warner's tenure of office as chief constable. These "orders and instructions" were bound in a sixty-five page, hardbacked, pocket size book, and formed a remarkably comprehensive guide to all aspects of police work in the 1870s.

The first part of the book dealt with the conditions of service for constables. Some of the early police regulations were similar to those still in existence. "All persons are to consider themselves on probation for the first fifty-six days after entering the Bedfordshire Constabulary. Every constable will be furnished with a warrant card which is to be kept clean and not to be parted with on any pretext whatsoever."

Other regulations reflected the harsh conditions of police service in the Victorian era. "Any constable guilty of neglect of his duty shall be liable to a penalty of £10 and imprisonment with hard labour for one month. 5/- will be deducted from the pay due to each person on his quitting the Bedfordshire Constabulary for the purpose of having his uniform altered for his successor."

In prefacing the section of the instruction book dealing with constabulary duties, Major Warner outlined his basic philosophy of policing. "It should be understood at the outset that the principal object to be attained is the prevention of crime. It is imperative to protect the property and liberty of Her Majesty's subjects, not to infringe upon them."

More detailed instructions followed. Prisoners being transported to court or to the divisional station house were to be handcuffed. "Nothing reflects greater disgrace on a constabulary than the escape of a prisoner save that of any of the members acting or speaking falsely."

Constables were only permitted to ask questions to establish whether there was sufficient evidence to arrest a suspect. "As regards questioning prisoners whilst in custody, it has been well observed that no practice is more censurable and unjust than that so common amongst officers of justice of putting questions to parties in their custody with the view of obtaining answers that may afterwards be used in evidence against them. It should be borne in mind by constables that it is no part of their duty to make evidence. It is an abuse of power and authority in any police officer to question an accused person."

Miscellaneous instructions governed the conduct of police officers. "The members of the force must practice the most complete sobriety, one instance of drunkenness will render any of them liable to dismissal." The constables were to "frequently report themselves to every magistrate residing in their beat and also call on the clergymen and farmers." They were "not to impart any information to the press" and were always to take the outward side of the footpath when passing fellow pedestrians. "It is particularly desired that constables when walking along the street should not shoulder past respectable people but give way in a mild manner. The more respectful and civil the constabulary are, the more they will be supported and respected by the public in the proper execution of their duty."

As far as practicable superintendents were to arrange the duties of the men "as to permit the attendance of the constabulary at divine service at least once a day on Sundays and other Holy Days."

The "instructions and orders" contained a wealth of practical information such as "the hours during which public houses may be open. In populous places from 6 a.m. till 11 p.m. on weekdays, and on Sundays, Christmas Day and Good Friday from 12.30 p.m. to 2.30 p.m. and from 6 p.m. to 10 p.m." In rural areas closing time was one hour earlier on weekdays. Detailed instructions were given as to the action to be taken in relation to various crimes. "In cases where a sheep is slaughtered in the field and the carcase skinned and carried off, the thieves almost invariably reside close at hand, the constable will therefore consider who are the most likely persons and unknown to them will set a watch at night upon their houses to discover whether they leave them for the purpose of bringing home a portion of the meat."

At a burglary, or a "house robbery" as it was then known, a constable was to "judge from the manner in which it has been effected, whether the thief appears to have been acquainted with the premises or is a stranger." Further he was to observe "if an entrance has been at once effected, or if the doors and windows have been in the first instance ineffectually attempted to be forced. He must then closely examine the ground under the windows and around the house for footmarks, which are carefully to be observed, and after being measured must be securely covered with boards or other means of protection in order to preserve them. The direction taken by the thieves, both in coming to and going from the house, is if possible to be ascertained, and for this purpose an examination must be made in the fields and lanes around the place at the distance of fifty, one hundred and two hundred yards. The constable will then enquire at all the beer shops and public houses in the neighbourhood as to what persons have called or have been lodging there. In the event of very recent information and where there is any likelihood of overtaking the guilty party, the constable will be justified in hiring a horse or other conveyance and proceeding in pursuit."

The final part of the "instructions and orders" was concerned with the constable's powers of arrest. "The principal felonies are murder, manslaughter, rape, robbery, cattle, horse and sheep stealing, also setting fire to any house, outbuilding, stacks or crops. Minor offences are called misdemeanours, such as frauds, riots, and assaults." The distinction between a felony and a misdemeanour determined the constable's power of arrest. "The constable must arrest anyone whom he sees in the act of committing a felony, or anyone whom another positively charges with having committed a felony. He may arrest one whom he has just cause to suspect to be about to commit a felony. Though no charge be made, yet if a constable suspect a person to have committed a felony he should arrest him, but the constable must be cautious in thus acting on his own suspicions. A constable in a case of assault (or other misdemeanour) which has not been committed in his presence, or within his view, is not authorised to arrest." Such cases were proceeded with by way of summons.

Major Warner's comprehensive instructions and approved guide to official letter writing typified his attention to detail and his concern for thorough training. The Bedfordshire Mercury praised the chief constable for his exceptional administrative abilities, his firm but temperate maintenance of discipline and for his principal achievement, "the cohesion which he effected in the force." Warner maintained the high standards set by Captain Boultbee but ensured that the force adapted itself to the changing requirements of Victorian society and parliamentary legislation.

Unexpected Death of Major Warner.

Tragically Major Warner's first wife and child died shortly after he assumed command of the Bedfordshire Constabulary. He remarried and started a second family but unfortunately he did not live long enough to see his four children grow up.

On Wednesday, 19th November 1879 Warner spent a day's shooting with a friend at Flitwick. He contracted a chill during the hunting expedition and was confined to bed for ten days with a severe chest infection. It may have been that Major Warner had never fully recovered from the damage done to his health during the suffering and privation at Lucknow and on Friday, 29th November 1879, at the age of forty-four years, he died from acute haemorrhaging of the lungs.

The funeral was conducted at St. Peter's Church, Bedford, on the following Thursday when the six superintendents of the county constabulary acted as pallbearers. Other officers from the county and borough forces lined the path leading to Major Warner's final resting place in Bedford cemetery.

Major Warner's untimely death was totally unexpected and Superintendent Shepherd of the Leighton Buzzard division was placed in temporary charge of the constabulary until the 21st February 1880 when Colonel Josselyn assumed command of the force. Josselyn's tenure of office was to extend well into the twentieth century.

LIEUTENANT-COLONEL FREDERICK J. JOSSELYN

CHAPTER FOUR

1880 – 1910
LIEUTENANT-COLONEL JOSSELYN

FREDERICK John Josselyn was born on 4th December 1840 at Market Weston Hall, Suffolk, and spent his early life in Bury St. Edmunds. His ancestors came from an Essex family whose line of descent dated from the reign of Henry III. At the age of eighteen Josselyn joined the Army as an ensign in the 96th Foot Regiment but quickly gained promotion to lieutenant and later to captain. A keen cricketer, he was captain of the regimental eleven and whilst serving in South Africa at the Cape of Good Hope and in India he took advantage of the opportunity to go big game hunting. The trophies from these shooting expeditions abroad later adorned the walls of Colonel Josselyn's home in Bedford.

In December 1875 Josselyn was appointed adjutant of the Bedfordshire Light Infantry Militia and consequently he was left in command of the regiment for eleven months each year. When Josselyn applied for the chief constableship of Bedfordshire he was already an established and respected figure in the county. His application was supported by testimonials from R. T. Gilpin, MP, of Hockliffe Grange, Leighton Buzzard, and William Stuart of Tempsford Hall, Sandy, who was both Josselyn's commanding officer and the chairman of the Bedfordshire Court of Quarter Sessions.

Josselyn's only serious rival for the post was a man named Beauchamp St. John but in the voting at the adjourned Epiphany quarter sessions in February 1880 Josselyn received the votes of twenty-nine of the justices against just twelve votes cast in favour of St. John. Josselyn was duly appointed Chief Constable of Bedfordshire and within a few months he had retired from the Army with the rank of lieutenant-colonel. Superintendent Shepherd received payment of £20 for his services as acting chief constable after the death of Major Warner.

In the months immediately following Colonel Josselyn's appointment an acrimonious dispute arose between the county quarter sessions and the Luton town council concerning the Luton station house. Her Majesty's Inspector of Constabulary had criticised the Luton borough police premises established in the Plait Hall as "very small for a police office." The authorities at Luton had approached the county magistrates with a view to purchasing the county police station situated in the borough and the sale had been agreed upon in principle. However, the negotiations stumbled on the question of the purchase price. The borough offered £1,000 for the buildings, approximately half the sum asked for by the county.

A conference held in 1881 to resolve the dispute illustrates the cool relations between the county and borough officials. Sir John Montagu Burgoyne spoke on behalf of the county magistrates. "I must remind the gentlemen representing the borough of Luton that they come to us and ask us to give up our police station for their convenience and then offer us a sum which is about £1,000 less than our valuer advises. I don't think the borough of Luton have met us at all in the spirit in which we have met them." Alderman Gilder on behalf of the Luton delegation replied: "We do not come here to be stigmatised as trying to catch the county authorities out." The mayor of Luton proceeded to offer £1,500 for the purchase of the police station but when this initiative was flatly rejected the conference ended in deadlock.

In June 1882 the borough of Luton raised their offer to £1,600 but the quarter sessions declined to re-open negotiations on the purchase. The long running dispute reached near farcical proportions in 1883 when the Luton authorities finally agreed to meet the full purchase price of £2,070 asked by the county. At a meeting held to finalise the details of the sale it became apparent that the Luton delegation believed the court house adjoining the police station was included in the purchase. When the mayor of Luton discovered the mistake he led his delegation from the meeting stating "the negotiations are at an end." The county force retained possession of the Luton station house for a further seventeen years.

During the dispute concerning the station house at Luton the county authorities had occupied the newly constructed Shire Hall in the St. Paul's area of Bedford. The chief constable was allocated offices in the new building and his old offices at Gadsby Street were converted into a constable's residence. The Gadsby Street station continued to act as the headquarters of the Bedford division of the county force but the new offices in the Shire Hall became the headquarters for the county constabulary as a whole.

The Shire Hall also contained a photographic room for the use of the county police. A camera and other photographic equipment was purchased from Mr Roberts, the governor of Bedford prison, for £17 and Colonel Josselyn notified his superintendents that, when necessary, prisoners could be brought to headquarters for photographing. This early experiment with the use of cameras was only of limited success and within ten years Josselyn reported that "the photographic plant which was purchased from Mr Roberts has become obsolete. I do not find it is often necessary to take these photographs and it would require not only new apparatus but frequent supplies of fresh chemicals to continue the work. I am of the opinion that it would cost the county much less if authority were given me to have photographs taken by some private person when the occasion arises."

Murder and Election Riot.

The two most serious crimes dealt with by the Bedfordshire Constabulary during the first years of Colonel Josselyn's chief constableship were both violent domestic murders. One of the cases involved the death of a ten month old baby at Tilbrook on 8th November 1881. Tilbrook did not become part of Huntingdonshire until 1896 and the Bedfordshire police were called to the village by Thomas Haines, a corporal in the Royal Engineers and the father of the murdered child. Police Sergeant Clarke attended the scene and detained Jane Haines, the twenty-five year old mother of the child who admitted killing her baby son. Sergeant Clarke later testified: "I went into the house and Mrs Haines said she got the child to sleep, took it upstairs, laid it on the bed, and then cut its throat. I went up into the bedroom and found the deceased lying on the left hand side of the bed with its throat cut. When I came down Mrs Haines went to a work basket and took out a razor, saying to me, that's the razor I cut the child's throat with. I don't know whatever made me do it. I think the devil must have got hold of me. It was a dear little thing, I did love it."

At the trial on Monday, 16th January 1882 evidence was given that Jane Haines had acted strangely ever since the birth of her son and on one occasion had made a serious attempt at suicide. She was found not guilty of murder on the grounds of insanity and ordered "to be detained during Her Majesty's pleasure."

A second domestic murder was reported to the police in May 1882 and subsequently George Battams, aged sixty-five years of age, was indicted for the wilful murder of his wife at Heath and Reach. George Battams had been off work for seven months with severe headaches at the time of the murder and had frequently quarrelled with his wife over her leaving him alone in the house when he was so ill. Early in the morning on Saturday, 6th May 1882 Battams fetched a billhook from an outhouse at his home address. Then as his wife lay sleeping, he struck her in the head with the pointed end of the billhook, killing her outright. At the trial on July 6th 1882 Battams' son stated: "Father's brother died in a lunatic asylum and he has another brother who is now an imbecile at the Ampthill Union Workhouse. His sister tried to commit suicide and died shortly afterwards. They were going to take her to an asylum." George Battams was also found to be insane and was detained at Her Majesty's pleasure.

Towards the end of the nineteenth century the police were frequently called upon to deal with public disturbances at election times. A police manual of 1883 contained the following advice on the action to be taken on polling days. "In those towns and villages where rioting is expected and where a large force is placed, the main body of the men should, if practicable, be kept under cover in the police station, a few constables being placed about the streets to keep order and give warning in case of riot. A few men in plain clothes should be employed to detect rioters and stone throwers."

The franchise for parliamentary and local elections had been progressively extended and the passion and excitement of politics was experienced by a larger proportion of the population resulting in occasional disorder. The third Reform Act of 1884 gave some agricultural workers the vote and in November the following year there was rioting on election day at Potton in rural Bedfordshire.

A mob of approximately one hundred and fifty persons assembled during the late afternoon of Friday, November 27th 1885. It appears that most of the rioters were predisposed towards the Conservative candidate, having been treated to free beer during the day by some wealthy supporters of that party. The Bedfordshire Mercury reported that "a body of roughs paraded the town doing a great amount of damage to property as well as injury to several individuals." The homes of prominent Liberal householders were stoned and many of their windows were smashed. The treasurer of the Liberal Association armed with a cudgel and poker was forced to repel rioters attempting to climb the wall at the back of his shop. A local Justice of the Peace read the Riot Act and when a detachment of constables from Biggleswade arrived at Potton the police attempted to intervene. The Mercury related: "Mr Edwards, a farmer living in Market Hill left his house to see what the row was about when he was set upon and knocked down. The police went to rescue Mr Edwards when they were all attacked. Sergeant Vincent was knocked down and lost his helmet. Pc Hull went to assist him when he was so seriously injured with sticks that he remained insensible for some time. The sergeant had his thumb put out of joint. Pc Bird was punched in the face and Pc Gilbert was hurt on the arm and mouth."

The police, only six in strength, were too heavily outnumbered to suppress the disorder which died down about midnight. The following day a large contingent of the county police arrived in Potton and there was no recurrence of the trouble. Subsequently eight men were convicted of assaults or acts of damage committed during the rioting although sentences were lenient. The election was won by the Liberal candidate, Charles Magniac of Colworth House, who duly became the Member of Parliament for North Bedfordshire.

Communications.

In August 1886 Colonel Josselyn issued an order establishing a code of police whistle signals. One long whistle requested the location of a constable and was answered by two long whistles. A rapid succession of short whistles indicated that a constable was in urgent need of assistance and was answered by two short whistles.

By 1886 the police were also beginning to make greater use of a more sophisticated means of communication, the telegraph system. Major Warner's instructions to the Bedfordshire force, issued in 1875, had authorised the use of the electric telegraph on occasions of urgency and importance. In 1886 the police almanac promoted an idea to make more economical use of the telegraph and explained the calculation of charges for a sixpenny telegram. "Up to twelve words are charged sixpence, and a halfpenny per word thereafter. Every word is charged for and five figures or under are counted as one word." The almanac published a list of chief officers of police, allocating each of them a number. "The object of numbering each name is to save words in sending a telegram. Instead of giving the name and address of the sender just the number opposite his name will be sufficient, as on reference to the list in the almanac the number will indicate the name and address of the sender." Bedfordshire was the first in the alphabetical list of county forces drawn up by the almanac and consequently Josselyn headed the list of chief officers. "No. 1. Beds. Lt.-Col. F. J. Josselyn, Bedford."

Within five years the almanac published a comprehensive police telegraph code which allowed detailed descriptions of wanted persons to be circulated by telegraph in just ten or eleven words. Each telegram was to follow carefully an agreed sequence using code words for thè most frequently used phrases. The established sequence printed in the almanac was as follows.

1. Offence or reason of message.
2. Person wanted.
3. Age, height and build. (To be conveyed in five figures).
4. Complexion, hair, eyes, whiskers and shape of face (five figures).
5. Peculiarities and distinctive marks (five figures).
6. Description of clothing (five figures).
7. Where likely to be found.
8. Instructions.
9. Code number of chief officer sending wire as in police almanac.

Using the code words listed in the almanac the phrase "wanted at this office on a charge of murder" was represented by the word "capital." The phrase "wanted at this office on a charge of shopbreaking" was represented by the codeword "banana." The almanac listed all the different likely offences, each with its own distinctive codeword.

Frequently used instructions were dealt with in the same way. The phrase "pawnshop to be searched" was represented by the codeword "lurch" whilst "if found apprehend and wire" was conveyed by the use of "nutmeg." Sequences of five figures were used to compile comprehensive descriptions of wanted persons. In considering build the almanac listed various types of build and allocated each one a number. "1. Stout, 2. Proportionate, 3. Slender, 4. Medium." A third "word" describing a suspect, aged 36 years of age, 5' 9" tall and of slender build would have read 36593. Numbers were similarly allocated to various hair styles, hair colouring, eye colouring, different types of clothing and so on until all the various facets of a description could be conveyed through numerical sequences. The message had to be decoded by the receiver using the almanac but the economics of the system ensured its success. By the time the police telegraph code was published in the almanac of 1891 the local administration of county police forces had been fundamentally reformed.

Administrative Reform.

A minor change in the financing of the Bedfordshire force occurred in January 1888 when the quarter sessions decided "that the present division of the county into six separate rating districts for police purposes should be done away with and one uniform police rate levied over the whole county." The force remained in six divisions for operational purposes.

Major changes in the administration of the force resulted from legislation contained in the Local Government Act of 1888. This Act provided for the creation of elected county councils similar to the town councils established under the Municipal Corporations Act of 1835. The administrative powers of the county Courts of Quarter Sessions were transferred to the newly formed county councils, but in considering the position of county constabularies the question arose as to whether the management of the police should be a judicial function performed by local justices or an administrative function performed by councillors. The Bedfordshire magistrates, in common with justices elsewhere, felt "that so long as the magistrates are responsible for keeping the peace of the county they should have full and undivided control over the means of preserving it." Those who sought greater power for county councils argued that borough councils had proved perfectly adequate in exercising control over borough police forces.

The Government reached a compromise, concluding that "The management of the police should be considered as partaking partly of the judicial and partly of the administrative character." A standing joint committee composed of equal numbers of justices and county councillors became responsible for the "raising and management" of county police forces. Further, the standing joint committee was to be financially independent of the county council. The administration of borough forces was unaffected and the management of county and borough constabularies remained very different in character.

In April 1889 the Bedfordshire magistrates assembled at the Easter quarter sessions in order "to conclude and generally wind up the administrative business of the county." The transfer of power to the county council was less dramatic than might have been expected as many of those elected to the council were Justices of the Peace who had previously taken an active role in the Court of Quarter Sessions. Ten county councillors were appointed to serve on the standing joint committee together with ten justices. The committee met for the first time on May 2nd 1889 when "It was resolved unanimously that this committee do elect William Stuart, Esquire as chairman." Stuart was the chairman of the quarter sessions and the new committee was anxious to secure continuity in the management of police affairs.

The first decisions of the standing joint committee concerned the amalgamation of the Dunstable borough police force with the county constabulary. The Local Government Act of 1888 abolished borough forces in towns with populations of less than 10,000 persons. Luton and Bedford had grown beyond this size and were unaffected, but in his report of 1889 Her Majesty's Inspector of Constabulary reported that on the 1st April that year "the police force of Dunstable, consisting of three officers was transferred to the county. An inspector was appointed in place of the head constable." Subsequently the standing joint committee secured the purchase of the police station at Dunstable for use by the county constabulary at a cost of £600.

Further Government legislation concerning the police was enacted in 1890. The Police Act of that year finally gave police officers the legal right to a pension provided they had completed twenty-five years' service or, in cases of retirement on grounds of ill health, fifteen years' service. The Police Act stipulated the maximum and minimum scale of pension awards and within this framework police authorities were free to choose their preferred scale. In Bedfordshire the standing joint committee adopted a pension scale just below the maximum allowed. The county constables were granted a pension equal to two-thirds of their salary after twenty-seven years' service. This was a generous award compared with the minimum scale under the Act which deferred the full two-thirds pension until thirty-five years' service had been completed. Constables who retired from the Bedfordshire force with less than twenty-seven years' service received proportionately smaller pensions. Contributions to the pension fund amounted to two and a half per cent of each officer's pay.

One of the first constables to be superannuated under the new arrangements in the county was Pc 17, Sturges. Colonel Josselyn certified that the constable "has served in this force for thirty-one years and is fifty-three years of age. His character has been good and his pension will amount to £47.13.0d per annum." The pension was granted from 4th August 1892.

In 1898 the standing joint committee of Northamptonshire sought "to call the attention of neighbouring counties to the present scale of pensions paid to the police and to confer with them with a view to adopting a uniformly lower rate of pension." The Bedfordshire standing joint committee replied by resolving "that the Northamptonshire county council be informed that this committee sees no occasion to alter the scale of pensions now in force in this county."

The legal entitlement to a pension was a significant advance in improving the conditions of service of police officers. Other improvements included the right to vote in parliamentary and local elections, granted in 1887 and 1893 respectively, and a better career structure. In 1889 the Bedfordshire Constabulary consisted of "one chief constable, five superintendents, one chief clerk with the rank of superintendent, four inspectors (one of whom has charge of the Sharnbrook division), ten sergeants and seventy-seven constables."

The larger establishment of the force provided more opportunities for promotion and a divisional command post was possible for a man in the rank of inspector. The working day had also been shortened. Bedfordshire constables had "as a rule to do nine hours duty in each twenty-four hours." However, each officer was still expected to be readily available for work at all times and there were no rest days. Annual leave was granted at the discretion of the chief constable who also decided whether leave would be paid or unpaid. Similarly, "if any member of the Bedfordshire Constabulary shall be absent from duty in consequence of ill health, the chief constable will exercise his pleasure as to stopping any portion of his pay during such absence." Further reform of police working conditions was to come early in the next century.

The Police Act of 1890 was not concerned solely with police pensions. It also sought to encourage greater co-operation between police forces with regard to mutual aid and on 7th September 1893 Colonel Josselyn received "an urgent application for assistance from the police authority of Derbyshire on account of the strike among the coal miners in that county." Josselyn despatched an inspector, two sergeants and twenty-two constables to Derby the same day. The officers were away for over six weeks and did not return to duty in Bedfordshire until the 21st October. A letter was sent to Colonel Josselyn containing "a most gratifying report on the conduct of the men. The chief constable of Derbyshire said that he had nothing but praise to say for them. Their conduct, their smart appearance, and the manner in which they had performed duties which had been difficult, were highly satisfactory."

Tales from the River Bank.

Earlier in 1893 there had been a considerable public outcry concerning unseemly behaviour on the banks of the river Ouse and Colonel Josselyn was eventually forced to bring the matter before the standing joint committee. "Constant complaints have been made to me of the nuisance to ladies boating on the river in the neighbourhood of Bedford, caused by persons bathing at all hours and places, and frequently without any bathing dress. I have instructed constables in plain clothes to patrol the banks of the river as frequently as possible but in the absence of any local regulations they are powerless to act unless in cases of indecent exposure."

The standing joint committee secured the passage of new bye-laws through the county council and during the following summer the constabulary brought several successful prosecutions for "indecent bathing." One of the first defendants to appear before the divisional petty sessions was Sidney Potter, an eighteen year old youth from Clarendon Street, Bedford, charged with "exposing his person in view of the river whilst bathing near the village of Goldington." The clerk of the county council prosecuted the case himself, in order to explain to the bench the circumstances under which the bye-laws applied. "It was a very serious case. The youth was seen to stand absolutely naked on a willow tree, then dive from the tree and swim across the river. For twenty minutes he disported himself on the bank playing with a ball with more grown men." The clerk of the council asked the bench to impose the maximum fine of £5 "to mark their sense of this disgusting conduct because, if it was not put a stop to, it would be absolutely impossible for ladies to go boating." The magistrates were less than convinced by this argument, noting that no one had passed along the river during the incident in question. Potter was fined the nominal sum of 1/- together with costs of 7/6d. The bathing nuisance proved a surprisingly emotive issue but the enforcement of the bye-laws and some cooler summer weather eventually caused the controversy to die down.

Colonel Josselyn was keen to build on Major Warner's work in the development of training and between 1892 and 1893 he purchased a number of new reference books for the use of the constabulary. "It would be advisable that the superintendents and inspectors of this force should be supplied from time to time with 'Stone's Justices' Manual' and the sergeants with 'Snowden's Constables' Guide'. Some detailed knowledge of the law is required and they often have to take responsibility upon themselves and I am certain would find these books of the greatest assistance." First aid training was also encouraged and in 1893 Her Majesty's Inspector of Constabulary reported that "seventeen members of the force hold certificates from the St. John Ambulance Association."

Biggleswade Polling Day Riot.

On Friday, 19th July 1895 there was another serious election day riot in the north of Bedfordshire. The disturbance occurred in Biggleswade where the Conservative Lord Alwynne Compton was standing for Parliament against George Russell, the Liberal candidate. The Bedfordshire Standard reported that the mood in the town turned ugly at an early stage. "A rough looking group of labourers displaying yellow Liberal favours congregated about the market square and behaved in a most rude manner to any who wore the colours of the Conservative Party." A Conservative banner had been tied high above one end of the square and "some of the roughs procured a sickle tied upon a pole with the idea of cutting it down but the appearance of Superintendent Cain upon the scene with a threat to take into custody any man who committed any damage caused them to slink away."

Later in the day the same mob attempted to enter the local Conservative campaign headquarters and "would probably have created a disturbance had not the sudden appearance of half a dozen policemen had a salutary effect on them." In the evening the Liberal candidate addressed a large crowd of his supporters outside the Biggleswade town hall. After his departure the crowd did not disperse, inflammatory speeches were made and fighting broke out. The police tried to restore order but "the crowd was too strong for them and they were compelled to retreat to the police station." They were attacked with sticks and some members of the five hundred strong mob shouted "kill them if you can." The angry rabble followed the police to the station house. "Here Superintendent Cain armed his men with cutlasses and they stood on the defensive behind the low wall in Station Road, the police station being literally besieged for some time. The sight of the cold steel rather dampened the ardour of the besiegers."

The mob gradually began to disperse but disturbances broke out again in the centre of town and several windows were smashed. At

10 p.m. Superintendent Cain telegraphed to Bedford for reinforcements. Colonel Josselyn had anticipated election day trouble somewhere in the county and had a sizeable contingent of constables standing by. However, the post office did not deliver the telegram until 8 a.m. the following morning and Superintendent Cain's request for assistance went unanswered. In the meantime the superintendent had sent for a local Justice of the Peace and twenty special constables were sworn in. Supported by the special constables the police regained control of the town and "by their tact and persuasion succeeded in dispersing the rioters without resorting to extreme measures." The following day a strong force of police arrived in the town and Colonel Josselyn travelled over in the early evening. There was no recurrence of the rioting and subsequently the police brought a number of prosecutions connected with the disturbances of the previous day. The standing joint committee received Colonel Josselyn's report of the events in Biggleswade and resolved that "strong representations be made to the Postmaster-General concerning the delayed telegram." Lord Compton, of Castle Ashby, won the election for the Conservatives.

New Transport.

In 1896 Colonel Josselyn approached the standing joint committee with a view to equipping each divisional headquarters with a bicycle. "I wish to bring to the notice of the committee the great use which bicycles have been in cases of robbery. In one instance in October last, information was received that a pony and cart had been stolen from Eastcotts, near Bedford. A bicycle was hired and a constable rode from Bedford through Ampthill, Silsoe, Barton, Luton, Hitchin, Shefford, and then back to Bedford warning all constables en route, and another constable went on his own bicycle from Cardington to Great Barford, Eaton Socon, Sandy, and Biggleswade, and on the day after to Stagsden, Newport Pagnell, Broadwell, Olney, and Turvey, the eventual result being that the pony and cart were recovered near Hitchin." The standing joint committee agreed to make funds available and on 11th April 1896 Josselyn reported that he had purchased six bicycles. "They were supplied by Mr Dan Albone of Biggleswade at £11 each and appear well built, serviceable machines." Josselyn also ordered that constables directed to use their own bicycles for police purposes should be paid an allowance of 3d per hour. Shortly after the purchase of the bicycles Colonel Josselyn acquired a Remington typewriter for the clerk superintendent at police headquarters at a cost of £21.7.0d.

On Tuesday, 22nd June 1897 Queen Victoria celebrated her Diamond Jubilee. Numerous parades, fetes and other events were held throughout Bedfordshire to mark the occasion and the standing joint committee resolved that "three days extra pay should be granted to each member of the county police force on account of the work imposed on them in connection with the celebration."

The Bedford Pig Fraud.

Later in the summer of 1897 the county constabulary successfully prosecuted a notorious case known as the 'Bedford Pig Fraud'. Bedford had long been an established pig breeding centre but some dishonest pig dealers had been carrying on a fraudulent business. The background history to the case appeared in one of Colonel Josselyn's reports to the standing joint committee. "For years past I have received letters from all parts of the country complaining that money has been sent for pigs in answer to advertisements by certain pig dealers living in Bedford and that no pigs had been sent and that they could not get their money back." Occasionally "a portion of the money might be returned or some pigs sent of much less value than those described in the advertisement. Otherwise the loss was total." Outbreaks of swine fever were common during this period and restrictions were frequently imposed on the movement of livestock. The restrictions were used as an excuse by the fraudulent dealers to explain delays in the transporting of pigs to their buyers. The Bedford borough police had investigated the case but their enquiries led them to believe that most of the cases involved should be dealt with through civil legal actions for breach of contract.

In June 1897 one of the crooked dealers left Bedford and bought a house in Kempston. Shortly afterwards he placed an advertisement in a farming magazine. "Pigs! H. Manton, Mabel Cottage, Battenberg Street, Kempston, near Bedford, has for sale forty pure Yorkshire pigs, eighteen weeks, 16/- each. Twenty-two weeks, 19/- each. Older, 25/- each. Berkshires, same age and price. Warranted healthy. Cash returned if not approved of."

Josselyn reported that "before long I received several complaints and instructed Superintendent Quenby to do his best to make out a case against Manton. Superintendent Quenby displayed not only zeal in the matter but caution so that there should be no loophole for escape if the man was brought into court." One of the difficulties of the case was that the victims of the fraud lived so far away from Bedfordshire. However, Quenby obtained evidence against Manton from three witnesses; a Glamorganshire farmer, a gardener from Staffordshire, and a smallholder from Middlesex. He was also able to prove that Manton "had no pigs at all when he advertised and owned no premises suitable for keeping pigs."

The case was tried before the county magistrates in November 1897 when the chairman of the bench, Lord St. John, of Melchbourne, found "that the prisoner had been carrying on a course of systematic fraud." Manton was convicted of obtaining money by false pretences and sentenced to two years' imprisonment with hard labour. Lord St. John commented that "the county police have been able to stop what the borough police apparently have not and great credit is due to them." The bench commended Superintendent Quenby, and the standing joint committee subsequently resolved to grant "to Police Superintendent Henry Quenby the sum of £10 in respect of the meritorious acts done by him." The reputation of the borough police was redeemed when they secured the convictions of two of Manton's associates and finally put a stop to the fraudulent pig dealing in the town.

Co-operation between County and Borough Forces.

As the turn of the century approached there was a marked improvement in the level of co-operation between the county and borough police forces in Bedfordshire. When the first generation of Luton borough police officers began to retire their pensions were paid jointly by the corporation of Luton and the standing joint committee of the county. In the case of David Jaquest, the chief officer of the Luton force, the clerk of the town council wrote to the county authorities: "I am directed by the watch committee to bring before the standing joint committee the question of the proportion of pension that should be paid by the county towards the amount payable to Mr Jaquest. His approved service in the county force was nineteen years and eight months." The standing joint committee resolved "that the corporation of Luton be informed that the county is willing to contribute the sum of £38.19.7d per annum towards the pension of Head Constable Jaquest." Similar arrangements were made with regard to all the officers who had transferred from the county constabulary to the Luton borough police.

Following the Police Act of 1890 Colonel Josselyn entered into agreements concerning mutual aid with both the Luton and Bedford borough forces. Two sergeants and nineteen constables from the county were loaned to the borough of Luton on the occasion of the parliamentary election in 1895. Three years later, in October 1898, forty officers from the county constabulary assisted the Bedford borough police during the visit of Barnum and Bailey's circus to the town.

In June 1899 the county police were again called to the assistance of the Bedford borough force during disturbances caused by the closure of the Old Priory recreation ground. The town council had decided to close the recreation ground after receiving complaints from residents of the nearby streets. The children who used the park, "many from the lowest part of town," were constantly making a nuisance of themselves. Further, young courting couples used the park to indulge in "flirtatious behaviour," playing on the swings meant for the children. "Not infrequently both sexes were on the same swing which was not only indecent but very demoralising and objectionable."

On Wednesday, 21st June 1899 a large crowd gathered in Priory Street to protest at the closure of the park. The demonstration was principally directed at the home of Mr F. Wiggins who was known to have complained to the borough council about nuisances in the park on several occasions. There was an incessant din outside the house as the protestors banged pots and pans together. There was also some stone throwing and several constables arrived in Priory Street "without, however, succeeding in abating the annoyance which continued until eleven o'clock at night."

The following evening the noisy protest resumed outside Mr Wiggins' house and the police were sent for again. "When the news arrived that a large body of police was appearing Mr Wiggins went into his front room to look, followed by his granddaughter, a girl of about fourteen years of age. At that moment a large stone came through the window and struck the girl on the temple with such force as to stun her and cut a gash from which the blood ran most profusely." The police were unable to identify those responsible for throwing the stone and though they tried to keep the crowd moving the demonstrators refused to disperse before nightfall.

On Friday evening the borough police sealed off the approaches to Mr Wiggins' house. Twenty constables were deployed in Priory Street as the protest resumed and when stones were thrown they moved in to make arrests. "Big crowds followed the prisoners to the police station trying to drag them away from the police, throwing more stones and whatever else they could get hold of. The same thing was repeated nine or ten times up to midnight." The next morning the whole of Bedford was alive with rumours of an even bigger disturbance planned for the coming night. The chief constable of the borough asked Colonel Josselyn for

Colonel Josselyn with veterans from the Boer War

Inspector Nottingham with the Sharnbrook division horse and cart in 1908

assistance and a force of thirty constables arrived in the town. Their presence acted as a deterrent to the demonstrators and there was no further trouble. The following week the council reluctantly re-opened the recreation ground to the public. The Bedfordshire Mercury succinctly described the entire affair as "a case of the classes against the masses."

Warmer relations between the county constabulary and the borough forces led the county into fresh discussions with the borough of Luton concerning the sale of the Luton station house. In September 1900 Her Majesty's Inspector of Constabulary reported on the success of the negotiations. "In the borough of Luton the purchase of the court house, police station and cells has been completed and the premises are to be occupied from 1st October." He also reported that the county force had built "a new station at Luton, comprising three cells and accommodation for a superintendent and married constable." This station house became the headquarters of the Luton division of the county police and stood directly alongside the old police station taken over by the borough force. Shortly after its construction the new Luton station house was connected to the public telephone exchange. The station telephone number was 90 and the installation cost £9. The Gadsby Street police station in Bedford had been connected to the telephone system just a few weeks earlier. The Bedford station house number was 21 and the telephone network provided the county constabulary with its first direct communications link between north and south Bedfordshire.

The Turn of the Century.

In 1900 fighting in the Boer War was at its height and several of the county constables had been called up from the war reserve to join the army in South Africa. Colonel Josselyn re-employed recently retired pensioners to make up the shortfall in the police establishment. Every member of the force contributed to a welfare fund which paid 2/- a week to the wives of officers serving in the war. These arrangements continued until the spring of 1902 when the Boers were finally defeated.

In the earliest years of the twentieth century the routine work of the police force came to include much tighter regulation of traffic on the highways. Horse drawn vehicles, bicycles and motor cars had all become the subject of Government legislation, and the summons register of the Leighton Buzzard and Woburn division of the Bedfordshire Constabulary gave details of the most common traffic offences. "Frederick Adams, Leighton Buzzard, timber merchant, aged forty years, summonsed for riding a bicycle on a highway without having a light attached at 10.20 p.m. at Leighton Buzzard on 27th March 1900. Fined 1/- and costs of 7/6d. Paid."

Drunkenness on the road was already a problem. "George Dixon, Leighton Buzzard, chimney sweep, aged thirty years, summonsed for being drunk in charge of a horse and cart on the highway at Leighton Buzzard on 25th October 1900. Fined 20/- with costs of 5/6d or one month's hard labour in default. Paid."

The Locomotives Act of 1896 abolished the earlier requirement for a man with a red flag to walk in front of a motor car and raised the maximum speed limit on the roads from five to twelve miles an hour. Delighted motorists held a special 'emancipation run' between London and Brighton. The anniversary of the run is still celebrated in the modern London to Brighton vintage car rally. Motor cars were rarely seen in Bedfordshire before the turn of the century but once they appeared the law was strictly enforced. "Robert Lievier, Toddington, gentleman, aged forty years, summonsed for being a person in charge of a light locomotive and unlawfully driving the same at more than twelve miles an hour on the highway at Hockliffe on 15th May 1901. Fined £5 with costs of £3.14.6d. Paid."

The speed of a locomotive was calculated by measuring the time the vehicle took to travel a set distance. "Arthur Du Cros, Regent Street, London, gentleman, aged thirty years, summonsed for driving a light locomotive at a speed greater than twelve miles an hour at Eastcotts, near Bedford, on October 4th 1902." The Bedfordshire Mercury reported this case in which Du Cros pleaded not guilty and conducted his own defence. During Du Cros' cross examination Constable Pedley explained the exact procedure he had followed in ascertaining the speed of the offending vehicle.

Pc Pedley: "I timed you four hundred yards in thirty seconds."
Du Cros: "Did you use a stopwatch?"
Pc Pedley: "No, my wristwatch. It has a second hand."
Du Cros: "Did you measure the road before I drove along it?"
Pc Pedley: "No, after you had gone by I measured the road to where I first saw you. I gave you the benefit of thirty or forty yards."

Du Cros lost the case and was fined £5 and costs.

Following the death of Queen Victoria in 1901, Edward VII succeeded to the throne at the age of sixty. The King fell ill just a few days before the date set for his Coronation on June 26th 1902 and the celebrations which had been planned across Britain and the Empire were postponed at short notice. In Bedfordshire the decision to delay the festivities led to two days of rioting in Dunstable. The Bedfordshire Standard reported that on the evening of Wednesday, June 27th 1902 a large crowd assembled outside the mayor's house in Dunstable demanding that the coronation celebrations go ahead as planned. When the mayor rejected their demands "the crowd proceeded to throw stones at his windows, shouting and using the most disgusting language. The streets were soon in a state of riot and after venting their anger at the mayor's house the crowd went in hundreds to the rectory."

Canon Macaulay had served on the committee organising the local coronation festivities and had been a leading advocate of the decision to postpone the celebrations. The mob "assaulted the reverend canon with filthy remarks and threats when the venerable parish priest left St. Peter's Church on Wednesday evening and he had to be escorted home by two constables." The rioters then set about stoning the windows at the rectory until the building "presented a forlorn appearance, almost every window being wrecked." The small force of police was powerless to intervene and "several respectable people who remonstrated with the crowd were roughly assaulted and kicked." The mob rampaged through the streets until just before midnight, when "a shout was made to light the bonfire. A mighty roar of approval went up and hundreds made their way to the downs where the coronation bonfire had been erected. The enormous stack was lighted and soon burned fiercely." When the flames eventually died down the fervour of the crowd subsided and they dispersed without further incident.

On the following morning "the town was perambulated by bodies of men threatening to cause more damage, and free beer was distributed from barrels in the open streets." Twenty constables from the Luton borough police force arrived at Dunstable police station and special constables were sworn in. Disturbances broke out again on Thursday evening when the mayor's house was stoned for a second time. The police managed to arrest some of the stone throwers but could not disperse the crowd. As darkness fell "the town was again made hideous with noise but in the face of extra police the scenes of wrecking of the previous evening were not repeated." The riot had been contained but not suppressed.

On Friday morning Colonel Josselyn arrived in Dunstable and special measures were taken. Beerhouses were placed under the close supervision of the police and extra patrols in the centre of the town prevented crowds from gathering. Later in the day a carefully controlled peaceful protest meeting was held, after which the town returned to normality. After recovering his health Edward VII was Crowned on August 9th 1902 at Westminster Abbey.

Double Murder.

Three months after the coronation riot at Dunstable the county constabulary investigated a double murder at Eversholt. The case involved an electrician named William Chambers, and his wife Emily. The couple had been married for fourteen years but Chambers had a history of violence towards his wife. Eventually, on 13th September 1902, Emily Chambers decided to leave her husband and went to her mother's house at Eversholt. Eight days later she instructed her solicitor to commence divorce proceedings. On Tuesday, 23rd September William Chambers sent a message to Emily asking her to return home but she refused. Later that day she was sitting in the kitchen at her mother's house with her sister and mother when William Chambers came to the back door. When the mother opened the door Chambers pointed a shotgun at her and said "now you old sod" before shooting her dead. He then turned towards his wife without saying anything further and fired a second time, killing Emily.

The murderer then turned his attention to the sister, saying "now I've one for you." The terrified woman ran to the next room and tried to shut the door. Chambers attempted to follow her and the barrel of the shotgun became wedged between the closing door and the doorpost. The sister held the door against Chambers' weight for a minute or two before fleeing through the front door of the house. She survived to give an eyewitness account of the two murders at Chambers' trial in November 1902. When Chambers left the cottage containing the bodies of his wife and mother-in-law he walked to the Falcon Inn at Eversholt. On the way there he attempted suicide by shooting himself under the chin with the shotgun.

Constable Whinnet was called to the scene of the double murder and arrested Chambers at the inn. The prisoner was tried at the winter assizes held in the Shire Hall at Bedford. He pleaded not guilty, stating "I don't remember anything about it." The defence argued that Chambers had suffered from temporary insanity on the day of the killings but the jury took only five minutes to return a verdict of wilful murder. William Chambers was sentenced to death and the execution took place on Friday, 2nd December 1902 at 8 a.m.

An editorial in the Bedfordshire Mercury carried a scathing

attack on capital punishment and reported that "a large number of the morbidly curious assembled outside the prison at the hour appointed but happily there was nothing to gratify their craving for sights which like the aforetime 'black flag' touch upon the gruesome."

The activities of the police attracted extensive coverage in the local press during murder investigations and incidents of rioting. At other times the professionalism and skill displayed by the constabulary in performing its regular duties went largely unnoticed. Crime detection rates were excellent. In the year ending 25th December 1903 thirty-three indictable offences were reported to the county police of which only two went undetected. One thousand, one hundred and fifty-one summary offences were reported during the same period and just six of these were undetected. Individual acts of bravery often received no recognition outside the courtroom and the ranks of the police force. In January 1904 Colonel Josselyn reported to the standing joint committee on one of many such instances. "On January 9th the Bedford divisional magistrates directed the conduct of Sergeant Nicholson to my notice with a recommendation that some reward should be granted to him. He apprehended a man who was drunk and had a loaded rifle in his hand with which he threatened the sergeant, who closed with him and after a struggle overpowered him. The rifle was discharged whilst they were struggling. Sergeant Nicholson displayed considerable courage and undoubtedly risked his life. I have therefore granted him the merit badge and pay."

By the end of 1904 the chief constable's office in the Shire Hall had been connected with the telephone system and the following year Colonel Josselyn asked the standing joint committee to consider equipping more police stations with telephones. "I have had application from some of the inhabitants of Leighton Buzzard and Biggleswade that the police stations in these towns should be connected with the telephone exchange. I think that it will probably be of advantage to the inhabitants but I cannot guarantee that a constable shall be kept permanently at the stations to answer calls." The standing joint committee subsequently authorised the connection of the Biggleswade, Leighton Buzzard, and Dunstable police stations to the telephone network.

Brickyard Trade Dispute.

The Bedfordshire constabulary gained one of its earliest experiences of policing a trade dispute between the 5th and 17th May 1905 when two hundred of the county's brickmakers went on strike. The reasons for the strike were fully documented in the local newspapers of the time. "The workers at the Klondyke brickyard at Wootton Pillinge, owned by Messrs Forder & Company, recently received notice that a reduction of 2d per thousand bricks would be made in their wages, this being in consequence of the slackness in trade. As this, in many cases, is equal to a reduction of 5/- in a man's weekly earnings the employees have come out on strike."

The employers threatened to bring in labour from out of town while the strikers stated that they would mount a mass picket across the entrance to the brickyard. Superintendent Quenby and Superintendent Woods were sent to Wootton Pillinge with a detachment of constables to maintain order. On 9th May fourteen men from Peterborough arrived at the brickyard under a police escort. However, "after hearing the cause of the strike they refused to start work and returned home in the afternoon, their railway fares being paid by a collection made among the men on strike. There was no disturbance of any kind."

The strike continued for another week but time was on the side of the employers. The strikers eventually ran short of money and were forced to return to work at reduced wage levels. The police were widely praised for their handling of the dispute and Colonel Josselyn commended his officers to the standing joint committee. "I think it is mainly owing to the tact and good humour of all the men on duty there that the strike ended without any breach of the peace or damage."

In 1907, towards the end of Colonel Josselyn's chief constableship, the standing joint committee agreed to equip all county police stations with telephones. Ampthill was connected to the telephone system in 1909 and Sharnbrook in 1910. Other developments included the employment of matrons at all county station houses to supervise female prisoners. These duties, which had previously been performed by officers' wives, were becoming time consuming and a more formal approach was long overdue. Matrons were first appointed in the summer of 1908. In October that year Colonel Josselyn also made arrangements for the use of "a small kennel of bloodhounds, kept near London, for the detection of criminals." The dogs received constant training and were available at short notice for a charge of five guineas.

In 1909 in response to instructions from the Home Office, the Bedfordshire Constabulary established a mounted police section. The six constables selected by Colonel Josselyn for mounted police duties were all ex-cavalry or ex-artillery officers. They were not placed on permanent mounted duties but were only deployed on special occasions and during emergencies. The six horses kept at the divisional headquarters of the force were trained to work amongst crowds and the standing joint committee authorised the purchase of mounted police truncheons, holsters, bridles, breastplates, breeches, and boots and spurs for the use of the mounted officers.

Royal Visit to Wrest Park.

On 7th July 1909 Edward VII instituted the King's Police Medal for heroic acts of courage and instances of conspicuous devotion to duty. Later in the same month Colonel Josselyn commanded a strong force of constables at Silsoe during the visit of the King to Wrest Park. His Majesty had been invited to spend a weekend at the house by the American Ambassador, Mr Whitelaw Reid, who used Wrest Park as his country retreat away from the embassy at Dorchester House. Barriers were erected round the entrance to the estate to control the crowds who gathered there hoping to catch a glimpse of the King. The arrival of Edward VII at 5.40 p.m. on Saturday, 24th July 1909 "was heralded by cheers all along the Luton Road" but the King passed quickly through the entrance to the estate and did not reappear that evening. "The rooms allocated to His Majesty for his private use were those over the library, facing south, so that the King had a fine view of the well kept pleasure grounds with a glimpse of Barton Hills in the distance."

On Sunday morning there was an even greater air of excitement in Silsoe. "The weather was favourable and long before ten o'clock large numbers of people crowded round the barrier to wait for the King as he went to church. Every wall and garden within sight was utilised and it was a wonder there were no accidents." The King arrived for the morning service at eleven to tumultuous cheers and flag waving. However, "on His Majesty's reappearance from the church the crush at the barrier was very great and it was feared the crowd would rush the police in their anxiety to see all." Fortunately the police were able to contain the crowd, calm was restored and nothing untoward occurred. On Sunday afternoon the King visited the Grey mausoleum at Flitton before departing for Goodwood at 9 a.m. on Monday.

The American Ambassador conveyed his thanks for the efforts of the constabulary throughout the weekend and the standing joint committee commended Colonel Josselyn and his officers. "Resolved that this committee express its extreme satisfaction to the chief constable for the manner in which he and his men carried

The officers who performed duty at Wrest Park, Silsoe, during the visit of His Majesty, King Edward VII, 24th-26th July 1909

The Shire Hall contained the County Police Headquarters from 1881-1947. Circa 1930

out the arrangements in connection with His Majesty the King's visit to Wrest Park."

The royal visit was the last major incident that Colonel Josselyn dealt with as Chief Constable of Bedfordshire. He was perhaps the most admired of all the early chief constables of the county. After his death the Bedfordshire Mercury wrote: "He was a born administrator. No more capable chief constable could be found in the four corners of the kingdom." Josselyn was respected for his skilful handling of police finances, often avoiding increases in expenditure through adjustments in the disposition of the force. He readily allowed the press and public to attend meetings of the quarter sessions and standing joint committee called to discuss the work of the county force. This practice earned popular support for the Bedfordshire Constabulary and was in striking contrast to the secret proceedings of the watch committees who controlled borough forces.

Colonel Josselyn also enjoyed a reputation as something of a diplomat with a knack for deflecting confrontation. He retained his love of sports throughout his life and became an officer of several local football and cricket clubs. He was still a fair cricketer and occasionally joined in a match with his constables. For many years he was president of the Bedford Swimming Club, frequently attending pool meetings as a judge and he was a regular member of the Oakley Hunt. Josselyn also involved himself in local agriculture, taking the presidency of the Bedfordshire Shire Horse Society and of the Bedfordshire Chamber of Agriculture.

Fire at Tempsford Hall.

In 1898 Colonel Josselyn had courageously saved the life of Major Dugald Stuart during a devastating fire at Tempsford Hall, near Sandy. Major Stuart was a local Justice of the Peace and the son of the first chairman of the standing joint committee. Josselyn had been staying with the Major for a few days shooting and on the night of Friday, November 11th 1898 Mr and Mrs Stuart and their guests retired to bed at an early hour. Fire broke out in the house just after 1 a.m. The Bedfordshire Standard reported that "in an incredibly short time the fine modern English mansion was alight from end to end and the sight was a truly magnificent yet awful one. Colonel Josselyn, the Chief Constable of Bedfordshire and Mr Bulkeley Hughes, a brother of Mrs Stuart, rendered most valuable assistance during the fire. The coolness and heroism displayed by these gentlemen is beyond praise."

Mr Hughes discovered the fire when he was woken by a crackling noise in the hallway. "He hurriedly got up and rushed to alarm Major and Mrs Stuart. He then lowered Mrs Stuart from her window by means of blankets and sheets tied together and then followed himself. In the meantime Major Stuart ran down the corridor calling Colonel Josselyn by name, but before he reached the Colonel's bedroom door he was overcome by smoke and fell to the floor. Fortunately Colonel Josselyn had heard the alarm and proceeding from his room came in contact with the prostrate body of Major Stuart, almost tripping over him in the smoke. Colonel Josselyn picked the Major up and endeavoured to get down the main staircase but this he found an impossibility. Hurriedly retracing his steps the gallant Colonel dragged him as far as he was able down a passage leading towards the back stairs but had to leave him while he went on to the door at the end of the passage in search of fresh air. Having recovered himself he went back into the passage and finally succeeded in dragging Major Stuart out and onto the top of the back stairs where Mr Hughes came to his assistance and helped to carry Major Stuart out onto the lawn."

Sadly Tempsford Hall was gutted by the fire but no lives were lost and Colonel Josselyn's reputation in the county was further enhanced by the story of his brave and determined rescue of Major Stuart.

Though he was happily married for many years Colonel Josselyn had no children. He was, however, very active in charity work for the young and founded the association between the Bedfordshire police and Miss Catherine Gurney of the Christian Police Association and Redhill Orphanage.

Declining Health of Chief Constable.

Towards the end of his life Colonel Josselyn's health was failing. In September 1910 he went to North Banffshire on a shooting holiday hoping that the air would improve his constitution. Unfortunately he contracted a chill in Scotland and when complications arose he was admitted to an Aberdeen nursing home. His wife travelled to his bedside from their home in Goldington Road, Bedford, and on 8th October 1910 Colonel Josselyn passed away.

The news of his death was greeted with great sorrow in Bedfordshire. In Bedford the church bell at St. Paul's tolled as a mark of respect whilst the Union Jack at the Shire Hall was lowered to half mast. Josselyn was cremated at Leicester and his ashes were interred in the family vault at Rougham, near Bury St. Edmunds. A memorial service was held in Bedford on 12th October 1910.

On Wednesday, 17th July 1912 a stained glass window erected

to the memory of Colonel Josselyn was unveiled in the Chapel of the Holy Trinity in St. Paul's Church, Bedford. Mrs Josselyn commissioned the superb window which depicted Joshua, the Good Centurion and St. Michael the Archangel, all typical soldiers from the scriptures. The Josselyn coat of arms and family motto 'Faire Mon Devoir' were also featured in the design. Colonel Josselyn was true to the motto throughout his life and it made a fitting memorial. The tribute paid to the county's third chief constable by the Bedfordshire Mercury was also particularly appropriate. "Colonel Josselyn was never given a title or degree by others but he had earned for himself the right to the highest title a man can attain, a C.E.G. – a Christian English Gentleman."

Colonel Josselyn is commemorated by a stained glass window in the Chapel of the Holy Trinity at St. Paul's Church, Bedford

LIEUTENANT-COLONEL SIR FRANK A. D. STEVENS

CHAPTER FIVE

1910 – 1939
LIEUTENANT-COLONEL SIR FRANK STEVENS

LIEUTENANT-Colonel Sir Frank Augustus Douglas Stevens was born in 1877, the eldest son of Colonel F. F. Stevens of Marlow in Buckinghamshire. Following in the military traditions of his family he joined the second battalion of the Bedfordshire Regiment as a second lieutenant in 1897. Stevens was promoted to lieutenant in 1899 and saw active service in South Africa during the Boer War, fighting at the battle of Diamond Hill and at the relief of Kimberley. He was mentioned in despatches during the campaign and was awarded the Queen's South African Medal with five clasps.

In April 1903 Stevens became the adjutant of the third battalion of the Bedfordshire Militia with headquarters at the barracks in Kempston. He also became the regimental recruiting officer which gave him a detailed knowledge of Bedfordshire as well as bringing him into regular contact with members of the county constabulary.

Stevens' term of office as adjutant was twice extended on the favourable recommendation of his commanding officer. He was promoted to captain in 1906 and that year, envisaging a later career as a chief constable, Stevens arranged to study under Colonel Josselyn at the county police headquarters at Bedford. Stevens attended the meetings of the standing joint committee and familiarised himself with police procedures and the workings of the law courts. In addition he attended an instructional course on the detection of crime at New Scotland Yard. In January 1910 Stevens resigned from the Bedfordshire Regiment intending to pursue his police career. At the same time he was gazetted a major in the Bedfordshire special reserve.

In October 1910 Stevens was one of eighteen candidates applying for the position of Chief Constable of Bedfordshire. His references included one from the late Colonel Josselyn written nine months earlier. "Major Stevens evinced great interest in all that he saw and learnt, and the experience which he gained cannot fail to be of use to him should he obtain a chief constableship."

On 22nd October 1910, the standing joint committee of Bedfordshire considered a short list of four of the candidates and quickly resolved, "that Major Frank Stevens be, and is hereby appointed, chief constable of this county." The Home Secretary confirmed the appointment on the following 19th November. Although Stevens was a major at the time of his appointment as chief constable, he later became a lieutenant-colonel as the result of the military duties he performed during the First World War.

The Police Forces Weekly Rest Day Act was passed through Parliament in 1910 and one of Colonel Stevens' first tasks as chief constable was to consider how to implement the legislation in Bedfordshire. The Act provided that "every constable shall be allowed at least fifty-two days in a year on which he is not required to perform police duty, save on occasions of emergency, such days being distributed throughout the year with the object of securing, as far as practicable to every constable, one day's rest in every seven." Sergeants and inspectors were also to receive weekly rest days and the legislation applied to ninety-seven officers of the Bedfordshire Constabulary. Stevens calculated "that the increase of constables required to bring this force fully within the operation of the Act will be seventeen."

Full implementation of the legislation was not compulsory until July 14th 1914 and Stevens proposed "that the Act be gradually brought into operation in the following manner:

Date.	*Increases in establishment.*
By 1st January 1912	Seven constables.
" " " 1913	Six constables.
" " " 1914	Four constables.
Total:	Seventeen constables."

Stevens' proposals were endorsed at a meeting of the standing joint committee held on October 21st 1911.

Industrial Unrest.

In the summer of 1911 there was widespread industrial unrest in Britain and a detachment of Bedfordshire police officers was sent to Liverpool where strikes by transport workers and dockers had resulted in serious disturbances. Stevens reported that "on August 15th I received a telegram from the Chief Constable of Bootle asking for police assistance as soon as possible. Inspector Bliss, one sergeant and thirteen constables immediately left for Liverpool. Owing to the railway strike I was obliged to recall these men on August 19th. I have received a letter from the Chief Constable of Bootle in which he says 'the detachment were a splendid lot of well behaved men and we are extremely sorry to have to part with them'."

The general railway strike called in August 1911 meant that Stevens required all his officers for duty in Bedfordshire. "On the evening of August 17th I received a telegram from St. Pancras asking me to protect the signal boxes on the Midland line. I also received a letter from the Home Secretary stating that it was the duty of the police force to give effective protection to all railway men within their jurisdiction who wished to work. This placed very heavy and anxious work on the police force."

The railway strike led to widespread attacks on signal boxes and serious rioting took place at Chesterfield and Llanelli. Troops were deployed during the disturbances resulting in some fatalities. The mood in the country was tense and Stevens prepared for trouble in Bedfordshire but there were no incidents of violence. "I made all the necessary arrangements for swearing in special constables. However, I am glad to report that throughout the strike everything was quiet in this county."

The strikes of 1911 and other instances of unrest in the early twentieth century led the Home Office to consider the need for a police reserve which could be called upon to assist the regular constabulary in times of crisis. A letter examining the options for establishing a police reserve was circulated to all forces and Stevens presented his response to the letter at a meeting of the standing joint committee held on 20th January 1912. "At present I have a list of fifty men willing to serve as special constables in time of emergency and I propose to increase this number to one hundred so that in the event of an emergency I could probably rely on obtaining the services of fifty. These men are equally distributed throughout the county so that if they were required, all the superintendents would have to do is to have them sworn in before one of the divisional magistrates. I am strongly in favour of this reserve as it will cost the county nothing until the men are actually sworn in when an emergency arises, but it will be necessary as soon as possible to inform these men what their pay will be when called out for duty as many have already asked. I recommend that the committee agree to pay 6/- per diem."

The standing joint committee resolved that, "the chief constable be authorised to organise a special police reserve for the county in accordance with the suggestions contained in his report." The police reserve was the forerunner of the special constabulary.

Chicken Thieves.

In March 1912 Colonel Stevens was delighted by the success of the constabulary in breaking up a fowl stealing ring. The Bedfordshire Standard reported that during the first two months of the year, "twenty cases of fowl stealing occurred in the Shillington district and could not be cleared up." Stevens related that, "the case in question was a most intricate one. The fowl stealing seemed to be systematic. I decided to send Sergeant Pedley into the neighbourhood from Leighton Buzzard to try and arrest the thieves. After working under the very greatest of difficulties for over a month Sergeant Pedley eventually brought to justice nine men who were implicated in fowl stealing and in thefts of hay and straw."

The cases were heard at the Ampthill petty sessions on Thursday, 29th February 1912. The principal thieves were James Kitson and William Arnold of Lower Stondon who were charged with stealing thirteen fowls, value £1.12.6d. Both men were sentenced to three months' imprisonment with hard labour. "Arthur Trumpton of the Three Horse Shoes Inn, Lower Stondon, was charged with receiving two fowls, value 5/-, well knowing the same to have been stolen." He was found to be at the centre of the fowl stealing ring and was sentenced to four months' hard labour. All nine men charged in connection with the case pleaded guilty and the chairman of the magistrates stated that the bench "wished to compliment Sergeant Pedley on the very able manner in which he brought to justice a gang of thieves whose depredations seemed to have been going on for a very long time." The chief constable also received many letters from the residents at Shillington "praising Sergeant Pedley's excellent work." Pedley had frequently been commended by the magistrates of the

Leighton Buzzard division for good detective work and had been awarded the merit badge on a previous occasion. For his work at Shillington he was granted a gratuity of £4. In May 1912 Colonel Stevens appointed detective sergeants in each of the six divisions of the force to investigate serious cases of theft and robbery.

Advances in Technology.

In January 1913 Colonel Stevens reported that the county constabulary had obtained its first motor car. "I have the honour to inform the standing joint committee that I have purchased an 11.9 h.p. four seater, Arrol Johnston car complete with hood, screen, head lamps, side and tail lamps, horn, spare wheel and tools, for the sum of £290. I should like to add that Doctor Bower, a motoring enthusiast, most kindly accompanied me to the motor exhibition and after we had seen all the cheaper cars we came to the conclusion that the above mentioned car was the best that could be bought for the money. Owing to the accident to the Luton horse and the condition of the horse at Leighton, I am stationing the motor in Bedford to work the Bedford and Sharnbrook divisions and I am transferring the horses at Sharnbrook and Bedford to Luton and Leighton. I hope therefore to make the motor do the work formerly done by two horses." The car travelled 7,164 miles during the first year of service and "proved to be of the very greatest use."

In the summer of 1913 Woburn became the last of the eight county police stations to be connected to the telephone exchange. The chief constable reported that, "the telephone system is being brought to Woburn. I have signed the necessary agreement to connect the police station with the telephone lines. The cost including an extension bell will be £5.5.0d per annum."

The following year, in April 1914, Colonel Stevens confirmed, "that the additional constables necessary to carry out the Weekly Rest Day Act of 1910 have all been obtained and the Act is now in full working order." Within four months the entitlement to a weekly rest day was suspended. On 4th August 1914 war was declared on Germany and the regular army was mobilised the following day. Nineteen constables belonging to the army reserve rejoined the colours on August 6th.

War Duties.

The declaration of war led to immediate problems for the police in maintaining order. There was panic buying of foodstuffs coupled with a sharp increase in food prices. Some traders behaved unscrupulously and the Leighton Buzzard Reporter carried an article outlining the grievances of consumers. "A good deal of criticism and anxiety has been caused locally by the rapid advance in the price of food which is pressing very hard on the inhabitants in the poorer districts. The ground for complaint is that grocers and provision merchants have sold at enhanced values, goods which they had purchased at the ordinary rate and thus doubled their normal income at the expense of the customers."

Discontent over food prices led to a riot at Hitchin on Wednesday, August 5th 1914 and there was a serious disturbance at Dunstable five days later. At 10.30 p.m. on the night of Monday, August 10th 1914, a crowd of up to two thousand people gathered outside the premises of Ernest Mowse, family grocer, tea dealer and provision merchant of 81, High Street North, Dunstable. "There was a strong feeling amongst the people against Mr. Mowse on account of his having raised the prices of goods and it having been reported that he said he could do without the trade of the lower classes." The gathering was intended as a protest demonstration but when the grocer refused to hear the grievances of the protestors, stones were thrown, the shop windows were smashed and the shop blinds torn down. Inspector Purser and a small force of constables formed a cordon round the shop and managed to prevent the commission of more serious offences. Purser reported: "It was impossible to stop the stone throwing, all I could do with the four constables was to prevent the shop from being looted and Mr. Mowse being fetched out by the people." The stone throwing continued for two and a half hours and the protestors did not disperse until 2 a.m. Public indignation at exploitation of the food shortage moderated the excesses of the worst traders and there were no further instances of disorder in Bedfordshire.

In his quarterly report presented to the standing joint committee of Bedfordshire in the autumn of 1914 Colonel Stevens outlined the measures taken by the county constabulary in response to the war emergency. "I have filled up fourteen of the nineteen vacancies caused by the mobilisation of the army reserve and hope to fill the remaining five in due course." Six of the reservists were married men and Stevens had taken steps to secure the payment of police reservist allowances to the wives of these officers. In addition he reported that, "the chairman of this committee has given me instructions to see that the wives of the constables now serving at the front should not be worse off than if their husbands were at home." Colonel Stevens made a point of paying personal visits to the families of constables serving in the Army to check on their welfare.

On the 4th September 1914 Stevens received an urgent telegram from the Home Office asking for qualified drill instructors to be sent to the nearest army depot to train new recruits for the infantry. The chief constable responded by sending four instructors from the constabulary at once and a further three instructors a fortnight later.

The loss of another seven officers exacerbated the manpower shortage in the constabulary. At the outbreak of the war many constables had been removed from their normal policing duties when the Home Office ordered that "vulnerable points in the county were to be watched by the police." Colonel Stevens consulted with the Chief of General Staff for the district to identify the installations which required protection. "I have had as many as forty men on this duty since 4th August." The police were called upon to guard railway bridges, all other important lines of communication and the reservoir at the Biggleswade water works. They were assisted in these duties by a large force of special constables.

The Special Constables Act of 1831 permitted the magistrates to swear in special constables when there was the threat of rioting or during an actual riot. In 1914 the Government hurried through new legislation concerning special constables and circulated a memo to all police authorities explaining the changes that had been effected. "You will see that under the new order special constables may be appointed although no riot or tumult may have occurred and that they will be appointed not, as at present, for parishes or townships but for police areas."

Colonel Stevens reported that, "six hundred men have been sworn in to act as special constables, some of them have undertaken very arduous duties. I especially wish to bring to the notice of the committee the names of the following gentlemen whose help to me has been invaluable. Mr Harold Allen has organised a motor patrol which works the whole county. There are two hundred special constables willing to carry out this important duty. The duties of the patrols are to watch the telegraph and telephone lines and patrol the roads of the county. The members of the patrol are out night and day using their own motors. Charles Lindsell, since the declaration of war, has been in charge of a section of the Midland railway line. He and his men, assisted by the regular police, have watched this section of the line by day and by night."

Special constables also provided another valuable service later in the war when there was the threat of enemy air raids. Colonel Stevens considered that it was "absolutely necessary to employ special constables in possession of vehicles, in case of air raids in rural districts where there are no telephones or other means of prompt communication." Those specials who were called upon to perform important duties using their own transport eventually received a mileage allowance amounting to 4d per mile for motorcycles and two seater motor cars, and 6d per mile for four seater cars. Pedal cyclists received 2d per mile. A small number of paid special constables assisted the police on a full time basis. Five such men, who were paid 5/- a day, helped the county constabulary to protect the water works at Biggleswade.

The extra wartime duties of the regular constables also included the registration and supervision of alien enemies and of Belgian refugees. They were additionally responsible for the billeting of troops and the tracing and arrest of an increased number of deserters from the Army. One of the most unusual duties of the police during the war was the registration of pigeon fanciers and issue of permits to the breeders. Pigeons were regarded as a potential means of covert communication between enemy agents.

The chief constable reported, "all these supplementary duties mean many hours extra work but the men have carried out their tasks in a most loyal manner." The officers received a war bonus for their extra efforts. The standing joint committee resolved, "that temporary, non pensionable allowances of 3/- per week be granted to all superintendents, inspectors, sergeants and constables and 2/- per week to all unmarried officers for the additional services rendered by them on account of the war." The bonuses were part of a national scheme and were increased from time to time in keeping with rising prices.

Colonel Stevens' own contribution to the war effort was immense. At the start of the war he informed the standing joint committee that, "The Duke of Bedford, with the sanction of the War Office, is about to raise and train a force in Ampthill Park to act as drafts to the regular battalions of the Bedfordshire Regiment now at the front. The Duke is very anxious for me to help him in the training of these men and has asked me to put the matter before the committee. It will not interfere with my duty as chief constable and I have obtained the sanction of the Home Secretary. I consider at this critical time that it is the duty of all officers with a military training to assist in their spare time in the training of recruits. I therefore trust that the standing joint committee will give me the necessary sanction."

The Duke of Bedford had written to Samuel Howard Whitbread, the chairman of the standing joint committee, concerning the matter. "I am very anxious to obtain the assistance of the chief constable, not as adjutant but as second in command." The police authority resolved that Colonel Stevens "be granted such leave of absence as may be necessary to enable him to assist in the training of the force at Ampthill Park." At the end of 1918, at the Swan Hotel in Bedford, Stevens was presented with a silver cup in recognition of his military services during the war. In presenting the cup the Lord-Lieutenant remarked that, "every day for the last four years Colonel Stevens has done four and a half men's work."

Serious Offences.

Although the police were concerned with civil defence and national security during the war they were still responsible for maintaining public order and dealing with incidents of crime. On the evening of July 5th 1915 Harriet Reeve was found murdered at her home in Plantation Road, Leighton Buzzard. She had been killed with a shotgun and one witness who attended the scene of the crime later testified, "the bottom part of her right cheek had been blown away exposing the jaw and there was a large hole at the base of her neck. Behind her the plaster on the wall was shot away and the curtains were saturated with blood."

At 7 p.m. the same evening Police Constable Clark was on duty in Leighton Buzzard when he saw William Benjamin Reeve, the husband of the deceased woman, stagger into Church Street with blood on his hands and neck. Reeve had attempted to cut his own throat. Pc Clark took the injured man into a nearby house and administered first aid. He was subsequently called to Reeve's house in Plantation Road where the body of Harriet Reeve had been discovered. He found a double-barrelled shotgun and a blood stained razor lying in the rear yard of the house. The shotgun had been loaned to William Reeve some months previously. Both barrels of the gun had been recently discharged but Reeve claimed that he could not remember anything that had happened at his home that evening. Police enquiries revealed that Reeve was unemployed and had spent the day drinking with a man named Major. Indeed, he had drunk nearly a gallon of strong beer before deciding to return home in the evening.

On his way back to Plantation Road Reeve stopped at his cousin's house where he had allegedly said to one of his relatives, "I am going to do my old gal in tonight," and complained that his wife never gave him any money. Harriet Reeve, in addition to bringing up five children, worked for a local firm of upholsterers and had been working all day on July 5th. She sent the children out of the house to the pictures when Reeve returned home, realising that he was the worse for drink. A short time later at 6.30 p.m. several neighbours heard the sound of two shots being fired from the direction of Reeve's home.

William Benjamin Reeve was tried at the Bedfordshire Assizes held in October 1915. He still maintained that he was too drunk on the evening of July 5th to remember anything that had happened. After hearing the evidence the jury took twelve minutes to return a verdict of wilful murder. The execution was subsequently carried out at Bedford at 8 a.m. on Tuesday, 16th November 1915.

Earlier in the autumn of 1915 Colonel Stevens had reported to the standing joint committee on a serious instance of disorder at Flitwick arising directly from the conflict with Germany. "I regret to inform the committee that on the night of Sunday, 12th September there was a disturbance at Flitwick caused by twenty-five soldiers who marched out from Bedford to attack the house of a man called Adolf Knuttel who is a German by birth but who had taken out naturalisation papers in 1899. The disturbance was caused by the troops seeing an article in a paper called 'John Bull' which stated that Knuttel had danced in the street when Warsaw fell and had laughed at a train load of wounded soldiers. There is not the slightest truth in either statement."

The soldiers broke several windows at Knuttel's house before forcing an entry and smashing up furniture inside the building. They searched every room for Knuttel but found that the only person in the house was his terrified mother hiding in a cupboard. Stevens reported that "the local constable was quickly on the scene and managed to a very great extent to calm the soldiers." He prevented any harm coming to Mrs Knuttel but was unable to stop further acts of damage. When the soldiers left Flitwick the police telephoned the military authorities in Bedford to have them arrested on their return to barracks. Subsequently there were problems in identifying those men responsible for specific acts of damage and there were no criminal prosecutions. The Knuttels received £36.7.0d in compensation under the Riot Damages Act.

Expenditure on police equipment was necessarily limited during the First World War. However, the Bedfordshire Constabulary did succeed in obtaining three new motor vehicles before the end of

1918. In 1915 Colonel Stevens purchased a Triumph two speed motorcycle at a cost of £48 for the use of the inspector at Sharnbrook. In the following year the force acquired two Allday & Onions two seater motor cars for £210 each, to be stationed at the Luton and Leighton Buzzard divisions.

Peace Day Riot.

The Armistice of 11th November 1918 ended the fighting in the First World War but Germany did not sign a final Peace Treaty until 28th June the following year. In Britain 19th July 1919 was designated as a holiday for a national peace celebration but at Luton, Peace Day came to be remembered for one of the most destructive riots in the history of Bedfordshire.

The borough council at Luton angered many of the townspeople when it published its proposed programme of celebrations for the 19th July. There was to be a procession, a sumptuous banquet for the mayor and a select group of invited guests, and the town hall was to be illuminated. There were no plans to hold a mass thanksgiving celebration and the guest list for the banquet did not include any war veterans. The veterans set about organising an alternative programme of events and proposed to hold a rally and thanksgiving service in Wardown Park. To their dismay the town council refused to allow the park to be used for such a purpose.

On 19th July the official procession set off as planned and stopped outside the town hall to be addressed by the mayor. He was received with jeering by many sections of the public and was unable to make himself heard. There were calls for him to explain the council's decision with regard to Wardown Park but no answers were forthcoming. Instead, alarmed by the increasing hostility of the crowd, the mayor and other officials retreated inside the town hall.

A section of the crowd surged forward in an attempt to storm the main doors of the building but a detachment of constables from the Luton borough police force was guarding the entrance. The Luton News and Bedfordshire Advertiser reported that "for some time Police Sergeant Matsell and his police colleagues held their ground. Finally, overpowered by sheer weight of numbers, the police were rushed and the door was forced open." Several police officers were injured during the fracas. Having entered the town hall the crowd streamed into the room set aside for the banquet where furniture was smashed and thrown through the windows into the street below. This first instance of disorder ended after

The remains of the Town Hall at Luton after the Peace Day riot

Officers taking refreshment at the Ceylon Hall in Luton during a lull in the disturbances following the riot

several ex-servicemen made speeches attacking the council from the steps of the town hall and the crowd dispersed.

Between 10 p.m. and 11 p.m. that night the crowd gathered again in the town centre. The borough police had anticipated further trouble but had been unable to obtain reinforcements from neighbouring forces who were fully committed in policing the celebrations held in their own areas. However, the regular police were supported by a number of special constables.

The crowd advanced on the town hall and showered it with bricks and other missiles, breaking every window in the building. "The doors of the town hall food office in Manchester Street were completely wrecked and Inspector Janes and his comrades repeatedly ejected from the room men who had gained entry and were endeavouring to set the place on fire."

Shortly after midnight the rioters succeeded in setting the town hall alight and the police, exhausted by their defence of the building against a succession of vigorous assaults, temporarily lost control of the situation. "The fire brigade arrived on the scene by way of Guildford Street but were prevented from attacking the flames owing to the fact that their hosepipes were severed in all directions." Shops were looted and petrol taken from a nearby garage was used to fuel the flames.

The police and the fire brigade eventually restored some semblance of order when they got a hosepipe working and turned it on the rioters before attempting to douse the fire. Subsequently troops were called out from an army camp at Biscot Mill. They arrived at the town hall at 3 a.m. and formed a cordon round the burning building, allowing the fire brigade to work unhindered and extinguish the blaze.

On July 20th police reinforcements arrived at Luton from neighbouring forces, including a large force from the Bedfordshire Constabulary and a smaller contingent from the borough of Bedford. The extra numbers of police proved to be the decisive factor in preventing further rioting. "That evening saw a fresh attempt to start a disturbance. There were threats to burn down the corn exchange and to rescue a marine who was allegedly in custody at the borough police station. An excited crowd went to the station house and gathered outside the gates where violent speeches were made." The crowd were warned that their gathering was illegal but "refusing to comply with a police request to disperse the mob found themselves attacked by a very strong force of police who charged down Dunstable Place and along Stuart Street with batons drawn, causing a number of casualties in routing the crowd.

Tackled in such a summary fashion the rioters soon faded away and after a wide sweep of the streets, in the centre of town, had been carried out by the police with complete thoroughness, order and decorum again reigned." Further attempts to start trouble on the following night were firmly dealt with in a similar manner.

Over £200,000 worth of damage had been caused on the night of July 19th but the police emerged with a good deal of credit for their handling of the riot. They were praised by both the local press and by the judge who heard the criminal cases against the rioters at the Bedfordshire Assizes held in October 1919. Seventeen of the defendants appearing at the assizes were given gaol sentences ranging from three months to three years.

Pay and Conditions.

At the end of the First World War police pay, though differing from force to force, had gradually fallen well below the average industrial worker's wage. This was despite the payment of the war bonus, and some policemen and their families were suffering genuine poverty. Discontent over pay led to the creation of an unofficial union and, in some parts of the country, to police strikes. Bedfordshire was unaffected by the strike action but a Government committee of enquiry appointed in response to the general discontent, and headed by Lord Desborough, recommended that police pay and conditions of service should be improved and standardised for all police forces in England and Wales. Subsequently these recommendations were adopted in the Police Act of 1919 which empowered the Home Secretary to issue regulations governing both the wages and working conditions of the police. Wages were dealt with first.

In November 1918 a new recruit in the Bedfordshire Constabulary received 40/- a week and his pay could rise in increments to 50/- a week after twenty years' service. Sergeants received between 53/- and 57/- a week according to length of service and inspectors between £160 and £180 per annum. Superintendents were paid between £220 and £280 a year whilst the chief constable's annual salary amounted to £600 plus £100 for travelling expenses.

The national pay scales recommended by the Desborough committee resulted in substantial wage rises for Bedfordshire police officers. The standing joint committee of the county resolved that the increases should be effective as of 1st April 1919. From that date constables were to receive 70/- a week on appointment rising by increments to 90/- after ten years' service and finally through further increments to a maximum of 95/-.

Under the new pay scales sergeants received between £5 and £5.12.0d a week, inspectors between £310 and £350 a year and superintendents between £400 and £460 per annum. The vast differences in size between the various police forces made it impossible to fix a uniform rate of salary for chief police officers although general guidelines were given. The Bedfordshire standing joint committee set the starting annual salary of the chief constable at £750 to rise to a maximum of £800 plus travelling expenses of £150 per annum.

In addition to these wage rises police officers were also to receive a rent allowance, and in Bedfordshire it was resolved that "the rents, rates and taxes of all houses occupied by the police with the approval of the chief constable be paid by the county within the limits specified in the table below:"

Rank	*Amount per annum.*
Constable	£15
Sergeant	£18
Inspector	£21
Superintendent	£30
Chief Constable	£100

The large increase in expenditure on the police resulting from improved wages and the new allowances led the Government to increase the exchequer grant paid to local police authorities. Under the 1919 Police Act the exchequer grant was to cover fifty per cent of the total cost of policing, not just fifty per cent of the cost of pay and clothing.

Apart from the question of pay, the discontent in the ranks of the police service had been fuelled by the lack of any representative body or union to promote the interests of ordinary police officers. The Police Act also rectified this situation through the creation of the Police Federation.

Colonel Stevens reported to the standing joint committee that: "Section one and the schedule to the Act provide for the establishment of an organisation which will include all members of the police force in England and Wales below the rank of superintendent and through which the various ranks will be able, by means of their selected representatives, to bring to the notice of the authorities all questions affecting the welfare and efficiency of the police other than questions of discipline. In each force there will be branch boards elected by the men. These boards will choose

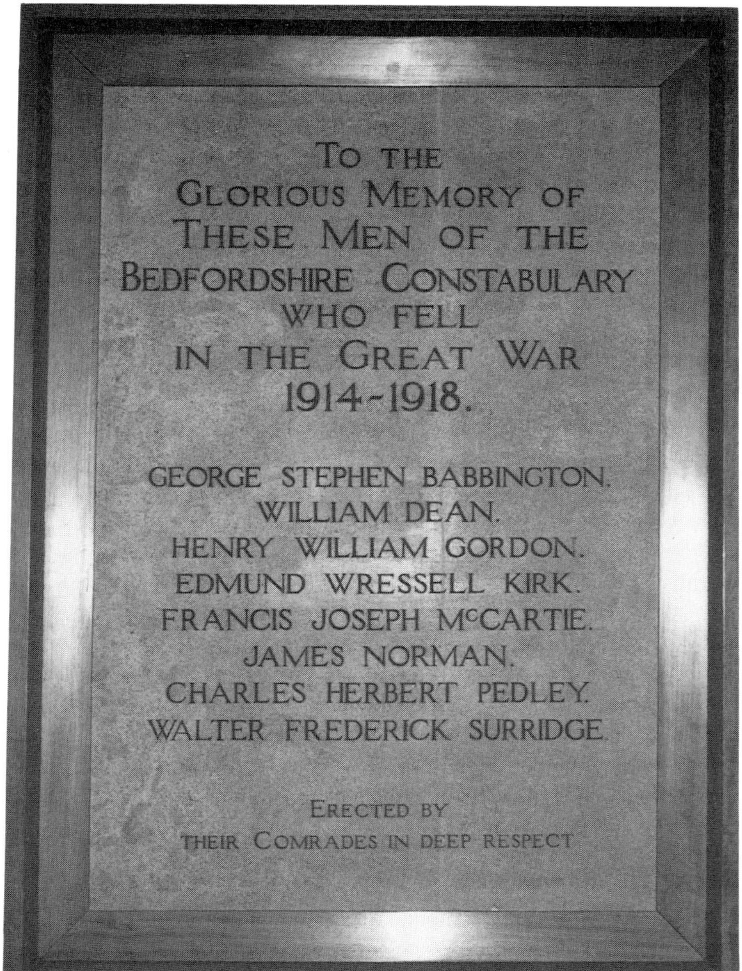

The Bedfordshire branch of the newly established Police Federation requested a memorial stone for the county constables killed in the First World War

delegates to attend the central conference, which is to meet annually, and the central conference will appoint a standing central committee. I have formed a branch board in Bedfordshire consisting of one inspector representing the inspectors, two sergeants representing the sergeants and one constable from each of the six divisions. The board meets quarterly a few weeks before the quarterly meeting of the standing joint committee. The delegates on the branch board have elected the following officers to represent them at the central conference: Inspector Vincent, Sergeant Church and Constable Pickering."

The first meeting of the branch board was held on 22nd December 1922 and one of the earliest resolutions passed by the board requested that a Roll of Honour be fixed in a conspicuous place at the Shire Hall "to the memory of our fallen comrades in the Great War." Colonel Stevens supported the resolution and the standing joint committee duly commissioned a memorial stone.

The nationally elected representatives of the police federation formed part of the 'Police Council' which met for the first time in the summer of 1920. The council, which also comprised delegates from the Home Office, local authorities and the senior ranks of the police service, was an advisory body constituted "for consideration of general questions affecting the police." Its first major task was to consider the recommendation of the Desborough committee concerning standardisation of the conditions of service of police officers. The council spent four days in discussion, finding areas of agreement between all the various parties concerned in the operation of the police. Subsequently the Home Secretary, using his powers under the Police Act of 1919, issued new police regulations which came into force on 1st October 1920.

The regulations established an eight hour working day for police officers, rates of overtime pay, a uniform discipline code and a statutory entitlement to twelve days' annual leave for constables rising to forty-two days' leave for chief constables. The regulations also stipulated that no one without previous police experience should be appointed as a chief constable unless they had exceptional qualifications. This was to prove significant when the standing joint committee of Bedfordshire eventually sought to appoint Colonel Stevens' successor.

The Desborough committee had also recommended slight alterations in the administration of police pensions. The suggested changes were implemented in the Police Pensions Act of 1921 which established pension awards of half pensionable pay after twenty five years' service and two-thirds pensionable pay after thirty years' service. These pension scales have remained in force up to the present day although contributions have now increased to more than one tenth of officers' pay.

There were a number of other significant developments affecting the police service in the aftermath of the First World War. The Police Federation was only one of a number of representative bodies to emerge between 1918 and 1921. A series of district conferences of county and borough chief constables had been established during the latter part of the war to co-ordinate the police response to civil defence. Each district sent delegates to a Central Conference of Chief Constables chaired by officials from the Home Office. At the end of the war these arrangements were kept in being and adapted to a peacetime role. A separate Association for County Chief Constables was established in 1920 and the regional conferences of superintendents held to elect officers of that rank to the Police Council eventually evolved into the Superintendents' Association. The Bedfordshire Constabulary fully participated in all of the new organisations.

Special Constabulary.

The post-war period also saw important changes in relation to the special constabulary. A Home Office circular urged that "every possible endeavour should be made to strengthen the special constabulary organisation established during the war and to maintain it in being as a permanent police reserve. The special constabulary should continue in the future, as in the past, a voluntary and unpaid body of men who are ready to undertake the duty, which rests on all citizens, of maintaining law and order in time of difficulty."

Colonel Stevens reported that he intended to maintain a special constabulary of 1,400 officers in Bedfordshire and the standing joint committee subsequently sanctioned the purchase of blue and white armlets, costing 1/8d each, and truncheons, costing 5/- each, for the use of the specials. The Special Constables Act of 1923 laid down regulations governing the organisation of the special constabulary in each force but Colonel Stevens reported that the new orders were virtually identical to the rules he had drawn up for the Bedfordshire Special Constabulary in 1919.

The special constables' regulations laid down various conditions of service and the qualifications for appointment. "Only persons who are of good character, healthy and physically fit shall be eligible for enrolment. The appointment of every special constable, unless otherwise specified, shall be without limitation as to period.

A special constable may resign on giving one month's notice in writing to the chief constable." The special constabulary established during the emergency at the start of the First World War had developed into a permanent auxiliary force of volunteer constables who were available to assist the police at any time.

The contribution made by women employed in munitions factories and other industries during the war led to calls for the employment of women police officers. A very small number had already been enrolled in some parts of the country but not in Bedfordshire. In 1920 a Government committee set up to report on the employment of women on police duties came to the following conclusion. "We consider that the experience of the war has proved that women can be employed, with advantage to the community, in the performance of certain police duties which before were exclusively discharged by men. However, police authorities must be left free to decide whether and how far the circumstances of their respective localities require the employment of women as constables."

The report accurately reflected the attitude adopted by the Home Office which had no objection to the appointment of policewomen but left the final decision to local chief officers and police authorities.

In Bedfordshire the Biggleswade branch of the Women's Co-operative Guild wrote to Colonel Stevens pressing for the introduction of women police officers into the county constabulary. The chief constable remained opposed to the employment of policewomen throughout his term of office and the standing joint committee supported Stevens' view, resolving: "That this committee do concur in the opinion expressed by the County Councils' Association that so far as county areas are concerned the employment of women police is unnecessary."

In 1920, apart from the residential quarters attached to the police stations in the county, the standing joint committee of Bedfordshire owned just two police houses – one at Silsoe and the other at Kempston. Colonel Stevens reported that "the remainder of the houses occupied by the police are rented. This is not satisfactory. I am continually getting notice to quit from landlords who want these houses for their own employees. Many of the houses are not satisfactory for occupation by police officers."

The standing joint committee subsequently embarked on a long term policy of buying suitable residential properties for the use of the police. In the next twelve months they obtained cottages at Caddington, Kensworth, Podington and Potton. The small fleet of

Point Duty

The county force obtained its first motor car, an 11.9 h.p. Arrol Johnston, in 1913

motor vehicles used by the constabulary was also expanded through the purchase of a Ford motor car for use at Biggleswade and a Talbot Daracq car which was stationed in the Bedford division.

Financial Crisis.

By 1922 the post-war economic boom had petered out and the country faced a deepening financial crisis. The Government made drastic cuts in public expenditure and spending on the police service suffered as a result. Police forces were directed to reduce their establishments by five per cent through a freeze on recruitment, and officers' wages and allowances were cut. The standing joint committee instructed Colonel Stevens to take what measures he could to effect further economies in the county. The chief constable reported that: "It has for some considerable time been the custom in this force for all the men to assemble at divisional headquarters once a month for instruction on drill, first aid, police duties, dictation, arithmetic and the making out of reports. The younger constables, in addition, have been accustomed to assemble at headquarters once a week for instruction by the superintendents. To save expense I have cancelled this instruction and all the men attend at divisional headquarters once a quarter."

By June 1922 the constabulary had reduced its establishment from 127 to 123. Colonel Stevens regarded the reduction in manpower as particularly serious as it came at a time of growing demand on the resources of the constabulary. "The greatly increased amount of motor traffic now necessitates constables being placed on point duty at various dangerous crossings to prevent serious accidents. Police supervision is also most necessary to check dangerous driving. Accidents, I regret to say, are of frequent occurrence and the investigation and reporting of such incidents entails hours of work."

Spending on the police was kept on a very tight rein throughout 1923. In Bedfordshire the house purchase programme was suspended and the annual issue of uniform was cancelled. However, Colonel Stevens did succeed in replacing one of the Allday & Onions motor cars, which had worn out, with a new Ford motor vehicle. The following year the force obtained its second motorcycle for £45 and a Gestetner copying machine for £40. The county constabulary was producing a growing number of intelligence bulletins and other documents for circulation in the divisions, and prior to the purchase of the duplicating machine the headquarters staff produced copies of documents in batches of six using carbon paper. The saving in time to the officers at headquarters more than justified the expense involved. The first half of the 1920s was a difficult time for the Bedfordshire Constabulary during which development of the force was undoubtedly restricted by the severe financial constraints imposed on the standing joint committee.

By 1925 the recession had eased and more funds were made available for expenditure on the police. In Bedfordshire the policy of purchasing housing for the use of the police was reinstated and the county embarked on a modest building programme. Colonel Stevens reported that "Sandy is a parish which is now urban in character. It is a growing parish in the centre of the market gardening industry of this county and has a population of 3,409. A police station with the necessary accommodation is urgently required." The standing joint committee commissioned the building of a small police station at Sandy and the construction of police cottages at Upper Dean, Sundon and Caddington. The committee hoped to build up to three new police houses each year.

In 1926 Colonel Stevens reported that "from the 1st January to 31st December 1925 there were 335 persons injured in motor accidents in the county and a further 17 persons were killed. It will be seen from these figures how very essential it is to have a police force very highly trained in first aid. The knowledge of first aid has become a very important part of the work of the police." Stevens recommended that stretchers should be supplied to as many police cottages as possible to improve the efficiency of the police in dealing with injured persons. The standing joint committee resolved to purchase twenty stretchers for £50 to be distributed throughout the county at the discretion of the chief constable. It was also decided that the constabulary should obtain a motor vehicle which could accommodate a stretcher, and Colonel Stevens subsequently purchased an Essex motor car for £225. "By removing one of the front seats and putting a small mattress on the floor a person can easily be placed with a considerable degree of comfort in the Essex car on a stretcher. I might add that within forty-eight hours of the purchase the police attended two accidents with the new motor."

Kempston Balloon Disaster.

The constabulary gained a great deal of public goodwill through its good offices in treating injured persons and when necessary, conveying them to the nearest hospital. During the period between

Four of the eight Royal Enfield motorcycle combinations purchased in 1930 for use as the first road traffic patrols. On the far left is the Leighton Buzzard divisional solo motorcycle, a BSA 3.49 h.p. machine

the two world wars, as society became increasingly mechanised, the police were called on to deal with a growing number of major accidents and disasters. One of the most unusual incidents of this nature, which occurred in Bedfordshire, involved the crash of a hot air balloon at the Kempston Flower Show on Tuesday, 3rd August 1926. The balloon had been one of the principal attractions at the show and many visitors had taken the opportunity to enjoy the view of the surrounding countryside from a height of several hundred feet.

The Bedfordshire Times reported that the balloon was attached to a hawser which wound onto the roller of a motor winch on the ground and that the accident occurred after a dozen or so trips had been made earlier in the day. When the descending balloon was about one hundred feet from the ground the rope drawing it in fouled in a tree. At the request of the pilot, as the strong wind buffeted the gondola, a large number of people seized the rope to try to pull the balloon down and during a particularly strong gust several men were lifted into the air. "Then the disaster occurred. A sharp crack was heard and the netting by which the basket was suspended was seen to break away. A second later the basket itself broke away and came hurtling to the ground pitching out the four passengers and pilot on impact."

The pilot and one of the passengers were killed instantly. The police attended to the three remaining casualties and held back the crowd of spectators who gathered at the site of the crash. Unfortunately none of the injured could be saved. One died on the way to hospital and the two others expired shortly after being admitted as patients. There was widespread praise for the police who were described as "very smart and efficient in tackling the unexpected tragedy."

Over two thousand mourners attended the funerals of four of the victims held at Kempston parish church and cemetery on 7th August 1926. A force of nearly forty constables was on hand to ensure that the arrangements for dealing with the crowds went smoothly. Colonel Eugster, the chairman of the flower show committee, later wrote to Colonel Stevens "to express the grateful thanks of the vicar, churchwardens and parishioners of Kempston for the services of the police at the sad ceremonies. The services were conducted in a very solemn manner and much of this was due to the presence of your officers."

Mutual Aid.

The General Strike called in May 1926 in support of a stoppage in the coal industry caused few problems for the Bedfordshire Constabulary. Colonel Stevens reported that: "A large number of pickets were placed at railway stations during the strike but they were well behaved and created no trouble. A number of special constables were called out to assist the regular force and carried out their work most efficiently."

Later in the year, on October 20th 1926, the county constabulary sent a detachment of twenty constables and two sergeants to the north of England on mutual aid concerning the coal strike which had continued even after the collapse of the General Strike. The youngest of the Bedfordshire constables, sent to the West Riding of Yorkshire, later recalled that officers received an allowance of 3/6 per day for being away from home. "On arriving at Wakefield, after spending a few days at police headquarters, the contingent divided, Sergeant Leist and ten men being posted to Hemsworth where they were billeted at the police station and Sergeant Bradshaw and his ten men were posted to Fitzwilliam where they slept in offices at the pit head. All the men at Fitzwilliam were expected to be up at 4 a.m. each morning to escort the safety men to the pit head to keep the safety pumps working. These men would not turn out from their houses or leave the pits unless under escort as they were looked on by their striking colleagues as blacklegs."

The detachment of police returned to Bedfordshire on 3rd November when they were expecting a week's leave promised them by Colonel Stevens. Unfortunately they found that the county constabulary was in the grip of a flue epidemic, many officers were off sick and all leave had been cancelled.

Rising Crime Rates.

By 1928 crime rates were rising across the country and Colonel Stevens reported that, "the methods employed by criminals today are quite changed. Motor vehicles of all sorts play a very important part in this and the following methods must now be used by the police to counteract the new phase of crime. (1) The police must be in possession of motor cars and motorcycles so that criminals can be followed with the least possible delay. (2) As many police officers as possible should be on the telephone. (3) The numbers of police should be such as to prevent crime by better supervision and more constant patrolling."

Each division had already been equipped with a motor car by this time but over the next eighteen months the standing joint committee increased the number of motor vehicles used by the force to twelve. Some of the new machines were stationed at the smaller centres of population such as Eaton Socon, Riseley, Silsoe and Streatley, whilst others were based at county police stations, including the newly opened station at Sandy. Many constables had purchased their own motorcycles and these men were granted an allowance of 2d per mile when using their machines for police duties.

Colonel Stevens also reported, "I have instituted a scheme by which police officers in this county can get into quick communication, not only with each other, but also with officers in neighbouring counties, and which has proved to be very successful." The chief constable cited one case in particular in which the scheme had secured the arrest in Derbyshire of one of two men wanted in connection with garage breaking at Dunstable. The second offender was subsequently taken into custody through the excellent detective work of Pc 31, Copperwheat. "A fair description of the two men who were seen in the vicinity of the garage was obtained and circulated to various police forces. Subsequently a message was received of the detention at Chapel-en-le-Frith, Derbyshire, of one of the men answering the description given. Pc Copperwheat was instructed to fetch this man but instead of travelling by train he did the journey by lorry so as to give him an opportunity of making enquiries en route concerning the other man.

"At a refreshment hut at Talke o' th' Hill, Staffordshire, the constable observed a youth enter who answered the description of the second person. He kept him under observation, listening to his conversation with other drivers and later saw him produce from his pocket some of the stolen articles. The arrest was then made." Both offenders were subsequently convicted of the burglary at Dunstable.

In April 1929 the Home Office issued a circular letter concerning the provision of motor ambulances. "Where the ambulances already provided are insufficient for local requirements the Secretary of State would suggest that police authorities should consider supplying an ambulance."

The position in Bedfordshire varied from district to district. In Bedford and Luton the respective town councils maintained an ambulance which was allowed to operate outside the borough boundary within a reasonable distance. A Red Cross ambulance was stationed at Dunstable and there was a privately owned ambulance in Leighton Buzzard. Biggleswade, however, was poorly served and the standing joint committee resolved "to purchase one Morris motor ambulance for use in the Biggleswade division, at a total cost of £370 and that such motor ambulance be used for police and accident purposes."

The ambulance was large enough to carry ten men in an emergency and the police occasionally made use of it as a personnel carrier. In cases of accident the committee approved of a tariff of charges to govern the use of the vehicle. "1/- per mile, and if the ambulance is called out between the hours of 10 p.m. and 6 a.m. an additional charge of 2/6d shall be imposed." At the same time the chief constable was authorised to waive the charges if he was satisfied that the person concerned could not afford payment. The police ambulance continued in operation until 1937 when the district council took over responsibility for the ambulance service.

In the summer of 1929 Colonel Stevens informed the standing joint committee that "the time has now arrived when it is absolutely essential that a new police station be built at Dunstable. The present station which was built over sixty years ago is out of date. The office is very small and there is no parade room. There is no lavatory accommodation for the men who have to use the facilities in the cells and in the event of any persons being in custody the constables have to go to the town hall and use the public lavatory." The committee obtained a piece of land on High Street South, close to Friars Walk, and ordered the construction of a new station house at a cost of £8,755.

The chief constable also reported that a central training school for police recruits had been established in Birmingham. "On his last visit to this force, Sir Leonard Dunning, His Majesty's Government Inspector suggested that we should send recruits from this force to Birmingham for training as he considered the course admirable in every way. I took his advice and sent three recruits. The result has been very successful. I received a letter from the Chief Constable of Birmingham referring to the three recruits as follows. 'They are sharp, intelligent and good workers. They have made very good progress, all are able to swim, their conduct has been exemplary and they should make efficient constables'. The course extends over a period of ten weeks and comprises instruction in police duties, arithmetic, dictation, general knowledge, swimming, life saving, boxing, ju-jitsu and first aid. The charge is only £5 per recruit." The standing joint committee subsequently resolved "to enter into a standing agreement under which members of the Bedfordshire police force can be accepted for training at the police school of the Birmingham authority."

The R101 Airship.

In October 1929 the Bedfordshire Constabulary was called on to control the huge crowds of spectators who gathered to witness the launch of the R101 airship at Cardington. The local newspapers reported that "from dawn until sunset on Sunday, 13th October there was dense and continuous traffic on all the main roads leading into the county." One queue of traffic to the south of Cardington was reported to have stretched almost all the way to Hitchin. "Nearly a hundred policemen had to be called out to deal with the situation and there was a constable on duty at nearly every crossing. So busy were the police that they had to snatch hasty meals of sandwiches at their posts." Colonel Stevens received letters from the Air Ministry and the airship works at Cardington thanking him "for the assistance of the police during the launch weekend and commending the constabulary on the manner in which the traffic was regulated."

On the exact same weekend the following year, the Bedfordshire Constabulary used the experience it had gained at the launch of the R101 to deal with even larger crowds which gathered to pay their respects to the forty-eight passengers and crew who died when the airship crashed near Beauvais in France in the early hours of October 5th 1930.

The bodies of the crash victims were returned to England and on Friday, 10th October 1930 there was a memorial service at St. Paul's Cathedral and the deceased were laid in state at Westminster Hall. "On Saturday morning, under a blue October sky, the procession of the dead and of the bereaved set out on the last long journey from Westminster to the cemetery at St. Mary's Church, Cardington." The coffins were conveyed to Euston station in preparation for the rail journey north and when the train pulled into Bedford St. John's at 2 p.m. "the purple draped doors of the carriages were opened and one by one the nameless casks were lifted out." The grim task of unloading the train was completed within an hour and at three o'clock the funeral cortège moved slowly out of the railway yard and into St. John's Street.

"Colonel Stevens, the Chief Constable of Bedfordshire, and Mr Timbrell, the Chief Constable of the borough of Bedford, led the procession followed by a small force of police, a detachment of the Royal Air Force, the Royal Air Force Band, the firing party and trumpeters, all marching with a slow measured step. Then came the long line of grey wagons bearing the coffins, each covered with the Union Jack and piled high with flowers." The carriages were followed by local dignitaries and officials, the crew of the R101's

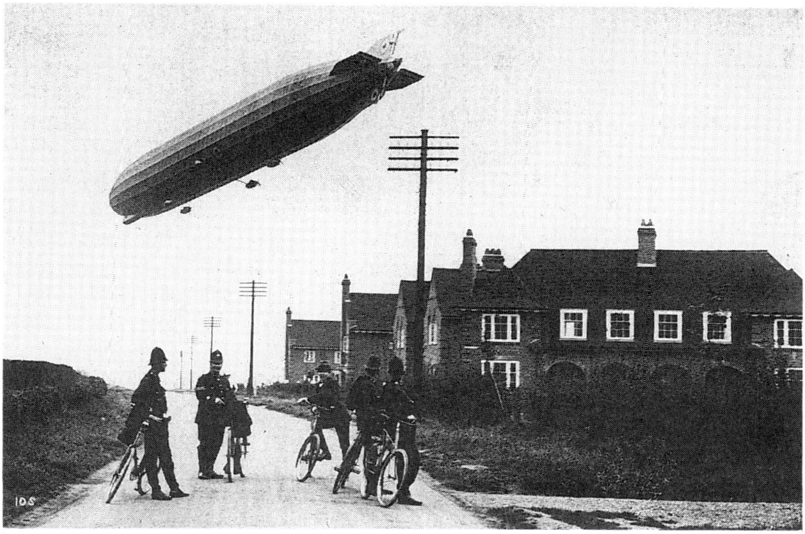

Constables at Cardington with airship overhead

The R101 funeral procession en route to St. Mary's Church, Cardington

sister ship, the R100, a detachment of the Bedfordshire Regiment and a convoy of motor cars carrying the mourners.

The great bell at St. Mary's Church tolled as the procession came into view at Cardington. A thirty foot square grave had been excavated at the cemetery and each coffin was carried along the gentle slope leading down into the burial place by six Royal Air Force pallbearers. When the coffins had been placed on the earth in four rows of twelve the Anglican burial service was conducted at the graveside. At the conclusion of the ceremony "the first volley from the firing party cracked loudly in the still air. The second and third volleys came to the sharp orders of the officer in charge and there followed the long drawn out sadness of the last post." The waiting crowds were allowed to file past the open grave in the fading twilight of the evening and the task of filling the grave was completed by the light of flares during the night.

The police handling of the funeral arrangements attracted widespread praise. The Bedfordshire Standard reported that "the huge task of traffic control and the policing of the vast crowds which lined the roads en route from the borough boundary to Cardington Church was carried out with wonderful smoothness and despatch. The dispersal of the people after the funeral service was completed with equal facility." The Bedford Record was also impressed by the police operation commenting that, "the constables performed the very difficult task of controlling long stretches of road with remarkable precision."

Over 150,000 people were estimated to have gathered along the route to Cardington on the day of the funeral service but Colonel Stevens reported that he had always expected the attendance of large numbers of the public. "I could see from the very first that I would not have nearly sufficient men of my own to line the route, guard the crossroads and take up positions in the cemetery. I accordingly asked for fifty men of the Buckinghamshire Constabulary and forty men from the Luton borough police force. These men were sent me. A number of special constables were also employed and I received the very greatest help from the Royal Air Force which placed one hundred men and one officer at my disposal."

The standing joint committee resolved to "record its high appreciation of the arrangements made by the chief constable for the funeral of the victims of the R101 airship disaster on Saturday, 11th October 1930." The committee also noted the "admirably efficient conduct" of all the police officers involved in the arrangements.

Road Traffic Section & Detective Training.

On 25th November 1930 Colonel Stevens received a communication from the Home Office concerning the provision of road traffic patrols. "Payments will be made from the road fund in respect of the cost of providing and maintaining motor patrols for the supervision of traffic on the roads, and the detection of traffic offences. The Secretary of State will regard the organisation of an effective system of motor patrols as especially important in the county forces. As to the organisation of the patrols, it is, in the Secretary of State's view, important that arrangements should be made between neighbouring forces to secure that on the main roads a systematic patrol is maintained."

In Bedfordshire Colonel Stevens received Home Office authorisation to purchase eight Royal Enfield 9.76 h.p. motorcycle combinations and he reported that "the patrol scheme for the county was put into operation on 30th December 1930." The motorcycle combinations proved to be unsuitable for traffic patrol work and were replaced with four 12 h.p. six cylinder Vauxhall cars in 1933. The introduction of regular motor patrols dedicated to the proper regulation of traffic was a response to the growing number of motor vehicles on the road and the alarmingly high number of serious injuries caused by road accidents. The traffic patrol instituted in Bedfordshire at the end of 1930 eventually led to the formation of the Road Traffic Department.

In February 1931 Colonel Stevens reported on significant developments concerning the investigation of crime in the county. "I have realised for a long time that to enable me to combat the present day criminal I should possess men who have been specially trained under the most highly skilled and experienced officers in the work of criminal investigation. I have had specially selected men trained at New Scotland Yard and will continue this practice with, I am sure, most beneficial results in the future."

Three months later Stevens appointed a detective inspector to be stationed at the police headquarters office at the Shire Hall. "His duties will include taking charge of all criminal records, fingerprints, records of travelling criminals and photographs. He will also assist divisions in the investigation of crime and will be available to be sent into other counties to trace criminals who have committed crimes in this county. The detective inspector will also hold classes for the sergeants engaged in the investigation of crime. The officer I have appointed holds a criminal investigation certificate from New Scotland Yard and is very keen on the work." The detective inspector was subsequently sent for further training at West Yorkshire Constabulary headquarters, Wakefield, and the headquarters of the Derbyshire Constabulary.

Railway Accident.

In March 1931 several officers from the Bedfordshire Constabulary distinguished themselves at the scene of a train crash near the border with Buckinghamshire. At 12.21 p.m. on Sunday, 22nd March the Royal Scot express train was derailed just south of Leighton Buzzard, the engine was overturned and five coaches were wrecked. Miraculously only six people were killed and five others seriously injured. Colonel Stevens later received a letter from several prominent citizens of Leighton Buzzard, including the chairman of the divisional petty sessions, which spoke very highly of the actions of the police at the scene. "We, the undersigned eyewitnesses of the rescue work after the accident to the Royal Scot express train, wish to testify that the work done by the police under Superintendent Marrit's direction calls for the fullest praise. In view of the fact that the Bedfordshire police were the first on the scene and were working for nearly three quarters of an hour before any other organised help arrived, it is needless to say that Superintendent Marrit's promptitude in action caused the police to be of the greatest possible assistance to the doctors in attendance."

The letter went on to cover most aspects of the police operation mounted by the Bedfordshire and Buckinghamshire forces at the scene of the disaster. Many of the police officers assisted in the rescue work and one of the constables from Bedfordshire was singled out for particular praise. "On arriving at the wreck Constable Turner at once commenced work on the removal of the body of the driver from the engine. In doing this it was necessary to work in the escaping steam and whilst shovelling away the coal which covered the driver, Turner cut his left arm against the side of the engine. After the body of the driver had been recovered the constable immediately went to a spot where several passengers were pinned under the wreckage and took a large part in their release. From the time he arrived on the scene until he was relieved, Constable Turner was working for seven hours without a break and many times endangered his own life."

Other police officers were deployed to control the crowds of onlookers. At one stage so many people gathered on the footbridge at Leighton Buzzard station it was believed it might collapse causing further casualties. The police cleared the bridge in the interests of public safety and to prevent damage to the structure.

One spectator was arrested for attempting to steal property which had been thrown clear of the train at the time of the crash.

A final aspect of the police operation concerned the identification of the dead and injured. Leighton Buzzard police station was inundated with telephone calls from anxious members of the public enquiring about the welfare of relations who might have been involved in the accident. The sympathetic and tactful handling of these enquiries was commended in the letter sent to Colonel Stevens which concluded that the "conduct of the police merited the praise and thanks of the community in general."

In the summer of 1931 Colonel Stevens reported to the standing joint committee on the opening of Whipsnade Zoo. "From 22nd May to 2nd July this year no less than 128,914 persons have paid for admission into the new zoological gardens." The force establishment was increased by two to accommodate the policing of the large crowds of sightseers and to regulate the increased traffic in the Whipsnade area.

In 1932 Colonel Stevens transferred the headquarters of the Luton division to the new police station at Dunstable and the county station house at Luton was sold. A further internal reorganisation took place in April 1934 when the chief constable reduced the number of divisions in the force from six to just four. The new divisions were known as Bedford, Biggleswade, Leighton Buzzard and Luton. Bedford now incorporated Sharnbrook, and Biggleswade incorporated Ampthill. Colonel Stevens also reported that he had withdrawn certain officers from their beats to form a small detective staff to assist the detective inspector in his duties. The new detective staff became known as the Criminal Investigation Department.

The following year King George V celebrated his Silver Jubilee and as part of the anniversary celebrations His Majesty inspected a parade of the nation's police in Hyde Park on 2nd July 1935. The Bedfordshire Constabulary and the Luton and Bedford borough forces all sent a small contingent to participate in the parade which comprised eight thousand serving police officers.

In 1936 the standing joint committee reviewed the progress of the police housing programme. Colonel Stevens reported that "At present the force are housed as follows:

Police cottages built to standard type – 17
Police cottages purchased by the committee – 24
Council houses rented – 24
Other houses rented – 36"

The chief constable strongly urged the construction of further residential accommodation and the standing joint committee agreed to erect up to six new police cottages a year. The committee also approved plans to build new police stations at Kempston and Biggleswade.

The Kempston station house was to include a constable's cottage, large living quarters for an inspector and a separate superintendent's residence. The building work, which cost £12,000, was quickly put underway at a site in Bedford Road, Kempston, opposite Farrer Street. The station at Biggleswade occupied the site of the old Biggleswade Boys' Home between Back Street and Station Road. The committee employed a Letchworth builder to construct the station at a cost of £13,476.

In 1937 the standing joint committee commissioned the building of a third new police station to replace the ageing divisional headquarters at Leighton Buzzard and the county force was also provided with enlarged accommodation at the Shire Hall.

Murder Investigation.

On Monday, 12th April 1937 the constabulary began its investigation of the murder of Ruby Keen. The body of the twenty-three year old factory worker was discovered in The Firs, a sandy lane running off Plantation Road on the outskirts of Leighton Buzzard. Superintendent Folkes and Detective Inspector Kitchener attended The Firs and closed the footpath to the public. They were assisted in a detailed examination of the scene of the crime by a detective chief inspector called in from New Scotland Yard. The victim was found lying on her back, her clothing had been torn and a blue silk scarf was tied tightly round her neck. There were signs of a violent struggle on the ground and a post mortem examination later confirmed that Ruby Keen had been strangled with her own scarf. Two shallow impressions on the sandy footpath indicated that at some stage during the commission of the crime the murderer had knelt over his victim.

Throughout Monday and Tuesday the police interviewed witnesses who had seen Ruby Keen on Sunday, 11th April. One of the witnesses who came forward was a young man named Leslie Stone who had first met Ruby in 1931 while serving in the Army. He had been posted to Hong Kong the following year and had not returned to Bedfordshire until January 1937. He renewed his acquaintance with Ruby Keen on Sunday, April 4th when he met her in the High Street at Leighton Buzzard and invited her to the Golden Bell for a drink. They met again on the following Sunday and Stone told the police that on the night of her murder he had left Ruby Keen at 10.15 p.m. near the Stag public house. He claimed that he had walked along Heath Road and that Ruby had carried on down Plantation Road alone. Stone's account of the evening was contradicted by the statements of other witnesses interviewed by the police who said that they had seen Stone walking together with Ruby Keen in Plantation Road near to the entrance of The Firs.

It was established that Stone had been wearing a brand new blue suit on Sunday evening and the police subsequently examined his clothing. A piece of silk thread was found on his jacket which was later found to match the material of Ruby Keen's torn dress. The knees of Stone's trousers were impregnated with sand of the type found in The Firs even though the nap of the cloth had been lost through vigorous brushing in an unsuccessful attempt to remove all the evidence. Stone was subsequently arrested and charged with murder before being sent for trial at the Old Bailey on Monday, June 29th 1937.

At the trial, confronted by the overwhelming evidence against him, Stone conceded that he had lied in his previous statement to the police. He admitted that he had gone into The Firs with Ruby Keen but alleged that a quarrel had broken out between them and that she had slapped him across the face. This, he claimed, had thrown him into a rage, he seized her scarf, he thought he had knotted it and then Ruby had collapsed. Stone swore that he had not intended to murder her but admitted manslaughter. The jury retired to consider the evidence and apparently concluded that the torn clothing of the murder victim was evidence of the defendant's true intent. After twenty-five minutes the jury asked the judge to direct them on a point of law. "If as the result of an intention to commit rape a girl was killed, even though there was no intention to kill her, is a man guilty of murder?" When the judge replied that the answer to the question was, "undoubtedly yes," the jury returned a verdict of guilty and Stone was sentenced to death.

The judge expressed his appreciation of the skill and professionalism with which the police had presented their case and particularly commended the work of seven of the Bedfordshire officers involved in the investigation. The standing joint committee was informed of the judge's comments by Colonel Stevens and resolved: "That this committee do record with satisfaction the excellent work performed by the police in bringing Leslie Stone to justice." Stone was executed at Pentonville gaol on the morning of Friday, 13th August 1937.

On 16th July 1938 one inspector and nineteen constables from the county were sent to Luton to assist the borough police on the occasion of the official opening of the Municipal Airport. The air pageant held to celebrate the opening involved over one hundred aircraft and featured a guest appearance by Amy Johnson. Thousands of spectators were attracted to the event and the extra police were drafted in to help control the large crowds. By now the county and borough police forces in Bedfordshire were on the friendliest terms and the standing joint committee endorsed Colonel Stevens' recommendation that the borough of Luton should not be charged for the loan of the officers.

New Equipment.

During the final years of Colonel Stevens' tenure of office as chief constable there were a number of developments which affected the road traffic patrol section. By 1938 there were five traffic patrol cars operating in Bedfordshire. Two of these concentrated their patrols on the main Watling Street trunk road while two more were responsible for policing the Great North Road. The fifth vehicle covered the centre of the county, paying particular attention to the heavy brickyard traffic.

In February 1938 Colonel Stevens arranged for all the traffic patrol vehicles to be equipped with cameras. "The cameras will be fitted in special brackets immediately above the driver's eye-level so that the driver's view can be reproduced in a photograph. With these cameras the controls are extended to the driver's hand so that he has only to press a button to operate the shutter. The photographs can be enlarged to 15″ × 12″ to assist the courts in deciding cases of dangerous and careless driving."

In November 1938 the chief constable reported that a school for the training of motor patrol drivers had been opened at Preston in Lancashire. "The training includes instruction both in motor driving and in educating the motoring public with regard to road safety. The principal object is to secure the highest possible standard of driving by motor patrol officers and to equip them for the task of improving, by precept and example, the general standard of road behaviour." The sergeant in charge of the motor patrol section was sent on the course and on his return he instructed the other patrol drivers in the new techniques he had learned.

One of the most effective ways in which the constabulary promoted road safety in 1938 involved the use of a new 10 h.p. two seater MG equipped with a public address system. Colonel

Stevens reported, "it affords an easy, inexpensive means of reaching the public and special attention is given to children leaving school in an attempt to impress on their minds the dangers of the roads."

Colonel Stevens was also anxious to obtain the best possible training and equipment for the criminal investigation department. At the beginning of 1938 there were two detective officers based at headquarters, including the detective inspector. In addition one detective constable was stationed in each of the four divisions of the force. In February 1938 the chief constable appointed a detective sergeant to the criminal investigation department at headquarters and sent him on the Home Office course for senior detective officers at Wakefield. Later in the year Stevens arranged for the detective inspector to attend a new six week course at New Scotland Yard in the classification of fingerprints.

One of the principal duties of the criminal investigation department was to conduct scenes of crime examinations at all burglaries reported in the county and in November 1938 the standing joint committee purchased the latest photographic equipment for the headquarters office including a fingerprint camera, a Kodak view camera, lighting and enlarging equipment.

By May 1939 the new police stations at Kempston and Biggleswade had become operational and the Leighton Buzzard station was nearing completion. The Kempston station house became the new headquarters of the Bedford division and the old Gadsby Street station in the borough of Bedford was left unoccupied. Later in the summer of 1939 the constabulary was equipped with an internal telephone network. Colonel Stevens reported: "I have arranged for the installation of a private line system connecting my headquarters with the divisional headquarters. My office will also be connected to the Bedford borough station via a loop line."

In the months leading up to the outbreak of the Second World War, Colonel Stevens took several measures designed to improve the civil defence arrangements of the county. The special constabulary strength was increased to 1,500 and each man underwent anti-gas attack and air raid precautions training with the regular force. Stevens also purchased 160 special constables uniforms reporting that "if these men should be called upon to carry out very important duties I consider that they should be supplied with proper uniform." Further measures involved the establishment of a reserve force of men who were willing to serve as special constables in time of war. Fifty such men were enrolled in the police war reserve at the Shire Hall on 19th June 1939. Colonel

Stevens also approached twenty police pensioners who were ready to rejoin the constabulary in the event of war.

Tragic Accident at Southill.

When war was declared on Germany on 3rd September 1939 the Bedfordshire Constabulary was ready to implement the emergency measures announced by the Home Office for the protection of the civilian population. However, Colonel Stevens' skilful handling of the civil defence arrangements was prematurely curtailed in October 1939 when he was injured in a tragic shooting accident.

On Saturday, 7th October the chief constable was invited to the Whitbread family estate at Southill for a day's shooting. The morning was wet and foggy and as the hunting party crossed a field of brussels-sprouts on the estate, the man acting as Colonel Stevens' loader slipped and fell in the mud. When the butt of the gun he was carrying struck the ground the firearm discharged itself and Colonel Stevens was critically wounded in the liver and kidneys.

The chief constable was immediately removed to Rye Nursing Home but the wounds were found to be inoperable. Gangrene set in and on the morning of Monday, 16th October 1939 Colonel Stevens passed away. The funeral was held on the following Thursday at St. Paul's Church, Bedford. Marching columns of police officers escorted the funeral procession on the route to the church from the Colonel's home at Biddenham and then from St. Paul's to the final resting place in Bedford cemetery.

Colonel Stevens' career as the Chief Constable of Bedfordshire was an illustrious one. He established a reputation as one of the leading chief constables in the country, representing the chief officers at the later meetings of the Police Council and serving on the national committees appointed to consider detective procedures and the standardisation of police uniform. He was awarded the King's Police Medal in 1928 and seven years later he was made an acting Inspector of Constabulary, conducting the annual inspection of forty-two county and borough forces. Colonel Stevens' loyalty to the Bedfordshire Constabulary led him to refuse a permanent position in the inspectorate and this decision further enhanced his stature and popularity in the county.

He was a man of immense energy and drive and he took an active role in many local organisations, becoming a Commander of the Order of the British Empire for his tireless work of twenty years as the director of the county Red Cross. Colonel Stevens was also a member of the Red Cross advisory committee in

London, chairman of the Bedford St. John Ambulance Brigade and vice-chairman of the Bedfordshire branch of the British Legion.

In January 1939 Colonel Stevens became a Knight Bachelor in the New Year's Honours List and he was formally knighted by King George VI at Buckingham Palace in the following month.

In his private life the chief constable was known as a family man. His first wife, by whom he had one daughter, had died in 1934. In November 1935 he married again and his second wife, from county Kerry, lived until 1989. The Colonel was a great patron of childrens' charities and shortly before his death he was elected president of the Southern Provincial Police Orphanage at Redhill.

The standing joint committee regarded the loss of Colonel Stevens' experience and qualities of leadership as a serious blow to the constabulary coming as it did at such a critical time with the county preparing for war. The committee was particularly anxious to appoint a new chief constable without delay but the choice of Colonel Stevens' successor led to a bitter dispute with the Home Office over what became known as the 'Bedfordshire Question'.

Colonel Stevens performed duty as a temporary Inspector of Constabulary in the late 1930s. He is pictured here with the Chief Constable of Warwickshire

COMMANDER WILLIAM J. A. WILLIS, RN, CBE, MVO, CGM

CHAPTER SIX

1940 – 1953
COMMANDER WILLIS

COMMANDER William John Adlam Willis was born at Fulham, West London, on June 27th 1894. He was educated at the Royal Naval Hospital School in Greenwich before joining the Navy in 1909. He was on active service with the British Fleet throughout the First World War, taking part in the naval actions at Heligoland, Jutland and Zeebrugge. At the Battle of Jutland, fought on 31st May and 1st June 1916, Willis was in command of a gun battery on board HMS Calliope. The light cruiser was involved in some of the heaviest fighting and suffered several direct hits during sustained enemy shelling which destroyed most of the ship's armament. Willis' gun emplacement was the last to be hit, his gun crew were injured and he was seriously wounded in the leg and chest. Despite his injuries he remained at his post, rallied his men, and succeeded in returning fire on the German Fleet. His courageous action during the battle was mentioned in despatches and he was subsequently awarded the Conspicuous Gallantry Medal.

Between 1918 and 1921 Willis was engaged in active service in Russia and following his return to Britain he spent two years at the Royal Naval College at Greenwich. He gained extensive experience at sea, first as a divisional officer and later as an executive officer on board His Majesty's ships, and further postings to training establishments took him to HMS Ganges at Shotley Gate, and finally to the Royal Navy barracks at Chatham where he was placed in command of the initial training given to new naval recruits. (Many years later HMS Ganges became a temporary police district training school.) In January 1936 Willis was second in command of the Royal Naval gun carriage used as the bier at the state funeral of King George V. In connection with this service he was made a Member of the Royal Victorian Order. Commander Willis retired from the Royal Navy in 1937 and on 1st December that year he was appointed Chief Constable of Rochester City Police Force in Kent.

The Bedfordshire Question.

In December 1939 Commander Willis was one of one hundred and fourteen candidates who applied for the office of Chief Constable of Bedfordshire in response to advertisements placed in The Times, The Daily Telegraph and The Police Chronicle. On 30th December the standing joint committee interviewed three applicants who had been short listed for the post. The three were Commander Willis, Captain J. N. Cheney of the Army and another retired naval officer, Lieutenant-Commander R. D. Coleridge. After the interviews had been completed, and following a lengthy discussion on the relative merits of each candidate, the committee resolved: "That subject to the approval of the Secretary of State for Home Affairs, Lieutenant-Commander Richard Duke Coleridge be appointed Chief Constable of the County of Bedford."

Richard Duke Coleridge, the son of Lord and Lady Coleridge of Ottery St. Mary, Devon, was thirty-four years of age and had been invalided out of the Royal Navy earlier in 1939 after an impressive maritime career. He had narrowly failed to secure the Chief Constableship of Hertfordshire just a few months previously and had studied police work and organisation under the Chief Constable of West Sussex.

The standing joint committee had anticipated that Lieutenant-Commander Coleridge would commence his duties as chief constable on 16th January 1940, but on 11th January the committee received an urgent communication from the Home Office: "With regard to the proposed appointment of Lt.-Commander Coleridge as Chief Constable of Bedfordshire, I am directed by the Secretary of State to say, for the information of the standing joint committee, that he is unable to regard the appointment as satisfying the terms of regulation nine of the police regulations.

That regulation prescribes that no person without previous police experience shall be appointed to the post of chief constable unless he possesses some exceptional qualification or experience which specifically fits him for the post or there is no candidate from the police service who is considered sufficiently well qualified.

"The Secretary of State regrets he will be unable to regard the selection as one which he could properly approve, under the terms of the regulations, and it will be necessary for him to ask the committee to submit for his approval, the name of such other candidate for the appointment as they may select."

On February 10th 1940 the standing joint committee met in special session to consider their rebuff at the hands of the Home Office. By this time the question of the appointment of Bedfordshire's Chief Constable had been raised in the House of Commons by the parliamentary spokesman of the Police Federation, Mr McEntee, the Labour MP for West Walthamstow. He voiced support for the Home Office interpretation of the police regulations and in reply Sir John Anderson, the Home Secretary, had confirmed his refusal to sanction Commander Coleridge's appointment. Samuel Howard Whitbread and Admiral Sir Lionel Halsey, in honour of whom Halsey Road, Kempston, was later to take its name, had been sent to the Home Office by the standing joint committee to meet with Sir John Anderson but they had been unable to persuade him to alter his decision.

At the special meeting of the standing joint committee, held on February 10th 1940, the councillors and justices drafted a final letter pressing the Secretary of State to reconsider his objections to the appointment of Commander Coleridge. The letter quoted from the findings of the 1929 Royal Commission on police powers and procedures. "Long experience and good service in the lower ranks are not the only, nor even the most important qualifications for the higher posts in the police service." The letter concluded: "The members of the committee respectfully ask the Home Secretary whether he would be so good as to interview Commander Coleridge, as was done by his predecessor in the case of a similar appointment, and let this committee know whether, in his opinion, the professional career of Commander Coleridge, and his wonderful, confidential reports from the Admiralty, are not of such a character as to afford reasonable grounds for approving the appointment already made by this committee."

On 16th February 1940 the Home Office sent an uncompromising reply to the letter. "The Secretary of State regrets that he finds no reason to modify the view which he has already expressed to the committee, that the proposed appointment of Commander Coleridge would not comply with the requirements of the police regulations. In these circumstances a personal interview with Commander Coleridge would serve no useful purpose and the Secretary of State can only repeat his request that the committee should submit the name of another candidate for his approval."

The standing joint committee was forced to admit defeat and on Saturday, 2nd March 1940 the committee interviewed five new candidates for the post of chief constable. In addition both Commander Willis and Captain Cheney were invited to re-attend for interview and at the conclusion of the proceedings the committee resolved to appoint Commander Willis as the new Chief Constable of Bedfordshire. The Home Secretary approved the appointment and Commander Willis commenced his duties on 8th April 1940.

The publishers of the Police Almanac had not anticipated the controversy surrounding 'The Bedfordshire Question' and had already printed the volume for 1940 which erroneously listed Lieutenant-Commander R. D. Coleridge as the chief constable of the county.

Preparations for War.

Nearly six months elapsed between the death of Colonel Stevens in October 1939 and the arrival of his successor at the Shire Hall headquarters in April 1940. During the intervening period Superintendent Setchell was appointed acting chief constable and at the end of 1939 he reported to the standing joint committee on the progress of the county's preparations for war. Most of these preparations concerned the provision of new equipment for the constabulary and the recruitment of auxiliary police officers.

The Government had believed that heavy air raids on mainland Britain would immediately follow the declaration of war on Germany and mindful of the role of the police in co-ordinating civil defence efforts, restoring communications and preventing looting in such circumstances, the authorities had deferred the call-up of military reservists from the ranks of the police and retained younger officers in the police service who would otherwise have been liable to conscription.

In fact the air raids had not materialised and in December 1939 Superintendent Setchell reported that "seventeen members of the Bedfordshire force who were Army reservists have been recalled for service with His Majesty's Forces." He also reported that the war reserve had been increased to one hundred and sixty-two officers and that some of the men had been deployed to guard vulnerable points. The war reservists were initially paid £3 per week. The special constabulary had also attracted new recruits and had been detailed to patrol important lines of communication. Those special constables using their own motor vehicles for police duties were paid allowances of up to 7/- a week and were issued with petrol for each twenty-five miles travelled.

Superintendent Setchell further reported that the Home Office was promoting a third source of fresh recruitment to the auxiliary police service through the formation of the women's auxiliary police corps. "As the committee are aware, they have resolutely refused to have anything to do with the appointment of women police in the past, and I beg to report there are no new circumstances to justify their appointment now." The standing joint committee resolved, "that no steps be taken to form a women's auxiliary police corps in this county."

At the request of the Home Office the force had purchased five wireless receiving sets at a total cost of £49.17.6d for the Shire Hall and the four divisional headquarters. "The sets were purchased in order that all the headquarters could listen to the broadcast of important Government announcements." The constabulary had also obtained extra stocks of torches, batteries and first aid dressings.

Air Raid Precautions.

Commander Willis presented his first quarterly report to the standing joint committee of Bedfordshire in the summer of 1940 when German air raids on Britain were becoming more frequent. The chief constable had issued special instructions to all members of the police force concerning their duties during air raids. "The primary aim of the police during an actual air attack will be to maintain that degree of order and steadiness which will allay panic, and generally reassure the public as to the measures being taken for their safety. In short, it will be for the police to keep order and to make it possible for the air raid wardens, first aid parties, ambulances, fire brigades and other ARP services to do their work."

To this end Commander Willis reported: "I have selected a number of officers in each police division to form an air raid incident squad and practices are being held. These officers will proceed to the scene of any air raid which may occur in the county police district and co-ordinate the necessary rescue work and any other necessary measures. In addition to these men I have selected the inspectors at Ampthill and Dunstable to act as senior incident officers. Each inspector will be responsible for two divisions." The officers selected for this work attended special training courses. "I have sent the two inspectors and eight sergeants in charge of the incident squads to the headquarters of the West Riding Constabulary at Wakefield for two or three day courses. These officers instructed the remainder of the force in air raid incident control. Five inspectors and five sergeants have attended a Royal Air Force course on the identification of bombs."

Commander Willis also set up an air raid control centre at his police headquarters in Bedford. In July 1940 he reported that "in view of the widespread air raids that are taking place I have caused the police room in the basement of the Shire Hall to be converted into an air raid control room. This room will be used in the event of bombing in the vicinity of my headquarters. It has been necessary to have extensions of all telephones, including the police private line system, installed in the control room. Two additional telephones have also been installed, one from the ARP control centre and one from the Observer Corps centre in Bedford." Further private lines which connected Bedfordshire with the headquarters of neighbouring police forces and with the eastern region civil defence headquarters at Cambridge were added to the control room in 1941.

The stocks of uniform, stored in the basement of the Shire Hall, were moved to the unoccupied Gadsby Street police station which also served as a repair depot for gas masks and ARP clothing. Commander Willis purchased bedding and blankets for the Shire Hall control room and ensured that a senior officer was on call there each night. Similar control rooms were eventually established at the county's divisional police headquarters at Kempston, Biggleswade, Dunstable and Leighton Buzzard.

Commander Willis also took steps to ensure that the constabulary was not totally dependent on means of communication which were vulnerable to enemy attack. The chief constable reported: "I have purchased seven Ariel motorcycles at a cost of £562.5.6d and selected seven constables to act as despatch riders. Their duties comprise patrol and carrying despatches to and from my headquarters to divisional headquarters and ARP centres. I have also arranged a link-up of despatch services with the chief constables of adjoining counties. This will facilitate the transmission of despatches in the event of ordinary communications being interrupted owing to enemy action."

In addition, in August 1940, Commander Willis "inaugurated a police cycle messenger service with a view to keeping open the lines of communication between the outlying stations, divisional headquarters and headquarters. The majority of messengers recruited to the service are members of cycling clubs and are between sixteen and eighteen years of age." By November 1940 there were over 370 youths employed on the cycle messenger scheme.

Apart from Luton, Bedfordshire did not suffer particularly heavy bombing raids during the war and the chief constable's extensive arrangements for dealing with air attacks on the county proved more than adequate. Although the Bedfordshire Constabulary was fortunate in not having to contend with destructive air raids locally, many of the officers were called upon to assist during the aftermath of devastating attacks in other parts of the country, most notably in Norwich in 1942. The city suffered heavy bombing on the night of Monday, 27th April and again on the night of 29th April. The number of casualties was estimated at 276 killed and 247 seriously injured. Another 374 persons were less severely injured and over 5,000 houses were destroyed. A number of officers from the Bedfordshire Constabulary, together with detachments from the county's other civil defence organisations, travelled to Norwich on mutual aid and the combined force rendered valuable assistance in mounting rescue operations, restoring water supplies and bringing many fires under control. In May 1942 the standing joint committee resolved unanimously "to convey to the chief constable their congratulations on the very admirable work carried out by a detachment of his force at Norwich on the occasion of the recent enemy air attack on that city."

All three of the county's police forces were commended in the Bedfordshire Times when the newspaper reported Winston Churchill's famous tribute to the nation's police for their unfailing efforts throughout months of enemy air attacks: "The police have been in it everywhere, and all the time, and as a working woman wrote to me in a letter, what gentlemen they are!"

The wartime role of the Bedfordshire Constabulary during the Second World War was much the same as it had been during the Great War. The police were responsible for the billeting of troops and keeping the highways open for use by military convoys. The constabulary was also responsible for enforcing the Emergency Defence Regulations designed to protect the internal security of the state. The regulations restricted the use of cameras in areas of military sensitivity and controlled ownership of homing pigeons.

BEDFORDSHIRE CONSTABULARY.

POLICE CYCLE MESSENGER SERVICE.

I Certify that John F. Barnett served without pay from July 1940 to June 1945 as a member of the Bedfordshire Constabulary Police Cycle Messenger Service and that throughout his service he was willing and competent and discharged his duties as a Police Cycle Messenger to my satisfaction.

Dated this 6th day of June 1945.

~~Commander,~~

Acting Chief Constable of Bedfordshire.

A certificate presented to a member of the Police Cycle Messenger Service

They also prohibited any activity prejudicial to the defence of the realm, such as attempting to cause disaffection amongst members of the armed services. The police were additionally responsible for the registration of foreign nationals and were empowered to control their movements inside the country. The Home Guard relieved the police of many of their guard duties in relation to vulnerable points although the special constabulary maintained a constant watch on a number of railway junctions and bridges.

Auxiliary Police Forces.

The role of the auxiliary police forces in Bedfordshire during the war years was particularly important in the light of the manpower shortage suffered by the regular constabulary. In February 1942 Commander Willis reported that "owing to the large number of vacancies in the regular force I regard it as essential that at least a proportion of the war reserve should receive training of the standard provided by the Metropolitan and West Riding police schools. Eight members of the war reserve are at present undergoing a four week course of instruction at the training school of the West Riding Constabulary at Wakefield. The fee for the course is £2 per man."

The use of the Wakefield training school was only a temporary measure however, and in July 1942 Commander Willis reported: "I have arranged with the chief constables of Luton and Bedford for a school of instruction to be set up in Bedfordshire at which the war reserve of the three forces will receive instruction similar to that given at the West Riding Constabulary headquarters."

Commander Willis also restructured the special constabulary as a separate force with its own supervisory officers. In the summer of 1942 the newly appointed special sergeants and inspectors attended at their local divisional headquarters for instructional classes and afterwards undertook the training of the rest of the special constabulary. Commander Willis recommended, "that an individual issue of uniform, comprising one jacket and one pair of trousers, be made to each member of the special constabulary. The total number of specials is approximately 1,350 and the cost of the uniform will be £3.10.0d each." The standing joint committee subsequently approved the purchase of 500 uniforms each year for a period of three years.

The shortage of regular police officers in Bedfordshire during the war years led Commander Willis to consider various means by which he could release officers employed on clerical duties for patrol work. In November 1940 the chief constable had approached the standing joint committee with regard to the employment of police cadet clerks and the idea was readily accepted. "Resolved that this committee do approve the scheme for the employment of police cadets to a number not exceeding five, that the salary to be paid to cadets be as set forth hereunder, and that such cadet clerks each be provided annually with a uniform jacket and two pairs of trousers.

Age 16	£40 per annum
Age 17	£50 " "

Rising thereafter by annual increments of £15."

In the summer of 1941 Commander Willis warned that yet more drastic measures would be needed. "There are thirty-four vacancies in the regular establishment. The clerical staff is already under strength and it seems inevitable that under present conditions additional men will have to be transferred to outside duties. When this occurs they will have to be replaced by women."

As a first step Willis recommended, "the employment of three women as unattested members of the women's auxiliary police corps, for telephone switchboard and clerical duties at police headquarters." However, the chief constable was at pains to reassure the standing joint committee of the temporary and limited nature of the appointments. "I make this recommendation only to enable me to maintain efficiency under wartime conditions and this does not mean the introduction of policewomen."

The employment of the three switchboard operators was approved and by January 1942 the authorised establishment of the women's auxiliary police corps in Bedfordshire had been increased to eight. The standing joint committee resolved "that five additional women be employed as unattested members of the corps at a wage of 47/- each per week, to act as divisional chauffeurs and relief clerks." Each member of the corps was issued with a jacket, skirt, cap and greatcoat. In addition, gloves were provided for the chauffeurs.

In the summer of 1942 the size of the women's corps trebled when Commander Willis employed a further sixteen women, "to take over the entire clerical and motor driving work now performed throughout the force by constables." He also reported that temporary canteens were being constructed at the four divisional headquarters of the force at a total cost of £600 and the chief constable added: "It is my intention, when it becomes possible to use the kitchen facilities, to call upon the women's auxiliary police corps to do the necessary cooking." Despite the patronising attitude adopted towards the members of the women's auxiliary police corps, the creation of the corps in Bedfordshire marked the first step towards the employment of women police constables in the county.

In 1943 the Home Office approached the standing joint committee on behalf of the War Office with respect to the Government's plans for re-establishing the civil administration in countries which, it was anticipated, would soon be liberated from Nazi occupation by the Allied armed forces. These plans included, "arrangements for the appointment of a number of British police officers to assist in the re-organisation of the local police administration." The police officers selected for such duties were to attend special courses of instruction at the Metropolitan Police training school at Peel House in London, and as Commander Willis had extensive experience of training procedures from his service in the Royal Navy, the War Office was anxious to utilise his expertise in connection with the proposed civil affairs training programme. The standing joint committee agreed to release the chief constable from his normal duties and on August 23rd 1943 Commander Willis was appointed as Commandant of the Peel House training school.

He remained in charge at the school for a period of six months, eventually returning to Bedfordshire on 1st March 1944, when the Home Office wrote to the standing joint committee to thank them for the loan of the chief constable's services. "The War Office has asked the Secretary of State for Home Affairs to convey to your committee their thanks for making Commander Willis available for this work since he has carried out a first class job, maintaining a high standard of instruction and promoting the utmost keenness among the students on all the courses for which he was responsible."

During the chief constable's absence, the Bedfordshire Constabulary was placed under the command of Chief Superintendent Ridd, who had been appointed as the county's first full-time deputy chief constable in February 1943 in response to general instructions issued by the Home Office. "It appears to the Secretary of State that under war conditions the officer acting as deputy to the chief constable should be in a position to act exclusively as his assistant and should have no other responsibilities." Ridd had previously been the clerk superintendent at headquarters but on becoming Commander Willis' full time deputy he was promoted to chief superintendent and his duties as clerk superintendent were taken over by a chief inspector.

Regular Officers, Specials, War Reservists and Police Cycle Messengers on parade in Leighton Buzzard High Street during the Second World War

Royal Visits.

On Tuesday, 9th November 1943 the deputy chief constable was present at Tempsford during an unofficial visit of King George VI and Queen Elizabeth to the nearby Royal Air Force base. This closely guarded airfield was used to drop agents and equipment inside enemy occupied territory on the continent. The King and Queen arrived in the north of Bedfordshire by train and there was tight security all along the railway line. Although the private nature of the occasion meant that the police were not required to deal with large crowds of spectators, Chief Superintendent Ridd was nevertheless thanked for his thorough and discreet preparations for the visit.

Queen Elizabeth paid a further visit to Bedfordshire on 23rd July 1944. In the morning she attended the Fairfield sports ground at Biggleswade to inspect the Second Bedfordshire Battalion of the Home Guard which was commanded by her brother, Lieutenant-Colonel, the Honourable Michael Bowes-Lyon. Thousands of people lined the roads leading to the sports ground and the police mounted a heavy presence along the route to maintain order. After completing her inspection of six companies of the Home Guard, Her Majesty proceeded to 'Gastlings', her brother's home at Southill, where she inspected a detachment of the Bedfordshire British Red Cross commanded by her sister-in-law. In the evening the Queen visited two American Red Cross officers' clubs in Goldington Road and Bromham Road, Bedford. When Her Majesty arrived at the Bromham Road club, twenty-five members of Captain Glenn Miller's United States Army Band played the National Anthem. At the conclusion of the visit the Queen returned to her brother's house before departing for London the following day.

Commander Willis escorted the royal convoy on the journeys between Biggleswade, Southill and Bedford and there were extra police on duty at Southill during Her Majesty's overnight stay at 'Gastlings'. The standing joint committee later expressed their satisfaction at the constabulary's unobtrusive and professional handing of the royal occasion, noting in particular the valuable contribution made by the special constabulary during the inspection at Biggleswade.

Campaign to Recruit Auxiliary Policewomen.

Earlier in the summer of 1944 the Home Office had published an influential circular which encouraged police forces to swear in women as attested members of the women's auxiliary police corps empowered to undertake police patrol duties. However, the thinking behind the circular was not the result of a new and liberal view of the role of women in society: "In the view of the Secretary of State for Home Affairs it is most important to maintain standards of order and decorum among certain young British girls and women which, in the absence of restraining influences, are apt in war time to be lowered and to bring British womanhood into disrepute.

"The Secretary of State realises that it is arguable that the police, as such, are not concerned with the prevention of acts of immorality or impropriety which do not constitute offences against the criminal law. However, apart from the fact that lax conduct between young women and troops may, if unchecked, bring breaches of the criminal law in its train, the matter is one of increasing importance to the maintenance of good relations between the civil population and allied troops, and on this ground alone the Secretary of State feels justified in regarding it as one with which the police must be prepared to deal.

"The Secretary of State is satisfied that for these purposes it is essential that the police forces in the areas concerned should include an adequate number of policewomen."

In May 1944 the standing joint committee of Bedfordshire passed a resolution approving "for the period of the existing national emergency, the appointment of seven attested members of the women's auxiliary corps." Ironically the recruitment of suitable women proved to be extremely difficult and two months later Commander Willis reported: "I have advertised the vacancies in The Times, The Daily Telegraph, three local newspapers and the weekly police journals and have approached the Ministry of Labour on two occasions in an endeavour to fill the vacancies. Only three applications have been received in response to the advertisements in the national press. The whole of the unattested members of the women's auxiliary police corps of the force have been approached but only one has expressed a desire to enrol as an attested member for patrol duties."

In fact the force was unable to fill any of the vacancies until 9th December 1944 when Edna Phyllis Farley was transferred from the WAAF through the agency of the Home Office. Unfortunately Miss Farley's police career proved to be a brief one. In February 1945 she attended a six week course for policewomen in London but within a fortnight of returning to Bedfordshire she was taken ill, and following thirteen weeks' paid sick leave, the maximum period permitted under the relevant Home Office regulations, she was automatically discharged from the women's corps. The constabulary did not succeed in recruiting any other attested members of the women's auxiliary police corps for the duration of the war.

Towards the end of the war the Home Office drew up plans for the training of the police service in the immediate post-war period. "On the basis of returns from all police forces, it is calculated that during the first two years after the end of hostilities in Europe, there will be some 10,000 vacancies for regular constables in the county and borough police forces of England and Wales. It is proposed that training schools should be organised within the Chief Constables' Conference districts and it is anticipated that the overall training requirement could be met by providing one residential training school in each of the eight districts."

As a preliminary step the Home Office planned to run courses at Peel House "in order to qualify police officers to act as instructors at the district training schools after the war." In October 1944 the Home Office wrote to the standing joint committee of Bedfordshire to ask whether they would release Commander Willis from his normal duties as chief constable to enable him to take charge of the instructors' training programme at Peel House. The committee acceded to the request and on 16th November 1944 Commander Willis was appointed Commandant at Peel House for the second time. The Commander did not return to his duties in Bedfordshire until June 1945 and during his absence Chief Superintendent Ridd again took charge of the constabulary.

Theft of Aviation Fuel.

Throughout the summer and autumn of 1944 the county police were investigating a serious and complex case involving the theft of aviation fuel. The case concerned a local firm of motor engineers, Howard Pyper Limited, of the High Street, Kempston. Pyper Limited operated a fleet of taxis in the north of Bedfordshire and it became noticeable that their vehicles seemed to be constantly on the road despite the strict regulations governing the rationing of petrol.

The police decided to keep observations on the most popular route used by the Pyper taxis, the eight mile journey between the United States Air Force base at Thurleigh and the American Red Cross club in Bromham Road, Bedford. The police logged every journey made by the Pyper taxis along the route over the period of a fortnight and found that the cars travelled a total of 4,575 miles. Allowing for fuel consumption at the rate of twenty miles to the gallon, it was calculated that the taxis would have used nearly 229 gallons of petrol during the fortnight.

Pyper Limited had been allocated 420 gallons of petrol for the quarter year in question and when the police inspected the records kept at the company's offices they found 396 gallons worth of petrol coupons. The company's directors, Howard Lynton Pyper and Donald Stanley Judge, were unable to account for the fact that their taxis had apparently travelled 4,575 miles on 24 gallons of petrol.

In a separate incident the police discovered five petrol drums containing 40 gallons of aviation fuel hidden in a spinney by the side of the Bedford to Rushden Road, near the Falcon Inn at Bletsoe. The police kept the location under covert surveillance for over a week before they eventually arrested a taxi driver by the name of Frederick Tracey as he attempted to collect the drums. Tracey was found to be an employee of Howard Pyper Limited and further police enquiries led to the arrest of two tanker drivers employed by the Petroleum Board. The drivers had discovered that the military personnel at certain air bases did not bother to check on the quantity of fuel being delivered before endorsing the receipt of delivery. Consequently the tanker drivers had been able to deliver less than the specified quantities of fuel and sell the remainder on the black market.

The police mounted prosecutions against Pyper, Judge, Tracey and the two tanker drivers on a variety of charges including conspiracy to steal petrol from the Petroleum Board. The committal trial at the Sharnbrook divisional court lasted for fourteen days and when the case was sent forward for trial at the Bedfordshire Assizes in May 1945 it became the longest trial to be heard at the court during the war. Over thirty witnesses were called to give evidence and their testimony was recorded on 160 sides of foolscap paper. The jury, which under special wartime conditions, consisted of just six men and a woman, took half an hour to return guilty verdicts against all five defendants. Pyper was sentenced to eighteen months in gaol and Judge was imprisoned for twelve months. The tanker drivers each received custodial sentences of nine months. Frederick Tracey had fought in the British Expeditionary Force at the start of the war; the court believed he had been manipulated by his employer and he was released after being bound over.

At the conclusion of the trial the judge, Mr Justice Macnaghten, congratulated all the police officers concerned in the case on their good work. Subsequently the acting chief constable received a letter from the Ministry of Fuel and Power referring to the successful prosecution of the offenders. "The Minister desires me to congratulate you and the officers concerned in the very satisfactory conclusion to this difficult and complicated case which, he is assured, was brought about by skill and pertinacity worthy of the highest commendation."

Post-War Developments.

By the time the Pyper trial was heard at the Bedfordshire Assizes, Germany had surrendered and the war in Europe was over. One of Chief Superintendent Ridd's last duties as acting chief constable was to oversee the policing of the VE Day celebrations held in the county on 8th May 1945. In the following month Commander Willis returned to his duties as chief constable and in July 1945 he reported to the standing joint committee with regard to the development of the force in the post-war period. "Detailed plans are already in being to enable me to deal with post-war police work, and apart from the normal functions of the police I will have to plan and make provision for police wireless, an expanded traffic section and an extensive programme of training. Photographic and fingerprint work are likely to develop further. I therefore beg to recommend, in view of the very cramped accommodation at the Shire Hall, that a more suitable building be purchased or rented by the police authority, for use as the county police headquarters."

The standing joint committee accepted the chief constable's recommendation and by October 1945 a suitable property had been found. The committee resolved "to purchase from the Broadway Milk Bar Limited of Bedford, the freehold property known as 'The Pines', 55, Goldington Road, in the borough of Bedford, for the sum of £5,000." Building work was undertaken to adapt the premises for police purposes, extra garage accommodation was added and 'The Pines' eventually became fully operational as the headquarters of the county constabulary early in 1947.

While the necessary alterations were being carried out at 'The Pines', the post-war developments envisaged by Commander Willis in his report of July 1945 began to take shape. In February 1946 the chief constable reported that the regional training schools, planned by the Home Office during the last part of the war, had started the work of training new recruits for the service. "Sergeant Nathaniel Martin, stationed at Sharnbrook, has been selected as an inspector instructor at the No. 5 district training school, Eynsham Hall, Oxfordshire. He commenced his duties on 11th January this year."

The Pines Headquarters, Goldington Road, Bedford

The control room at The Pines with early radio transmitting and receiving equipment

Commander Willis also reported an increase in the amount of time spent on routine in-force training for the regular constabulary, and outlined the special measures which were taken to retrain officers returning to the force after military service during the war. "Prior to the end of hostilities in Europe I arranged with the Chief Constables of Bedford and Luton for the members of our respective forces, on their discharge from H.M. Forces, to attend an eight weeks refresher course at the combined Bedfordshire police training school which was set up in 1942 to train members of the war reserve. The instructors are members of the three forces who have qualified at one of the police instructors' courses held at Peel House in London."

In 1946 the Home Office issued a circular instructing police forces to review their arrangements for the regulation of road traffic in their respective force areas. The Home Office indicated that it was willing to authorise increases in establishment to facilitate the introduction of Road Traffic Departments with responsibility for all aspects of road safety, including in particular, accident investigations, the prosecution of traffic offences, the production of statistics and the training and organisation of motor patrols. By 1946 the county constabulary's traffic section consisted of six vehicles, operated by fourteen constables and a sergeant. All the vehicles were equipped with police signs which had first been fitted to police cars in the county during the war. The signs were box type, could be illuminated at night, and had the word 'Police' written in white letters on a blue background.

In considering the proposed expansion of the traffic section in 1946, Commander Willis reported: "There are sections of three trunk roads, the A1, A5 and A6, passing through this force area and totalling 49 miles. Additionally there are 100 miles of first class road, 68 miles of second class road, and 597 miles of unclassified road in the county. There are 148 schools in the area, 114,000 motor vehicle licences have been issued in the area and at present there are approximately 880 road traffic accidents in the county each year."

On the basis of these figures the chief constable applied for an increase in establishment of twelve constables, a sergeant and an inspector for the purpose of upgrading the traffic section and creating a Road Traffic Department on the lines envisaged by the Home Office. The increase in establishment was granted but initially proved to be of limited value because of the difficulties the constabulary was experiencing in attracting new recruits. New vehicles were also in short supply but the department eventually built up a fleet of ten Humber 18 h.p. special police model patrol cars.

The Home Office programme for the development of police wireless in the post-war years included a plan to establish a joint wireless facility for the Bedfordshire, Hertfordshire, Bedford, Luton and St. Albans City police forces. The plan involved the construction of main transmitting stations at Baldock and Hatfield in Hertfordshire, and of a satellite station at Streatley in Bedfordshire. However, in 1946 Commander Willis informed the standing joint committee: "The Home Office has now indicated that it is possible for both Bedfordshire and Hertfordshire to have individual wireless schemes. The provision of an independent scheme in Bedfordshire will entail the installation of an additional transmitter upon a site, selected as high as possible, to the north of Bedford. The Home Office experts have chosen a suitable spot adjacent to Twin Woods where there already exists an RAF wireless station, on the redundant list, but which possesses a suitable building and one mast. It will be necessary to approach the Bedford and Luton authorities to obtain their agreement to participate in the scheme. So far eight police cars from this county have been fitted with wireless apparatus at the Home Office depot at Cheveley."

The borough forces agreed to take part in the new scheme but the change of plans delayed the introduction of wireless into the county and in the meantime there were other important developments affecting the constabulary.

One of the developments concerned the employment of civilians. At the end of the war the women's auxiliary police corps and the war reserve were kept in being to assist the police service during the transitional period between the end of hostilities and the re-establishment of normal peacetime conditions. When the women's corps was finally disbanded in March 1946 Commander Willis took immediate steps to engage women as civilian clerks. "The experience gained during the war has shown that the employment of women as shorthand typists and telephonists is essential for the efficient administration of the force. I therefore respectfully recommend that fourteen women be employed on clerical duties in the constabulary, that they be paid according to county council scales of pay, and included in the county council superannuation scheme."

The chief constable proposed to station four civilian clerks at the administration department at force headquarters and two more in the criminal investigation department. Two clerks were to be employed at each of the four divisional headquarters. The standing joint committee approved the appointments and by the end of 1946 the force had appointed further civilians both male and female, as cleaners, mechanics and storekeepers.

Women Police Constables.

The chief constable's more positive attitude towards the employment of women in the constabulary had largely been brought about by the highly competent work done by unattested members of the women's auxiliary police corps during the war. Subsequently Commander Willis proved to be more responsive to fresh overtures from the Home Office regarding the potential value of women police constables. Early in 1946 he reported: "With the release of women from the services, suitable women may now be obtained. I have given careful consideration to the matter and in view of the many police duties which require the presence of a policewoman when dealing with female and young offenders, and particularly in regard to juvenile delinquency, I respectfully recommend that seven regular policewomen be appointed, two to be stationed at headquarters (one of whom to hold the rank of sergeant), two at the divisional headquarters at Dunstable and one each at Kempston, Biggleswade and Leighton Buzzard."

The standing joint committee was prepared to accept the chief constable's view in such matters and in May 1946 Commander Willis informed the committee of his progress in forming a women's section in the constabulary. "I beg to report that following the receipt of Home Office approval for an establishment of seven policewomen, the following women, both former unattested members of the women's auxiliary police corps, have been appointed regular members of the county force and sworn in as constables: Policewoman Irene Constance Walters, stationed at Kempston and Policewoman Maud Valerie Lawrence, stationed at headquarters. With a view to obtaining suitable recruits to fill the remaining vacancies, a leaflet on the pay and conditions of service of policewomen has been completed and copies sent to a number of women's service demobilisation centres."

The recruitment leaflet sought to dispel popular misconceptions regarding the police service. "There is quite a wrong idea in the minds of many women that the daily life of a policewoman is similar to that of a woman serving in H.M. Forces. This is not so. The police service is a uniformed civilian body and a policewoman can resign if she wishes. She has fixed hours of duty after which she can, in civilian clothes, take part in amenities enjoyed by the ordinary citizen, and she would probably reside in lodgings with homely people instead of in quarters with a large number of other women. Women constables have the same powers as men and wear uniform which has greatly improved in style to the point of now being one of the smartest worn by women today." The document also set out the pre-entry qualifications needed for policewomen: "Candidates must be at least 5′ 4″ in height, must be unmarried or widowed and be between 22 and 35 years of age."

Despite the publication of the recruitment leaflet, obtaining suitable women proved to be very difficult and in November 1946 Commander Willis informed the standing joint committee that "on Thursday, 8th October last Miss B. M. Denis de Vitré, the staff officer to H.M. Inspectors of Constabulary, visited this force to examine the arrangements made in respect of policewomen. There are still five vacancies but Miss Denis de Vitré was satisfied that all possible avenues of recruitment were being exploited and that the programme planned for the women's section was on the right lines."

Several years passed before the women's section attained its authorised strength but the constabulary as a whole was also well below authorised establishment during the late 1940s. In 1947 Commander Willis was involved in a special police recruitment campaign sponsored by the Home Office. "I have to report having been invited by the Secretary of State to visit Germany on the 10th February this year for a period of about one month as a representative of a mission to the British Army of the Rhine for the purpose of stimulating recruiting for the police service from amongst the members of the armed forces serving there." Following the chief constable's return from Germany on 5th March 1947, the standing joint committee received a letter from the Home Secretary congratulating Commander Willis on the success of the mission.

Amalgamation with Luton and Bedford.

A further development which affected the policing of Bedfordshire in the post-war years concerned the abolition of smaller borough police forces. During the war, emergency legislation had empowered the Home Secretary to amalgamate police forces in the interests of co-ordinated military operations. Seven mergers were initiated under the legislation, all of which affected police forces in the south-east and south-west of England where military resources were concentrated. Subsequently the chief constables appointed to take charge of the merged forces reported that the amalgamations had benefited the economy and efficiency of policing in the areas concerned. The experience of the wartime amalgamations encouraged the Home Office to introduce further measures to abolish smaller police forces and merge them with their larger neighbours. The Police Bill of 1946 contained the necessary legislation to enforce the proposed mergers and, despite fierce opposition from the borough councils concerned, the Bill became law.

Commander Willis reported: "The police forces of the boroughs of Bedford and Luton were, by operation of section one of the Police Act 1946, transferred to the county constabulary on 1st April 1947. A conference took place between officers of the standing joint committee and representatives of the two borough authorities, prior to the date of transfer, in order that the arrangements for the merger might be made to run smoothly." All the powers of the borough watch committees, with regard to the policing of Luton and Bedford, passed to the standing joint committee of the county upon the mergers taking effect. Commander Willis reported further on the re-organisation of the county constabulary following the abolition of the borough forces. "I carefully considered the divisional arrangements for the combined force and approached the Home Office with my views which were as follows. The merging of the former Leighton Buzzard and Dunstable divisions to form one division, the merging of the former Bedford borough area with the former Kempston division to form one division, and for the former Luton borough area to constitute yet another division. The Headquarters and Biggleswade divisions to remain basically unchanged in the new internal structure consisting of five divisions.

'A' division	HQ		The Pines.
'B' division	Bedford/Kempston	DHQ	Bedford.
'C' division	Biggleswade	,,	Biggleswade.
'D' division	Dunstable/		
	Leighton Buzzard	,,	Leighton Buzzard.
'E' division	Luton	,,	Luton."

The old borough police stations were transferred to the county as part of the merger arrangements and at Bedford the Horne Lane police station became the headquarters of the combined Bedford and Kempston division. At Luton the borough council had constructed a new police station in Dunstable Place in 1937 and this building became the headquarters of the county constabulary's Luton division. Both the borough police forces had operated a beat system based on police boxes and this method of patrolling was retained after the merger. Luton's police boxes were found to be in a poor state of repair and by the end of 1947 all twelve had been refurbished.

The authorised establishment of the Bedfordshire constabulary was increased to four hundred and thirty-six in consequence of the merger and consisted of one chief constable, one assistant chief constable, six superintendents, five chief inspectors, nineteen inspectors, forty-six sergeants and three hundred and fifty-eight constables, including two women police sergeants and sixteen women police constables. However, there were over a hundred vacancies in the authorised establishment of the force and the actual strength of the constabulary was not much over three hundred officers. Mr Ronald Alderson, the chief constable of the Luton borough police force, became the assistant chief constable of the county constabulary and he was given supervisory control of the Leighton Buzzard and Luton divisions of the force.

Generally there was a good deal of ill-feeling regarding the enforced amalgamations and the chief constable of the Bedford borough police, Mr Edward Nugent Christie, refused to communicate with the county authorities on the subject. On 3rd April 1947 Commander Willis reported: "On 24th January last I wrote to Mr Christie offering him an appointment in the enlarged force. Up to date I have received no acknowledgement of this offer and consequently I assume that under the terms of the Police Act 1946 he has automatically retired from the force."

In fact, the Act provided that in such a case an officer was to be paid his normal salary for a period of three months from the date of the merger, during which time he would still be eligible to accept an appointment in the enlarged force. However, April, May and June passed by without any word from the ex-chief constable and consequently in July 1947 the standing joint committee resolved that "Mr E. Nugent Christie, having been deemed to have retired from 31st March 1947, in accordance with the Police Act 1946, be granted a pension as of 1st July 1946." The pension amounted to over £600 a year.

His Majesty's Inspectors of Constabulary had fully anticipated that the mergers might initially produce feelings of resentment among borough police officers. The general report of the inspectorate for the year ending 1947 reflected on the results of the amalgamations. "Naturally, in the boroughs affected, there had for some time been considerable heart burning amongst the members of the police forces and police authorities at the prospect of losing their own identities as separate police forces, and many were strongly opposed to the amalgamations. It is therefore with satisfaction that we can report that, in spite of this natural feeling of anxiety, the amalgamations have been carried out with a maximum amount of efficiency and good will, and in a spirit of collaboration which augurs well for the future of the enlarged county forces. We are satisfied that there is no justification for the continued existence of the very small police units of days gone by."

Mr F. T. Tarry, His Majesty's Inspector of Constabulary, conducted the annual inspection of the Bedfordshire Constabulary on the 10th, 11th and 12th November 1947. Subsequently Commander Willis informed the standing joint committee: "As the members of the committee are aware, this was the first inspection made of the force since the absorption of the former Bedford and Luton borough forces. Parades of personnel and vehicles were carried out at Kempston and Luton and Mr Tarry expressed complete satisfaction with all that he saw. At the end of the inspection His Majesty's Inspector informed me that it was most gratifying to see the complete smoothness with which the newly enlarged force was working." The standing joint committee congratulated the entire force upon the favourable report of the Inspector of Constabulary and entered the commendation in the official committee minutes.

Despite the apparent success of the mergers, by 1949 the Luton Civic Society was petitioning the Home Office for the reinstatement of an independent borough police force. "The position of the police control in this county under centralisation has now become ludicrous. Bedford, the county town of 54,000 inhabitants, has become the centre of police administration, while industrial Luton, with a population twice the size and carrying its proportionate increase in the number and complexity of police cover problems and duties, has been reduced to the status of a local parish. Practically all decisions must be referred to Bedford, twenty miles away. As a result of this anomalous position we submit there is a loss of efficiency in the conduct of police duties in Luton." The Home Office was unsympathetic to the petitioners' cause but the campaign to re-establish an independent Luton borough police force continued for many years and was eventually to prove successful.

Wireless Communication.

In November 1947 Commander Willis reported the successful introduction of police wireless into the county. "I am glad to be able to inform the committee that the wireless scheme for this county is now working on a skeleton basis. The master station at Twin Woods has now been equipped and is controlled by land line from the control room at headquarters. The ten traffic patrol cars and five divisional cars have been fully equipped. It is now possible to hold conversation in normal speech between control and cars almost anywhere in the county. Already good use has been made of the equipment on the occasions of the County Agricultural Show at Silsoe, the Sandy Flower Show, the reporting of a large factory fire and the re-taking of boys absconding from Carlton School.

"Contact cannot be established in every part of the county because the satellite station at Streatley is not yet functioning. Wireless aerial masts for the satellite station are expected to be delivered by the end of the year." The erection of the masts at Streatley appears to have caused some consternation among the householders in the village. "We, the undersigned residents of Streatley, wish to protest against the erection of the police radio station. We consider it would be a danger to lives and property and would also spoil the beauty of the district. We humbly request you to consider changing the site to a suitable position where we should have no cause to object."

The perceived danger of the wireless station included "the possibility of aircraft colliding with the masts in low clouds, fog or mist, and landing on adjacent buildings, and the possibility of the masts being blown down in high gales." The residents were reassured regarding the safety of the wireless masts and by the autumn of 1948 the satellite station was in operation.

The principal cause of poor recruitment to the police service in the late 1940s was the low level of police pay. By the end of the Second World War the wage levels established by the Desborough committee in 1919 had been seriously eroded and the pay of a constable had fallen well below average industrial earnings. In May 1948, in response to growing discontent in the police service, the Government appointed a committee under the chairmanship of Lord Oaksey to examine police pay and conditions of service. While the Oaksey committee proceeded with its enquiry, Commander Willis conducted a wide ranging review of policing in Bedfordshire in an attempt to anticipate the future demands likely to be placed on the resources of the constabulary. "With the development of industry, agriculture and housing schemes, the growing incidence of crime, the increase of traffic problems and the amount of time lost through leave, sickness, absence on courses, and for other reasons, it is to my mind, most important that plans be laid to develop the force and so keep in step with the above mentioned problems."

In 1949 the standing joint committee considered the findings of the Oaksey committee and the recommendations of the chief constable simultaneously but unfortunately the two reports proved to be incompatible. The standing joint committee accepted Commander Willis' contention that the county force should seek a substantial increase in its establishment by 1952. However, the disappointing pay award recommended by the Oaksey committee prevented the constabulary from recruiting up to strength and made any proposed increase in the authorised establishment largely academic. The effect of the chief constable's review of the force was consequently limited, although the standing joint committee did draw up long term plans for the provision of up to five hundred police houses over a twenty-five year period and for the modernisation and expansion of the vehicle fleet. The manpower shortage remained a constant problem throughout the 1950s and profoundly affected the future development of the constabulary.

Following publication of the Oaksey report the Home Office wrote to the standing joint committee drawing attention "to that part of the report which recommended that assistance should be given to foster sports activities in police forces." The Bedfordshire Constabulary Social and Athletic Club had been formed earlier in 1949 through an amalgamation of various existing athletic and social clubs, and the standing joint committee resolved "to contribute annually towards the expenses of the county police social and athletic club, a sum equal to the amount of the fixed subscriptions paid by the members of such club, subject to a maximum of 10/- a head."

On Saturday, 11th November 1950 the Queen visited Kempston to unveil the memorial erected to honour the men of the Bedfordshire and Hertfordshire Regiment who died in the Second World War. The Bedfordshire Times reported, "The new memorial takes the form of an obelisk similar to the one unveiled in 1921. The two obelisks stand in front of the shrine, facing the main entrance to the Kempston barracks. Her Majesty was met at the county boundary, near Henlow, by the Chief Constable of Bedfordshire, Commander W. J. A. Willis, who escorted the royal car along the route to Kempston."

A detachment of constables was on duty at the war memorial where large crowds had gathered to witness the ceremony. Further constables were deployed in the streets leading to the barracks to control the thousands of spectators who lined the route taken by the royal car on its journey through Kempston. Commander Willis later informed the standing joint committee: "On 16th November 1950 I received a copy of a letter, which the Lord-Lieutenant had received from the Queen's private secretary, in which Her Majesty conveyed her thanks to me for all the arrangements made and for the efficient way in which they were carried out by the force."

Tunnel Collapse.

In September 1951 the county constabulary co-ordinated the rescue work carried out at the scene of a tunnel collapse in Park Square at Luton. The chief constable related the circumstances surrounding the incident at a meeting of the standing joint committee held in the following January. "An excavation had been made in connection with the laying of a sewer from the premises of Messrs J. W. Green Limited, Luton, and this involved the sinking of a shaft some thirty feet deep, with a tunnel leading from the shaft. Shortly after 7 p.m. on 10th September last, six men were working along the tunnel about twenty feet distant from the bottom of the shaft when a collapse occurred and three men were trapped. The police were notified and Inspector Whiffen, with other officers, immediately went to the scene. Traffic was stopped to lessen the vibrations and the risk of further collapse; rescue parties were organised and urgent messages were sent to all firms in Luton asking for the assistance of persons with rescue and mining experience.

"Inspector Whiffen went into the tunnel and discovered that one workman was dead and two others trapped behind falls of earth. Several men, including Constable Bonner, worked unceasingly in the tunnel to reach the entombed men, and as a result of their efforts one of the men was rescued about an hour later and was found to be suffering only from shock and bruises. The other trapped man, however, was in a serious condition and had to be injected with morphia through a hole in the earth. All the time it was obvious that further falls of earth were imminent and the rescue operations were fraught with danger. Fresh falls did in fact occur and the tunnel had to be shored up before rescue work could continue. The body of the dead man was then recovered and renewed attempts were made to reach the third buried man. This work continued through the night and shortly before 9 a.m. the following morning the trapped workman was extricated alive.

"The rescue parties consisted of members of the fire and ambulance services, doctors, and civilians from the firms of

Vauxhall Motors, SKF Ball Bearing Company, George Kent Limited and Electrolux."

Commander Willis received a number of letters praising the police for their handling of the incident and the chief constable commended Inspector Whiffen and Constable Bonner. "Both men worked in the tunnel unceasingly and with complete disregard for their own safety."

In 1952 Commander Willis reported: "On 4th January I was asked by the Home Office, on behalf of the Secretary of State to act as Commandant of the police college during the absence through illness of Brigadier P. D. W. Dunn." The police college had been established at Ryton-on-Dunsmore, near Coventry, in 1948 for the training of the higher ranks of the police service.

The Home Office had previously written to the chairman of the standing joint committee to secure the release of the chief constable for temporary duty at Ryton. "There is no one who would be more fitted to undertake this task than Commander Willis, who is a member of the college advisory board, already has an intimate knowledge of the work being done there and who has, of course, a very wide background experience of the type of training which is undertaken at the college."

The chairman of the standing joint committee agreed to Commander Willis taking up the appointment and the chief constable was away from the force between 7th January and 7th April 1952. During his absence the county constabulary was placed in the charge of the assistant chief constable, Mr R. C. Machin. The former assistant chief constable, Mr Alderson, had taken up an appointment as the Chief Constable of Monmouthshire in 1950.

In the summer of 1952 the constabulary obtained its first police dogs. Commander Willis informed the standing joint committee: "I have gone thoroughly into the question of the usefulness of properly trained police dogs and I am satisfied that the acquisition of two dogs by this force would prove invaluable, not only in the war against crime generally, but in other ways, such as finding missing children and lost valuables. I have made initial enquiries and have been offered two suitable dogs at a nominal cost of not more than £5 each, and the cost of food for the animals is approximately 25/- a week per dog. The two constables to be selected as handlers can be trained at the Metropolitan dog training establishment. Police dogs have more than proved their worth in those forces which have gone ahead in this direction, and I am sure that the committee will be gratified to know this force is keeping abreast of the times by employing every aid in the discharge of its multifarious duties." The dogs purchased by the constabulary were both Alsatians and were named 'Rustler' and 'Laddie'. Rustler was the first to become operational and commenced duty with his handler, Pc 110, Norman, on 25th June 1952.

One of Commander Willis' final duties as the Chief Constable of Bedfordshire was to respond to a request from the Commissioner of the Metropolitan Police for assistance on the occasion of the Coronation of Her Majesty, Queen Elizabeth II, on Tuesday, 2nd June 1953 at Westminster Abbey. Commander Willis reported: "In common with other provincial forces I was asked to send a detachment from the Bedfordshire Constabulary to assist the Metropolitan Police on Coronation Day. This aid was worked out on a quota basis according to the size of the various forces and the detachment from this force consisted of two inspectors, four sergeants and forty constables, all of whom were carefully selected.

"The terms under which police officers should be loaned to the Metropolitan Police in this connection were considered by the executive committee of the Association of Chief Police Officers and it was unanimously agreed that it would be appropriate if, as an expression of their duty to the Crown, the services of members of the police forces concerned were loaned by their authorities free of charge."

The Association of Chief Police Officers had come into being in 1948 through the merger of the Chief Constables' Association, which predominantly represented chief officers from borough forces, and the County Chief Constables' Association, formed in 1920. The standing joint committee adopted the recommendation of the Association of Chief Police Officers and passed a resolution "approving the waiving of charges for police officers loaned to the Metropolitan Police for duty on Coronation Day."

Appointment as H.M. Inspector of Constabulary.

On 8th June 1953 the standing joint committee met in special session to receive official news of the appointment of Commander Willis as one of Her Majesty's Inspectors of Constabulary. The chief constable presented his last quarterly report to the committee on June 26th when the chairman, Lord Luke of Pavenham, and Sir Frederick Mander, the chairman of the county council, both paid fulsome tribute to the work done by the Commander. Subsequently it was unanimously resolved "that the standing joint committee do record their appreciation of the service and personal qualities of their chief constable, Commander W. J. A. Willis, and of his unfailing efforts on their behalf during his term of office which have made the county force second to none in the country."

Commander Willis commenced his new duties on 1st August 1953 and continued to work as one of Her Majesty's Inspectors of Constabulary until 1963 when he retired, first to Cockfield, near Bury St. Edmund's in Suffolk, and finally to Dovercourt, Harwich, in Essex. During his long and distinguished career of service to the Crown, the Commander received the O.B.E., the King's Police Medal, and just prior to his appointment as an Inspector of Constabulary, the C.B.E.

In private life Commander Willis was happily married for over fifty years and had a family of two sons and a daughter. He enjoyed a long retirement and in the early morning of Tuesday, 22nd June 1982, at the age of eighty-seven years, Commander Willis died peacefully in his sleep.

Commander Willis was the last Chief Constable of Bedfordshire appointed in the military and naval tradition established in 1840, when Captain Boultbee was engaged as the first chief constable, and carried on for over a century through the successive appointments of Major Warner, Colonel Josselyn and Colonel Stevens.

MR HENRY R. PRATT, OBE, QPM

CHAPTER SEVEN

1953 – 1971
HENRY RICHARD PRATT

HENRY Richard Pratt was born on 18th July 1911 at Cork in Ireland and received his education at the Portora Royal School, Enniskillen, in County Fermanagh. Between 1930 and 1933 he served as a second-lieutenant in the Royal Enniskillen Fusiliers, spending eighteen months at the Army college in Aldershot studying military strategy and economics.

In April 1934 Mr Pratt joined the Metropolitan Police Force serving for three years as a uniformed constable on beat and patrol duties. Subsequently he was selected for accelerated promotion and attended an eighteen months' course at the Metropolitan Police College established at Hendon in 1934 by Lord Trenchard.

Mr Pratt worked as a junior station inspector until 1941 when he was released from police duties during the Second World War to join the Royal Air Force as a navigator. Unfortunately in 1943 he was a crew member aboard a Wellington bomber which crashed on a routine training flight near Market Harborough in Leicestershire and the injuries he sustained resulted in a premature end to his service in the Air Force.

Mr Pratt rejoined the Metropolitan Police later in 1943 as a station inspector, and from 1945 to 1948 he was acting chief inspector at Cannon Row police station where he was in command of the Whitehall area during the peace celebrations of 1945, and also on the occasion of the Royal Wedding of Princess Elizabeth and Lieutenant Philip Mountbatten, RN, in November 1947. In September 1948 Mr Pratt was appointed Commandant at the No. 2 district police training centre at Plawsworth, near Durham, and in February 1950 he became Assistant Chief Constable of the North Riding of Yorkshire Constabulary.

In June 1953 the standing joint committee of Bedfordshire advertised the post of chief constable of the county and appointed a special sub-committee "consisting of the chairman and vice-chairman of the standing joint committee, the chairmen of the county council and quarter sessions, and Her Majesty's Lord-Lieutenant, to interview no less than six candidates for the post and to select at least two to appear before the committee for interview on 29th July next."

Fifty-nine applications were received by the sub-committee and eight of the candidates were invited to attend for interview. Subsequently, on 29th July, Mr Pratt and Mr A. U. R. Scroggie, the Assistant Chief Constable of Buckinghamshire, attended before a full meeting of the standing joint committee when it was resolved: "That subject to the approval of the Secretary of State for Home Affairs, Henry Richard Pratt be appointed chief constable of the county." Home Office approval of the appointment was received in a letter dated August 1st 1953 and Mr Pratt commenced his duties in Bedfordshire in the following October.

One of Mr Pratt's first duties as chief constable concerned a royal inspection of the police similar to that held in 1935 to celebrate the Silver Jubilee of George V. Mr Pratt reported: "The police forces of the United Kingdom were reviewed by Her Majesty the Queen in Hyde Park, London, on Wednesday, 11th July 1954. The parade included a contingent from Bedfordshire consisting of one superintendent, one chief inspector, three sergeants, thirty-nine constables and two women constables from the regular force together with one inspector, one sergeant and two constables from the special constabulary, and two cadets, a grand total of fifty-two officers. I attended with other chief officers of police as part of a guard of honour."

Another of Mr. Pratt's earliest duties was to oversee the running of an Attendance Centre which had been established at Luton just prior to his arrival in Bedfordshire. In March 1955 the chief constable reported on the progress of the centre. "Persons between the ages of twelve and seventeen years may be ordered by a court to attend the centre for periods not exceeding twelve hours in all, and not more than three hours on any day. The centre, which is being run as part of a national scheme, is only open on Saturday mornings and the aim is to maintain firm discipline throughout the period of attendance and to educate the boys in the proper use of leisure time. The Attendance Centre is available to the juvenile courts at Luton, Leighton Buzzard and Dunstable together with those at St. Albans and Hitchin in Hertfordshire. It is staffed by senior police officers, all of whom are stationed at Luton, and the whole cost of the scheme is borne by the Home Office.

"Since the formation of the centre thirty-four youths have attended and it is apparent that excellent results are being achieved. Only one of the youths has again come to the notice of the police and that was for a minor offence. This is very satisfactory and does reflect credit on the work being carried out by the staff at the centre." Attendance Centres have continued in operation to the present day and can now be used to deal with young offenders between the ages of ten and twenty-one.

At the end of May 1955 the Associated Society of Locomotive Engineers and Firemen, the train drivers union, called a national railway strike in support of a pay claim and the Bedfordshire Constabulary was asked to supply officers on mutual aid to the Metropolitan Police district. Mr Pratt reported: "On Friday, 3rd June I received a request from the Home Office for a contingent, on the basis of ten per cent of the authorised strength of the force, to be sent from the Bedfordshire Constabulary to assist the Metropolitan Police during the emergency consequent upon the railway stoppage. On Sunday, 5th June a contingent from this force comprising two inspectors, four sergeants and forty-four constables reported for duty at 'D' divisional headquarters, Metropolitan Police, Albany Street Station, London."

The strike was short-lived but the Bedfordshire officers acquitted themselves well and at a meeting of the county's standing joint committee held on 24th June 1955 "the chairman and other members paid tribute to the high standard of efficiency and conduct of the contingent from the county force during their tour of duty in the Metropolitan Police area."

Tracker Dogs.

In 1956 Mr Pratt reported on the re-organisation of the dog section which had enjoyed only limited success since its inception. "The committee will remember that in 1952 my predecessor advised on the usefulness of properly trained dogs and that subsequently two dogs were purchased. These dogs were not very suitable for tracking purposes but I am convinced that patrols made with them in parks and open spaces were a deterrent to possible offenders and did reduce the number of indecent exposures and assaults in such areas."

Dogs with a greater aptitude for tracking were purchased and trained by the force and the dog section received its own transport. "It will be appreciated that if the greatest benefit is to be derived from the dogs it is of paramount importance that they should arrive at the scene of the crime as soon as possible after its commission. I am quite certain that the only way this can be done is to provide a motor vehicle for the handler and his dog. With this in mind I have retained a Ford van which was authorised to be replaced by the committee some months ago. The vehicle has been overhauled at the workshops in Kempston and the interior converted for use as a dog carrier." Better training for the dogs and quicker response times brought improved results with regard to tracking. Pc Winter and 'Anna', the third dog deployed by the constabulary, became operational in February 1956 and in the following April they were called to Chiltern Green Crossroads at Luton where a stolen Ford Consul had been abandoned with the engine running. 'Anna' tracked from the nearside door into New Mill Lane where a man who admitted taking the car was found hiding under a hedge.

There were further successes in tracking offenders during the remainder of the year and by the summer of 1957 Mr Pratt was able to report: "The dog section now consists of one sergeant and five constables with six dogs. This section is really proving its usefulness and further expansion will be desirable in due course." Police dogs were stationed at Leighton Buzzard and Biggleswade in the following autumn.

Manpower Shortage.

In 1957 the chief constable approached the standing joint committee concerning the persistent problem of the manpower shortage in the constabulary. "The committee will remember that from 5th September 1955 all police officers below the rank of superintendent became entitled to an additional rest day per fortnight. By reason of the shortage of manpower I was not able to grant this leave day in practice but personnel are being paid in lieu. I had hoped by now, that the manpower position would have improved but we are still seventy-four men short of the present authorised establishment. However, I feel that with certain adjustments in duties I can arrange for all personnel to take one additional rest day per month. This will make a saving of £19,000 in overtime payments."

Mr Pratt's proposals concerning the redeployment of manpower in the county included the mechanisation of certain beats, the employment of more civilians and an expansion of the police cadet corps. "I am concerned by the growth of the residential areas on the outskirts of Luton and Bedford and the lack of police supervision of these new housing estates. I have therefore prepared a scheme for the merging of several beats in the two towns which will require the provision of silent, lightweight motorcycles in order that the constables may cover the whole of the area for which they will be responsible. It will be necessary for four such vehicles to be provided in Bedford and four in Luton with one spare machine to replace those undergoing repair." The standing joint committee subsequently agreed to purchase "nine Velocette special silent police model lightweight motorcycles at a cost of £183.15.1d each." The committee also approved the employment of five civilians – three to relieve police officers from vehicle cleaning duties and two more to work as wireless operators.

The benefit of increasing the authorised establishment of the cadet corps was twofold. "Not only has the employment of cadets released regular members of the force for other duties, the corps has also provided early training for youths who wish to make the police service a career. This source of recruitment is most profitable as the vast majority of the cadets are now joining the regular force at nineteen years of age. Another significant and important point is that wastage amongst constables who are ex-cadets is negligible compared with that arising amongst men recruited from outside the force." The standing joint committee resolved that "the number of police cadets employed in the county be increased from thirty-six to forty-three."

Despite the manpower shortages experienced by the constabulary in the 1950s, the county force still responded to an appeal from the Home Office for volunteers to perform duty with a British Police Unit operating in the crown colony of Cyprus during civil unrest caused by the 'enosis' movement which advocated union with Greece. Constables J. E. Lloyd and K. A. Hassall joined the unit in August 1956, and in May 1957 Woman Sergeant M. Clapperton and Woman Constable J. M. Childs were also selected for duty in Cyprus. Further appointments to the unit were made in the following years and the force also responded to a request for volunteers to serve with a second British Police Unit established in the protectorate of Nyasaland (Malawi) after demands for independence from Southern Rhodesia led to violent disturbances.

The extra fortnightly rest day granted to police officers in 1955 had been intended as one of a series of long term measures designed to improve recruitment to the police service and ease the manpower shortage. In introducing the additional rest day the Home Office explained: "The long hours worked by the police in comparison with industry represent one of the most serious obstacles to obtaining men for the service."

Further measures included the provision of good sports and social facilities and the provision of adequate housing for all police officers. In 1958 the standing joint committee agreed to co-operate with the town council at Bedford and the county education committee in funding the construction and maintenance of an athletic ground and pavilion at Newnham Avenue, Bedford. The first floor of the pavilion was allocated exclusively for the use of the police and the new recreational facilities were taken into use in 1960.

Poor housing arrangements contributed to the constabulary's recruitment problems and the standing joint committee supplemented the house building programme through the purchase of suitable existing accommodation. Increased expenditure on house building also benefited the level of local service offered by the constabulary. Many purpose built houses, erected in smaller towns and villages, included a police office and at Woburn a well equipped block of houses, with an office and garages attached, served as an adequate replacement for the old Leighton Street police station which was sold in 1957.

Unfortunately the measures designed to make the police service more attractive to potential recruits were of limited success and the number of vacancies in the authorised establishment of the county constabulary remained high. Significantly, police pay had not improved and by the end of the 1950s the minimum wage for a constable was only two-thirds of the salary typically on offer to employees in industry.

In addition to the house building programme the standing joint committee commissioned a number of major building projects to improve the network of police stations in the county's major towns. In 1956 the committee accepted a tender of £33,243 for the construction of a new police station at Ampthill and the building was officially opened two years later on 21st March 1958. A number of police sub-stations were also constructed during Mr Pratt's term of office as chief constable and the first of these, located in Putnoe, Bedford, opened in August 1958. In the following year Farley Hill sub-station in Luton became operational and Houghton Regis sub-station was occupied early in 1962.

Advances in Communications.

In the summer of 1958 the chief constable reported on developments concerning the use of wireless equipment in the county constabulary. "All of the four-wheeled vehicles owned by the police authority have been fitted with wireless receiving and transmitting sets but wireless equipment suitable for use on motorcycles has now become available. Four motorcycles were recently acquired for use by the road traffic department and wireless apparatus for these machines is very necessary if the best use is to be made of them. Nine other lightweight machines are being used for the supervision of the outlying districts of Bedford and Luton and they are proving invaluable, the only criticism being the loss of contact with constables in between their set points. It would add very considerably to the efficient policing of the towns of Bedford and Luton if the new lightweight motorcycles were also equipped with wireless." All thirteen vehicles were subsequently fitted with wireless apparatus.

The chief constable further reported on the progress of an experiment regarding the use of telecommunications by the force. "The committee will recall that I previously reported the purchase of one teleprinter on the telex service, which was taken into use in the information room at police headquarters, initially for an experimental period of twelve months. I am pleased to inform the committee that the value of this means of communication between forces has proved itself beyond dispute. The teleprinter is in daily use, the bulk of the calls being made to London. A three minute call by telex to London costs 9d whereas an ordinary telephone call to the same number costs 1/10d. There are now over thirty forces equipped with telex machines and although we are still the only force in our district connected with the service I have been informed that four other forces in the district are installing telex equipment before the end of the year. As more forces install this equipment we shall be able to further reduce the costs incurred in circulating information by telephone."

Policing the M1 Motorway.

During the late 1950s the Bedfordshire Constabulary played a leading role in formulating detailed plans for the efficient policing of the M1 motorway. The chief constable travelled to Germany and

Three Ford Zephyr Farnham estate cars were converted for police use on the M1 motorway which opened in 1959. The cars were the first to be painted white and fitted with flashing blue beacons

Holland as a member of a three man delegation sent to observe the policing techniques employed on the continent to regulate traffic on fast free-flowing highways. On returning to Bedfordshire Mr Pratt's first step was to secure the purchase of three cars suitable for motorway patrol work. "In November 1959 a nineteen mile stretch of motorway, part of the first major section of the new Yorkshire Highway, will be opened to the public in Bedfordshire. The patrol and supervision of the motorway will be a task which is different from any other we have undertaken in the past and I recommend that the establishment of the road traffic vehicle fleet (at present ten cars and four motorcycles), be augmented by three Zephyr Farnham conversion estate cars, to be used for the sole purpose of patrolling the new highway."

The three cars were purchased at a cost of £1,246 each and were converted for police purposes at the county workshops in Kempston. Estate cars were favoured because of the large amount of equipment to be carried on the motorway. "Inside, in carefully pre-arranged order, will be a series of warning signs and a number of two foot high traffic cones. There will also be white coats, which must be worn as soon as the police officers reach the scene of an accident, mountain rescue type stretchers for use on steep embankments, a shovel, broom, first aid kit and portable lighting equipment."

Up to 1959 police cars, by tradition, had been black in colour but the motorway patrols were intended to provide a particularly conspicuous police presence on the highway and accordingly the Ford Zephyrs were painted brilliant white. They also incorporated a number of other new features which were fully described in a special report on the cars carried in the Bedfordshire Times. "There is little doubt that the three motorway patrol vehicles will maintain a highly visible presence on the motorway. Not only do they carry a powerful blue flashing beacon on the roof but along the front bonnet in nine inch high letters is the word 'Police'. The lettering has remarkable reflective qualities and can be seen easily in the glare of headlamps at night. The cars also have reflective cream stripes on the coachwork.

"Lives may well depend on a patrol car reaching the scene of an accident as soon as possible and on such vital journeys a two-tone horn driven by a specially fitted compressor will herald its approach. The distinctive high pitched note, so different from the more usual warning bells of fire engines and ambulances, is guaranteed to command instant attention. Your correspondent, who travelled along the motorway in one of the patrol cars, can personally vouch for the incredulous gaze of the workmen who heard the horn's strange notes for the first time."

The motorway patrol cars were also fitted with a 'Stop' sign at the rear and a powerful loud hailing system. The Bedfordshire Times concluded that the innovation of white paintwork, blue beacon and two-tone horn showed "a bold and imaginative approach" to the problems of policing the new motorway.

The M1 was opened to the public on 2nd November 1959 at the Pepperstock junction by the Minister of Transport, Mr Ernest Marples. "There was loud cheering and applause when Mr Marples declared the road open. He then walked to a nearby police patrol car and gave a radio signal to the county police stationed along the route to open the motorway to traffic. Then the first of the many vehicles waiting on the slip road was allowed on to the motorway and soon a steady flow of traffic was seen passing in both directions."

The policing of the motorway produced a heavy workload for the county constabulary and in May 1960 Mr Pratt reported: "Since the opening of the M1, the nineteen mile stretch of motorway in Bedfordshire has been patrolled twenty-four hours a day. It has been found necessary to have two of the motorway patrol vehicles on the road between 8 a.m. and midnight and all three cars have already travelled between 31,000 and 34,000 miles. The crews of the vehicles, who have been specially trained for the work, are fully employed and have dealt with an average of 700 calls a month. The emergency telephones on the motorway, which are linked to Ampthill police station, have produced, on average, 550 emergency calls per month and the system is working very smoothly.

"Quite clearly the M1 will be very busy during the coming summer and in view of the very high mileage performed by our three cars, I have arranged for two of our motorcycles to be transferred to the motorway unit in the near future.

"We have worked in very close contact with the Ministry of Transport since the opening of the motorway and submit monthly reports which I understand have been of great use to the Ministry. I am pleased to inform the committee that the method of policing carried out on the M1 by the Bedfordshire Constabulary, in conjunction with neighbouring police forces, is to be adopted as standard operating procedure on all stretches of motorway constructed in the future."

In January 1960 increasing national concern regarding the accountability of the police led the Government to appoint a Royal

Commission under the chairmanship of Sir Henry Willink, Q.C. "to review the constitutional position of the police and to examine the arrangements for their control and administration throughout Great Britain." Subsequently Mr Pratt reported: "On the 14th, 15th and 16th February 1961 the annual inspection of the force was carried out by Her Majesty's Inspector of Constabulary, Commander W. J. A. Willis, who was accompanied on the first day of the visit by Sir Ian Jacob, vice-chairman of the Royal Commission reviewing the police, and also Mr T. A. Critchley, the secretary to the commission. Her Majesty's Inspector of Constabulary commented very favourably upon the standard of efficiency throughout the force."

The A6 Murder.

While the Royal Commission pursued its wide ranging enquiries into the administration of the police, the Bedfordshire Constabulary began its investigation of the A6 murder which led to the conviction and execution of James Hanratty.

On the evening of Tuesday, 22nd August 1961 Michael Gregsten and Valerie Storie were parked in a grey Morris Minor in a deserted cornfield at Dorney Reach, in Buckinghamshire, when they were disturbed by a gunman who told them, "this is a hold-up. I am a desperate man." He climbed into the back of the car and forced the couple to drive first to Slough then to St. Albans and eventually onto the A6 in Bedfordshire. Finally Gregsten was directed to pull into the lay-by at Deadman's Hill on the A6 near Clophill.

The gunman then shot Gregsten twice in the head at close range and Miss Storie was raped at gunpoint. The murderer subsequently ordered Valerie Storie to drag Gregsten's body out of the car and when she had done so she was shot five times. The gunman walked over to her to check that she was dead, and Miss Storie pretended that she was, by holding her breath. The murderer then drove away in the Morris Minor which was later found abandoned at Ilford.

The investigation of the case continued over a period of four months and Mr Pratt reported: "This murder and the enquiries consequent upon it have placed an enormous burden of additional work upon the force as a whole. Twenty-six members of the force have been engaged whole time in the 'Murder Room' at headquarters and an enormous amount of information has been sifted, checked and re-checked. The work has been arduous and sometimes monotonous, yet has been carried out with minute accuracy."

Two BSA 650cc twin cylinder motorcycles were used to supplement the Ford Zephyr patrols on the motorway

Commander Willis returned to Bedfordshire as an Inspector of Constabulary to carry out the annual inspection of the force

The enquiries made by the police soon led to James Hanratty becoming a suspect in the murder investigation and he was eventually arrested in Blackpool on 11th October 1961. He was charged with the A6 murder shortly afterwards and the highly publicised trial held in January and February 1962 proved to be controversial.

The murder weapon was found under the back seat on the top floor of a 36A London Transport bus on 24th August 1961, the day after the killing, and on 11th September two .38 calibre cartridges which had been fired from the weapon were found in room 24 of the Vienna Hotel in Maida Vale. At the trial the prosecution was able to establish that James Hanratty had stayed in room 24 at the Vienna Hotel on 21st August 1961 and that prior to that date he had been making enquiries about acquiring a gun. Another prosecution witness testified that Hanratty had once told him that the rear seat on top of a bus was a good place to hide things.

The defence was able to show that the manager of the Vienna Hotel had made contradictory statements to the police and that one of the statements which had been retracted contained incriminating evidence against another suspect in the case, a man named Peter Alphon who had also stayed at the hotel.

A further central feature of the prosecution case was the evidence of three separate witnesses who identified Hanratty as the murderer. On 14th October 1961 Valerie Storie picked Hanratty out at an identity parade at Stoke Mandeville Hospital. Each man on the line up was required to repeat the words "Be quiet, I am thinking" – a phrase which had been used by the murderer. Storie recalled that the gunman had not been able to pronounce the 'th' sound properly but had said "I am finking." Hanratty did in fact speak in this way.

The defence pointed out that Miss Storie had attended an earlier identity parade at Guy's Hospital on 24th September and that she had then picked out a man who had no connection with the case. Storie had only seen the murderer's face for a second in the light of headlamps from a passing car and the defence argued that her identification of Hanratty was unduly influenced by his mispronunciation of 'thinking' which was a commonly heard mistake.

A second witness named Skillet had also identified Hanratty during an identity parade at police headquarters in Bedford on 13th October. This witness had challenged the driver of a grey Morris Minor over his inconsiderate driving in Ilford early in the morning of 23rd August. Skillet positively identified Hanratty as the driver of the car, as did a third witness who had seen the Morris Minor being driven close to where it was eventually abandoned. The defence drew attention to the fact that a passenger travelling with Skillet, who had enjoyed a slightly better view of the murderer, had not been able to identify Hanratty. All three identifications, it was argued, were based on very brief sightings of the subject.

During the weeks preceding the trial James Hanratty was remanded in Brixton gaol and subsequently a convict named Langdale gave evidence for the prosecution alleging that Hanratty had confessed to the A6 murder in prison. Langdale's credibility as a witness was damaged, however, by the revelation that the story of the confession had been sold to the newspapers for personal gain.

James Hanratty had originally stated that he was in Liverpool at the time of the murder but that three men who could substantiate his alibi would not come forward because they were wanted by the police. During the trial Hanratty changed his alibi and stated he had in fact been at a guesthouse in Rhyl on the night of 22nd August. The landlady of a boarding house in Rhyl was called to the stand by the defence but her evidence as to the exact dates that James Hanratty had been in Rhyl was vague. The prosecution, by contrast, was able to produce three witnesses who had stayed at the guesthouse in question on the 22nd and 23rd August 1961. All three gave evidence that they had not seen Hanratty there.

The trial, which lasted twenty-one days, was at the time the longest murder trial on record. The jury took nine hours and fifty minutes to reach their verdict – also the longest retirement. The eleven jurors (one had been excused because of a tendency to faint at the mention of blood) returned a unanimous verdict of guilty and Hanratty was executed at 8 a.m. on Wednesday, 4th April 1962 at Bedford Prison.

Not everyone was convinced of Hanratty's guilt and the A6 Murder Committee was formed to try and establish his innocence. Controversy concerning the case was fuelled when Peter Alphon confessed to the murder in Paris in 1962. However, Alphon's credibility was undermined by the financial gain he made from selling his story, and critics further pointed out that he had taken part in an identity parade attended by Miss Storie during the original investigation and that she had not picked him out. Peter Alphon was one of four men who confessed to the murder after the trial and execution.

At the same time, witnesses, claiming to have remembered more about the facts in question, made statements which strengthened Hanratty's Rhyl alibi. Four books were written about the case and it was alleged that Hanratty had been framed by his criminal associates or had been the victim of a conspiracy by the authorities.

In 1974 public disquiet concerning the case led the Home Secretary, Mr Roy Jenkins, to ask Mr C. Lewis Hawser, Q.C. to re-examine the evidence. After a thorough review of the many reports and transcripts relating to the case Mr Lewis Hawser presented his report on 26th March 1975 and firmly rejected calls for a pardon. "My conclusion is that at the end of the day the case against Mr Hanratty remains overwhelming and that the additional material, set into the framework of the case as a whole, does not cast any real doubt upon the jury's verdict." Despite the Lewis Hawser report many people remained convinced of Hanratty's innocence and the A6 murder continues to be the subject of controversy.

On the morning of 2nd November 1962 Her Majesty the Queen and His Royal Highness the Duke of Edinburgh visited the borough of Luton, touring the new public library in the civic square before taking lunch in the assembly room at the town hall. The Luton News and Bedfordshire Advertiser reported: "It was the first ever official civic visit to the borough by a reigning monarch. Two police outriders and a green Bedfordshire police Jaguar escorted the Queen's maroon Rolls Royce to the new library from the borough boundary. The town was a blaze of colour for the royal visit and even though bunting and flags hung heavily in the rain, six thousand coloured fairy lights, decorating the town centre, twinkled through the gloom. Thousands of people waited for as much as three hours in the rain hoping to catch a glimpse of the Queen."

At the library Her Majesty was greeted by the Lord-Lieutenant of Bedfordshire, Major Simon Whitbread, and Mr and Mrs Pratt were among the local dignitaries presented to the Queen inside the new building. Mr Pratt later reported to the standing joint committee on the arrangements for the policing of the royal visit. "All the officers who could safely be spared from the various divisions of the force were moved into Luton for special duty. Additional assistance was rendered by the Chief Constable of Hertfordshire who supplied two sergeants and thirty constables under the police mutual aid agreement.

"The preparations made by the police worked very smoothly and I have since received a congratulatory letter from the

Lord-Lieutenant, Major Whitbread, your chairman, who forwarded an extract from a letter he received from Buckingham Palace. I have also received letters of appreciation from the Mayor of Luton and the chief regional officer of the Central Office of Information."

In 1963 the chief constable reported to the standing joint committee concerning the progress of the new underwater search and recovery section. "This unit was formed and became operational in May 1962. The present strength is one sergeant and seven operational divers with three novice divers at the moment in training. All members of the section perform normal police duties and are called together as a team when the need arises. During 1962 the section was called out on nine occasions. Eight calls were in connection with a search for property and in four of these cases the property was recovered. In the other four cases the section was able to confirm that the property sought was not in the search area. The ninth call was for the recovery of a body – which was successful.

"The underwater search and recovery section has proved itself a most useful addition to the force and a great deal of time, to say nothing of anxiety, is saved by using divers instead of the old fashioned method of dragging a river or pond with grapples and rope."

The Police Act of 1964.

In November 1963, the Government, having considered the findings of the Royal Commission on the police, introduced a wide ranging Police Bill into Parliament. The Government's proposals included wider powers for the Home Secretary to compel police forces to amalgamate in the interests of efficiency. This was particularly important in Bedfordshire where the borough of Luton had successfully applied to the Local Government Boundary Commission for county borough status. As a county borough Luton was to become an independent area for the purpose of local government, quite separate from the rest of Bedfordshire. A memorandum to the standing joint committee in 1963 further explained: "When Luton becomes a county borough, the appointed date for which is likely to be 1st April 1964, the corporation of Luton will automatically become the police authority for the town and an independent police force will be established unless other arrangements are agreed between the corporation and the county authorities."

Representatives from the Luton borough council and the standing joint committee met at the Home Office in 1963 to discuss the situation. The chairman of the delegation from the county subsequently reported: "The Secretary of State for Home Affairs referred to the recommendations of the Royal Commission on the police concerning the minimum size of police forces and said that in his view it would be unfortunate if a separate force were to be established in Luton which might have to be amalgamated with some other force soon afterwards. He suggested that the two authorities might consider a combined force on a temporary basis until Parliament had reached a decision on the commission's recommendations.

"Your delegation informed the Home Secretary that they would be willing to recommend such an arrangement to a full meeting of the standing joint committee but the representatives from the corporation of Luton intimated, that although the matter had not been considered by the borough council as a whole, there was a unanimous recommendation from the appropriate council committee that a separate force should be established for the county borough. The Home Secretary urged that very serious consideration should be given to at least the temporary establishment of a combined force under the joint control of the county and borough authorities and made it clear that if separate forces were created, this step must be taken in the face of his warning that early compulsory amalgamations might result from new legislation."

Despite this cautionary advice from the Home Office the corporation of Luton opted to establish an independent police force and on 1st April 1964 one hundred and fifty-four officers from the Bedfordshire Constabulary, most of whom were already serving in Luton, transferred to the new county borough force. The Police Act of 1964 received the Royal Assent in the following June and three months later the chairman of the standing joint committee reported: "I have received notice from the Secretary of State for Home Affairs of a proposed amalgamation scheme, to be made by him, by which the county of Bedford and the county borough of Luton will form a combined police area as from 1st June 1965." The borough of Luton immediately lodged an official objection to the proposed scheme which necessitated a public inquiry and in the meantime there were other important developments affecting the Bedfordshire Constabulary.

The Police Act of 1964 contained extensive legislation which implemented most of the recommendations made by the Royal Commission chaired by Lord Willink. The primary aim of the legislation was to reform the administration of the police and the Act defined and adjusted the respective duties and powers of the Home Secretary, local police authorities and chief constables.

The Home Secretary was placed under a duty to promote the efficiency of the police service and in order to carry out this obligation he was empowered to compel forces to collaborate in providing national or regional common services. Accordingly, in November 1964, Mr Pratt reported on the establishment of the No. 5 Regional Crime Squad, covering part of the Home and Eastern Counties. "The Bedford unit of the squad consists of a detective inspector in charge together with two detective sergeants and two detective constables. Detective Inspector A. S. Lucas of the county force has been seconded to command the unit."

The Home Secretary was further empowered to order amalgamation schemes such as that proposed for Luton and Bedfordshire; to require a chief constable to retire in the interests of efficiency; to demand a report from a chief constable on any aspect of the policing of his force area; and to set up a public inquiry to examine the policing of any locality. Finally the appointment of deputy and assistant chief constables was also made subject to the approval of the Home Secretary. The role of Her Majesty's Inspectorate of Constabulary was expanded to advise the Secretary of State for Home Affairs in the exercise of his powers.

The Police Act intended that police forces should be made more accountable to locally elected officials and on 1st June 1965 the composition of every local police authority was reconstituted on the basis of two-thirds elected councillors and one-third magistrates. The magistrates retained some representation because of their long experience of police matters. In addition, in county areas, the financial autonomy which the standing joint committees had enjoyed with respect to their local county council was removed from the newly formed police authorities. A Home Office memorandum explained: "Under the financial provisions of the Police Act any expenditure out of police funds, excepting payments for salaries, pensions and the like, will require the approval of the county council. It is anticipated that this will be given through the submission and approval of estimates."

The primary duty of a police authority was to "secure the maintenance of an adequate and efficient police" for the local area. This included the provision and repair of the buildings, vehicles and equipment required for police purposes and also the employment of any civilian staff needed. A police authority was also empowered "to require the chief constable to submit a report in writing on any matter connected with the policing of the area."

However, there was a proviso: "the chief constable may refuse to supply information which ought not to be disclosed in the public interest or which is not needed for the discharge of the duties of the police authority." The Home Secretary was given the right of intervention to settle any dispute arising between the police authority and the chief constable.

Under the terms of the Police Act chief constables were to exercise "direction and control" over their police forces, and they remained free from any direct political or outside influence on all operational matters, including issues of broad policy. Instead they were to be held accountable through the powers of the Home Secretary and the local police authority to demand reports from them and through the close supervision of Her Majesty's Inspectorate of Constabulary. The Police Act also required chief constables to prepare an annual report on the policing of their force area for the information of the Home Office and the police authority.

The overall effect of the legislation contained in the Police Act of 1964 was to strengthen the influence of central Government in the administration of the police. There had been widespread calls for the establishment of a centrally administered national police force, a view supported by one member of the Royal Commission on the police. The Government rejected such calls, believing that there was value in retaining police forces which were essentially local in character. In introducing the Police Bill to Parliament, the Home Secretary, Mr R. A. Butler, argued that the tri-partite arrangements for sharing the control of the police between chief officers and central and local government was a safeguard against the abuse of power based on the tried and tested system of constitutional checks and balances.

Mr Pratt published the first annual report of the Bedfordshire Constabulary in April 1965. The report contained a wealth of statistical information on the activities of the force during the previous year but also included sections on developments within the constabulary and incidents of note. The chief constable reported: "The building of the new six storey divisional headquarters at Bedford which commenced in June 1962 was completed in the summer of 1964 and the new police station was opened to the public in September. This magnificent building replaced a very old and inadequate station and provides much improved working conditions and first class facilities for recreation and sport in the gymnasium, the rifle range and the club premises." The design specifications for the new police station at Greyfriars included provision for the construction of further storeys to accommodate expansion at some future date. Mr Pratt further reported: "Mr A. Armstrong was appointed assistant chief constable of the force with effect from 27th July 1964 to succeed Mr R. C. Machin, M.B.E., who retired on pension."

One of the incidents dealt with by the Bedfordshire Constabulary in 1964 reflected a common public order problem experienced by the police in the 1960s. "An anticipated clash between elements of 'Mods' and 'Rockers' at Bedford on Sunday, 24th May 1964 was not allowed to develop. Following information of a planned disturbance similar to those which had previously occurred at seaside resorts, police reinforcements were drafted into the town. During the afternoon three hundred youths roamed around the riverside in groups. A strong force of police officers maintained a constant patrol of the embankment and parks and prevented the youths from gathering in large numbers. Five arrests were made for offences of obstruction, breach of the peace, and possession of an offensive weapon, and the culprits were severely dealt with by the courts."

Earlier in 1964 the county constabulary had been called on to police a record crowd at the Eyrie, Ford End Road, Bedford, the home ground of Bedford Town Football Club. The Southern League Club had been drawn at home in the fourth round of the F.A. Cup against Carlisle United after defeating Newcastle United 2–1 away at St James' Park in the previous round. The 18,500 tickets for the match were sold out and there was a heavy police presence both inside and outside the ground. There was a brief pitch invasion when Bedford, 1–0 down, had an equalising goal disallowed for offside. The Bedford Record reported: "Protesting fans rushed onto the pitch but were quickly ushered off by the police." In 1964 the primary concern of the constabulary at a football match was not the threat of hooliganism. Mr Pratt's report of the policing of the fixture focused on public safety and the regulation of traffic in the vicinity of the stadium. "The police arrangements enabled a steady flow of traffic to be maintained and vehicles were able to leave the parking areas with a minimum of delay." Carlisle United won the cup tie 3–0.

At twelve noon on 7th May 1965, at Greyfriars police station, the standing joint committee of Bedfordshire met for the last time and the chief constable paid tribute to their efforts over the years in support of the police. "I wish to place on record on behalf of all the members of the force, past and present, our gratitude for the very real interest the standing joint committee has always taken in the well-being and efficiency of the county constabulary." One of the final duties of the committee concerned the provision of mutual aid to the police in Oxfordshire. Mr Pratt reported: "A contingent of officers from the county force assisted on the occasion of the funeral of the late Sir Winston Churchill at Bladon in Oxfordshire on 30th January 1965. Most of the police authorities affording such assistance subsequently decided to waive any charges arising from the commitment." The standing joint committee similarly resolved to waive all charges.

The first meeting of the new Bedfordshire police authority took place on Thursday, 10th June 1965 at the Shire Hall in Bedford. The committee was composed of twelve members appointed by the county council, including Major Simon Whitbread, the chairman of the old standing joint committee, and six members appointed by the quarter sessions. Major Whitbread was duly elected chairman of the new committee.

Mr Pratt presented his annual report for 1965 to the police committee early in the following year. "A new divisional headquarters for the road traffic department at Kempston was taken into use on 8th June 1965. The building consists of a block of fourteen garages with office accommodation above and replaces the inadequate facilities used by the department in the house adjacent to Kempston police station." The chief constable also reported on a measure designed to ease pressure of work on the constabulary which was still sixty-two officers short of its authorised strength. "Traffic wardens were introduced in Bedford in May 1965, the complement of wardens being eight in all. The first parking tickets were issued in June and by the end of the year 2,744 offences had been dealt with in this way. The wardens have been accepted, and in the main welcomed, by members of the public."

Amalgamation with Luton.

The most significant event of 1965 concerned the proposed merger with Luton. "In February a public inquiry was held at the Shire Hall in Bedford. This arose from the objection made by the watch committee of the county borough of Luton to proposals under the Police Act of 1964 for the amalgamation, for police purposes, of the area comprising the county of Bedford and the county borough of Luton."

The Home Secretary was represented at the public inquiry as well as the two police authorities concerned and evidence was heard over a period of five days, with concluding arguments being presented on a sixth day at a later stage. The inquiry was conducted in an atmosphere of bitterness and the more contentious aspects of the evidence attracted national press coverage.

The principal witness on behalf of the Home Secretary was Her Majesty's Inspector of Constabulary, Mr P. E. Brodie, who presented a formidable case against the continuance of small police forces on the grounds of efficiency and economy. However, the case advanced by the authorities at Luton against the proposed amalgamation was based on two main elements and proved to be equally persuasive.

The first part of the case asserted that there were no social and economic ties between Luton and the county of Bedfordshire and that therefore there was no logical reason to combine the two areas. Mr Charles E. Scholefield who conducted the inquiry commented: "Throughout the evidence before me it was clear that Luton felt itself, to a greater extent than I have previously met in the case of any local government area, to be no part of Bedfordshire and to be anxious to shed every possible Bedfordshire connection."

The second part of the Luton case contained stinging criticisms concerning the policing arrangements which had existed in Luton when the town was a part of the Bedfordshire Constabulary between 1947 and 1964. It was alleged that the police buildings at Luton had been neglected, that the division had been kept short of manpower and equipment, and that officers at Luton had been passed over for promotion. This, it was contended, was in complete contrast with the situation in the new county borough force at Luton which was well equipped, well housed, offered excellent promotion prospects for promising officers, and consequently was also in a favourable position to recruit up to full strength.

Such allegations made for sensational reports in the newspapers and the inquiry was a disconcerting experience for the county force which had adopted a neutral stance regarding the proposed amalgamations.

The only evidence presented by the county authorities at the inquiry was offered in response to the specific criticisms made by the borough of Luton. Mr Scholefield dismissed the allegations against the county constabulary concerning the provision of buildings, manpower and equipment, accepting that other divisions of the county police force had laboured under difficulties similar to those experienced at Luton because of a general shortage of resources. The criticism regarding the small number of promotions given to men stationed at Luton was complicated by the terms of the merger between the county constabulary and the

Luton borough force in 1947. Former borough officers had received a guarantee that they would not be moved from Luton without their agreement. The county authorities submitted that subsequently many of the borough officers had refused promotions involving a transfer to another division while others had refused transfers which would have widened their police experience and made them better qualified for promotion. Mr Scholefield concluded that although the grievance felt by the Luton men was genuine it was not entirely reasonable.

Despite rejecting the criticisms made against the county constabulary, Mr Scholefield attached importance to the fact that they had been made. They reinforced his deep concern over the strength of the opposition to the amalgamation scheme at Luton. At the same time he expressed considerable admiration for the achievements of the small county borough force and fully accepted that the greater wealth of the council at Luton had brought substantial benefits to the force in terms of improved equipment and facilities.

The strength of the evidence presented on behalf of the Home Secretary and on behalf of the borough of Luton clearly left Mr Scholefield in two minds regarding the proposed amalgamation and this was reflected in the non-committal conclusion to his report of inquiry which was unsatisfactory to all the parties concerned. He recommended that the county and borough forces "should not be combined for the present but allowed to continue as they are for an experimental period," but, he added, "if it is not practicable to allow for such an experimental period the two forces should be compelled to amalgamate now."

The Home Secretary remained convinced that Luton was attempting to retain a form of police organisation that was outdated and he ordered that the amalgamation scheme should go ahead. Accordingly on 1st April 1966 the county and borough forces merged to form the Bedfordshire and Luton Constabulary. In his annual report for 1966 Mr Pratt, who was appointed as the chief constable of the new constabulary, outlined the structure of the combined force. "In spite of the misgivings which some people may have had, the new force was quickly into its stride and the problems which arose were soon ironed out. The constabulary is now organised in six divisions.

"'A' division comprises the administration and criminal investigation departments located at force headquarters in Bedford. 'B' division comprises Bedford and the north of Bedfordshire, the divisional headquarters are situated in Bedford and there are sub-divisional stations at Kempston and Sharnbrook. 'C' division constitutes Biggleswade and mid-Bedfordshire, the divisional headquarters are located in Biggleswade and there is a sub-divisional station at Ampthill. There are two divisions in the south of the county, 'D' division and 'F' division. The divisional headquarters for 'D' division are situated at Dunstable and there is also a sub-divisional station at Leighton Buzzard. The town of Luton has been designated 'F' division. 'E' division – Road Traffic – has been divided into a northern sub-division based at Kempston and a southern sub-division based at Luton."

The authorised establishment of the combined force was eight hundred and three officers although its actual strength was well below seven hundred men and women. The Bedfordshire and Luton police authority, the third police committee to be entrusted with the administration of the county force in the space of a year, met in full session for the first time at the Ampthill rural district council chambers at 2.30 p.m. on Friday, 17th June 1966. The authority consisted of twelve Bedfordshire county councillors and six magistrates from the county quarter sessions together with ten Luton borough councillors and five justices from the borough. Major Whitbread was elected as the chairman of the new authority to provide some continuity during the period of transition.

Mr Pratt prepared a special report for the members of the new police authority reviewing developments in the county force immediately prior to the amalgamation with Luton: "I have recently formed in the force a mobile operational group known as the Bedfordshire Flying Column and this became operational on an experimental basis on 12th February 1966. This operational unit allows resources to be concentrated on specific problems as they arise and so far has dealt with complaints of rowdyism, and checked on concentrations of unattended vehicles with a view to preventing larceny, arresting thieves, and detecting road fund licence offences. The column comprises one inspector, two sergeants, eight constables (two of whom are dog handlers), one woman sergeant and one woman constable." The experiment produced worthwhile results and the Flying Column continued to operate successfully for a number of years.

Mr Pratt also reported on the opening of a new sub-station at Stotfold on the 15th February 1966 and on the provision of summer uniforms for policewomen. "During the summer months when weather conditions are favourable policewomen are permitted to discard their jackets and to perform duty in their skirts and blouses, but even so these garments can be most uncomfortable to wear in hot weather. Earlier in the year I purchased thirty short-sleeved navy blue dresses in rayon and cotton material (with a belt and two imitation breast pockets) in suitable sizes at a cost of 59/11d each. These will be worn in hot weather during the summer months. The dresses will have epaulettes attached bearing the officers' rank and number."

Unit Beat Policing.

In September 1966 the chief constable approached the police authority with regard to developments in the use of police wireless. "The force has been testing a number of personal transmitter-receiver wireless sets and is at present equipped with twenty-five such sets. Fifteen Cossor sets with a control station have been installed at Bedford and ten Lancon sets with a control station are in use at Luton. Ten Pye sets are due to be delivered later this year with new control equipment and it is proposed to install these at Bedford and transfer the existing Cossor sets to Dunstable and Leighton Buzzard. These personal wireless sets enable police officers to remain in constant touch with their stations and greatly increase efficiency." The police authority resolved to make funds available for the purchase of further pocket wireless sets and their more widespread use allowed the county constabulary to adopt a new system of patrolling.

In his annual report for 1967 Mr Pratt informed the police authority: "The main feature of the year was the introduction of a new method of policing throughout the force area – the coverage of the whole county by UHF personal pocket radios on three separate wavelengths and the mechanisation of all beats both rural and urban. A system known as 'unit beat policing' was introduced to the larger urban areas of the force, i.e. Bedford, Luton, Dunstable and Leighton Buzzard on 1st September 1967. Patrols are mounted in 'Panda' cars on a twenty-four hour basis. A few months previously a similar method of policing was put into operation in the rural districts. The new rural scheme, in essence, is a modified form of unit beat policing which provides cover in 'Panda' cars for sixteen hours each day with a resident constable in some of the larger villages. The rural officers are provided with the extra high frequency Pye 'pocketfones' which operate on the same frequency as the unit beat policing schemes in the urban area. It is already clear that the new method of urban and rural beat policing is a success and I have no doubt that this will be the pattern for many years to come."

Unit Beat Policing. British Motor Corporation Minis were used in urban areas and Vauxhall Viva motor cars in rural districts

The advent of personal wireless sets led to a phasing out of the police box system and with the introduction of unit beat policing the last police boxes in the county were pulled down. The force purchased a fleet of British Motor Corporation Minis for use in the urban scheme while the rural beats were covered in Vauxhall Viva motor cars. Unit beat policing remains an integral part of the police patrol methods employed in the present day.

The new urban and rural patrol schemes provided good response times to incidents requiring the attention of the police and offered a partial solution to the constabulary's manpower shortage but Mr Pratt also recognised the potential disadvantages of the use of motorised patrols. The principal drawback was the loss of contact with the public which had always been one of the main benefits of patrolling on foot. The chief constable attempted to minimise the consequences of this loss of contact by promoting activities which strengthened the ties between the police and the community. He reported: "It is of the utmost importance that every encouragement should be given to police officers to make contact with the public in spheres other than in their official role as law enforcement officers. Leisure time activities which bring officers into closer contact with the public can do much to foster a good relationship with the wider community."

Mr Pratt included a section in each year's annual report which detailed the voluntary and charity work undertaken by police officers in the community and listed any other sporting or social activities which promoted better contacts with the public. In 1967 the chief constable made special mention of the force choir which contained both male and female members and was believed to be the first mixed voice police choir in the country. "The Bedfordshire Police Choir under its conductor, Sergeant Deeley, gave twenty-one concerts for women's institutes, schools and old people's homes. The choir had a particularly successful year, winning the premier trophy at the St. Albans Choral Festival for the second year running."

Other developments during 1967 included the reorganisation of the operational structure of the force. "On 1st July 1967 divisional boundaries were revised and this resulted in the disappearance of the Biggleswade division; the Biggleswade sub-division was absorbed by the Bedford division, and the Ampthill sub-division by the Dunstable division." Within a few months of the changes Sharnbrook police station was closed and put up for sale. There was also new legislation in the Road Safety Act of 1967 to combat the growing problem of drinking and driving. Mr Pratt reported:

"Since 9th October 1967, when the section of the Road Safety Act relating to the use of breathalyser equipment became operative, there has been a substantial reduction in the amount of traffic seen late at night in this county, particularly at weekends. It is also worthy of note that the number of road accidents between the hours of 9 p.m. and midnight involving personal injury during the last three months of 1967 show a twenty-five per cent decrease when compared with the corresponding period in 1966."

Crime Prevention Campaign.

In 1968 over ten thousand crimes were reported to the Bedfordshire and Luton Constabulary, an increase of twelve per cent on the previous year. The figures were in line with national trends which showed that the level of crime in England and Wales had doubled in the space of a decade. The steady rise in offences of theft and burglary, which represented over eighty per cent of all crime in Bedfordshire, led the county constabulary to devote more time and resources to promoting public awareness of simple crime prevention measures.

Mr Pratt reported: "A very ambitious crime prevention project was mounted in Luton between 26th February and 23rd March 1968 in conjunction with a national crime prevention campaign which used the trenchant slogan 'Watch out – there's a thief about!' The local project known as 'Crime cut – Luton' received financial support from both the Home Office and the police committee, and I am pleased to report that many business houses in Luton also supported us with cash donations and other services. A crime prevention exhibition was mounted which attracted 21,000 visitors, campaign literature was distributed throughout Luton and several competitions were organised.

"The campaign and exhibition were successfully launched by Mr Dick Taverne, MP, an Under-Secretary of State at the Home Office, and by that best known of Chief Superintendents – Barlow, now more familiarly known to us as the actor, Mr Stratford Johns. The project was an enormous joint effort by police and public, and an excellent relationship was fostered.

"The Home Office later suggested that in towns with populations of 150,000 people or more there would be advantages in establishing crime prevention panels, to bring together locally interested parties such as the police, local authorities, business and insurance companies, to co-ordinate crime prevention activities. Fortunately as a result of the 'Crime cut – Luton' campaign we had a ready made and experienced crime prevention panel and

I am pleased to inform the police authority that the panel is now operating in close co-operation with my officers at Luton." The crime prevention panel sponsored a number of successful campaigns at Luton over the following years and similar panels were eventually established throughout the whole of Bedfordshire.

In the summer of 1968 the chief constable approached the police authority with reference to developments which affected the policing of the municipal airport at Luton. "For many years the Metropolitan Police have assumed responsibility for the appointment of special branch officers to selected sea and air ports across the country. The Home Office have recently decided that special branch officers should be attached to an increased number of rapidly growing ports, including the airport at Luton. It has also been decided that the Metropolitan Police cannot possibly provide men to cover all the locations envisaged under the planned expansion and consequently the Home Office have asked provincial forces to undertake the responsibility for the ports in their own force areas."

In his annual report for 1968 Mr Pratt informed the police authority: "A special branch unit became operational at Luton Airport on 13th June this year and twenty-four hour cover has been maintained from that date by five detective constables working under the supervision of a detective sergeant and a detective constable from the Metropolitan Police. The Metropolitan officers will be withdrawn when our own detectives have gained sufficient experience of this type of work.

"During the second half of 1968 the special branch officers dealt with 513,000 passengers and 6,166 aircraft movements from outside the United Kingdom. It is anticipated that passenger traffic at Luton Airport will increase considerably in the next two years and extra officers have been trained in airport duties as a reserve for relief and replacement purposes."

The annual report for 1968 also included details of the first full scale exercise mounted to test the constabulary's ability to respond to major disaster. The chief constable reported: "The exercise was held on Sunday, 22nd September 1968 and revolved round the basic situation of a train crash. Invitations were sent to all organisations which would have a part to play in such a situation and the maximum co-operation was received. British Railways authorities had placed 'crashed' coaches at my disposal in a goods siding at Leagrave. More than 100 'casualties' had been put into these coaches when the alert call message was received. The response and subsequent efforts of all concerned were of a very high order.

"Briefing and de-briefing conferences were held and much of value was learned. The plans to deal with such a situation, now amended in the light of the exercise, are sound and workable. These plans have been dovetailed into the general pattern of the major disaster scheme prepared by the Bedfordshire County Council."

One of the developments which arose from the amended disaster plan was the provision of a casualty bureau at Bedford. Mr Pratt reported: "One of the problems which beset the police when dealing with a large number of casualties is the difficulty of identifying the dead and injured and answering enquiries from distressed relatives. In order to relieve the personnel engaged at the scene of the disaster from these difficulties a permanent casualty bureau has been established in the training department at force headquarters. The additional equipment necessary during such an emergency has been installed in the department including a specially designed set of blackboards and telephone jack points in order that ex-directory telephone lines can be utilised."

Specialist Departments.

During the final years of Mr Pratt's tenure of office as chief constable, the nature of police work was becoming increasingly complex and diversified and this in turn led to the formation of specialist departments to cope with some of the extra demands placed on the constabulary. The Drug Squad was established on 11th August 1969 in response to the growing incidence of drug abuse in the county. The squad initially consisted of just two detective officers but the number was increased to four in the summer of the following year. Fifteen arrests were made during 1969 and Mr Pratt reported: "One case of interest took place at a public house in Bedford when uniformed constables searched several youths for drugs whilst the drug squad detectives sat in a corner. After the departure of the patrol officers the detectives saw a youth place a packet of Physeptone on his head and dance round the bar celebrating his supposed escape, at which point he was, in fact, arrested."

In his annual report for 1970 the chief constable informed the police authority of the creation of the Juvenile Liaison Department. "Following a successful trial scheme in Liverpool a juvenile liaison scheme was inaugurated in this county on the 1st January 1970 to combat juvenile delinquency and to provide a nucleus of experienced officers for duties arising from the Children and Young Persons Act 1969. The team is divided into a northern

('B' division) and a southern section ('D' and 'F' divisions) co-ordinated by a chief inspector at force headquarters. One of the primary objects of the police is the prevention of crime and the work of this team is seen merely as an extension of this important function in trying by any legitimate means whatsoever to prevent children developing delinquent tendencies."

Under the scheme juveniles between the ages of 10 and 16 who committed minor criminal offences could be dealt with by way of an official caution given by the new department. In 1970, 723 juveniles were cautioned under the scheme and only 24 of these, or 3.3 per cent, had re-offended by the end of the year. "Due to contacts made under the scheme 569 indictable offences committed by juveniles were reported to the police and dealt with by the officers in the juvenile liaison department. There is no doubt that a large proportion of these offences would not normally have come to our notice and nothing would have been done to deter the child from committing further offences. The key to success in a scheme of this nature is the degree of co-operation between the police and social agencies and it is satisfying to record that a high standard of liaison has been established with the local authority children's department and head teachers."

In 1970 Mr Pratt further reported on a national measure taken "with a view to making police officers more distinguishable from other uniformed services. Diced cap bands were taken into use on 25th September this year and have quickly been accepted by all the members of the force and the public."

One of Mr Pratt's last duties as chief constable was to report the decoration of two members of the Bedfordshire and Luton Constabulary for gallantry. In March 1971 he was "pleased to inform the police authority that Her Majesty the Queen has been graciously pleased to award the British Empire Medal for Gallantry to Constable 438, Brendan Paschal Walsh of 'F' division, and Constable 572, Colin Arthur Jones of 'D' division. The circumstances leading to these awards are that at 9.30 a.m. on Thursday, 9th April 1970 an armed robbery occurred at the National Westminster Bank Limited, George Street, Luton, when staff and customers were held up by four men armed with shotguns and revolvers. The raiders stole £32,625 and made good their escape from the scene in a stolen Rover motor car. Later the car was seen in the Houghton Regis area and was eventually pursued into a field at Toddington by the two constables. Whilst in pursuit the two officers were fired on no less than five times but by their courage, persistence and devotion to duty, they succeeded in arresting one of the raiders and £29,000 of the stolen money was recovered.

"At Nottingham Assizes on 24th June 1970 the man who had been detained pleaded guilty to a number of offences connected with the robbery and was sentenced to ten years' imprisonment. The constables have been commended by the Director of Public Prosecutions and myself, and they were also commended in open court at the conclusion of the trial by Mr Justice Cusack."

Retirement of Mr Pratt.

Mr Pratt retired on 17th July 1971 after completing thirty-five years' service in the police force, nearly eighteen of which were spent as Chief Constable of Bedfordshire. His dedication and professionalism were recognised in the award of the Queen's Police Medal in 1963 and the O.B.E. in 1967. Mr Pratt brought a wife and two children to Bedford on his appointment and was well known as a family man who took a personal interest in the welfare of his officers. He inaugurated the force Family Sports Day, the first of which was held in July 1969 and also founded the Senior Officers' Dining Club. Standing 6′ 6″ tall the chief constable was equally well known for his impressive bearing and imposing physical presence.

Mr Pratt celebrated his Golden Wedding anniversary in 1988 and he and his wife, Brenda Mary, continue to enjoy a happy retirement in a small Devon village near the south coast.

Mr Pratt founded the underwater search and recovery section in May 1962. The section was eventually disbanded in August 1986

MR ANTHONY ARMSTRONG, OBE, QPM

CHAPTER EIGHT

1971 – 1979
ANTHONY ARMSTRONG

ANTHONY Armstrong was born on 29th January 1918 at Walbottle, in Northumberland, a small village lying on the route of Hadrian's Wall to the west of Newcastle. He was brought up in the Methodist faith and spent his early life at Newbiggin-by-the-Sea and on Tyneside before leaving school at the age of sixteen to work in the clerical department of a local transport company.

At the outbreak of the Second World War Mr Armstrong registered as a conscientious objector and volunteered for duty with the British Red Cross in Finland during the 'Winter War' with Russia. He worked as an ambulance driver and hospital orderly throughout the Finnish campaign and later received the Finnish Winter War Service Medal.

In April 1940 Germany invaded Denmark and Norway and Mr Armstrong's Red Cross Unit was sent to assist the allied forces fighting in support of the Norwegians. When the allies were forced to retreat from Scandinavia Mr Armstrong's unit was left behind and he was interned. He was subsequently released during a formal exchange of prisoners and resumed his duties with the Red Cross in the Middle East and North Africa during the desert campaign.

Mr Armstrong's experiences during the war led him to renounce his belief in pacifism and in 1943 he enlisted in the Lancashire Fusiliers. He was posted to India for the remainder of the war and spent much of his Army service in the Military Police at Rawalpindi. In 1946 Mr Armstrong decided to pursue a career in the civil police force and travelled to a British police recruitment mission in Karachi. He was flown back to Britain by the Army but found his applications to the Northumberland Constabulary and other provincial police forces were rejected on the grounds that he was too short. The Army referred the matter to the Home Office; Mr Armstrong was instructed to re-apply to the Northumberland Constabulary and in August 1946, after being demobilised in the rank of captain, he was finally sworn in as a constable.

Between 1946 and 1949 Mr Armstrong worked as a uniformed patrol officer before gaining experience as a detective constable and as a police instructor. He was promoted to sergeant in 1954 and inspector in 1958, taking charge of recruitment in Northumberland and the force building programme. In April 1960 he was appointed deputy commandant at the No. 2 district police training centre, previously commanded by Mr Pratt, and two years later he transferred to the Durham Constabulary on promotion to superintendent. Mr Armstrong joined the Bedfordshire police force as assistant chief constable in 1964 and in the summer of 1971 he was one of sixteen candidates to apply for the post of chief constable of the county on Mr Pratt's retirement. Two other applicants, Mr R. P. Boyes, the Deputy Chief Constable of the Mid-Anglia Constabulary and Mr E. H. Post, the Deputy Chief Constable of the Surrey Constabulary, appeared with Mr Armstrong before the Bedfordshire and Luton police authority at Ampthill on 4th June 1971 when it was unanimously resolved that Mr Armstrong should become the new Chief Constable of Bedfordshire.

Multiple Accident on M1 Motorway.

Within four months of Mr Armstrong's appointment, the county constabulary was called upon to deal with the first major accident on the M1 in Bedfordshire. The chief constable reported: "At 11.00 a.m. on Monday, 29th November 1971 two multiple road traffic accidents occurred on the M1 motorway in the vicinity of Luton. The first accident occurred on the northbound carriageway near the junction with the A.505 and involved thirty-nine vehicles. The second accident took place on the southbound carriageway, approximately four hundred yards north of the first incident, and involved fifty-six vehicles.

"Although the weather had been intermittent fog prior to the accidents, the sun had also been shining. Shortly before 11.00 a.m. a narrow belt of dense fog passed across the motorway and it was then that the accidents took place. Within twenty minutes the fog had completely cleared and the full extent of the disaster became apparent. Both carriageways were completely blocked and at 11.18 a.m. arrangements were made for the motorway to be closed. Extensive diversions were put into operation which affected the flow of traffic in the neighbouring counties of Hertfordshire, Buckinghamshire and Northamptonshire, but the level of co-operation we received from the police forces concerned was excellent.

"The northbound carriageway was not re-opened until 8.55 p.m. and the southbound not until 12.44 a.m. the following day. Taking both accidents, the cost of the tragedy in human terms is as follows:-

Deaths	9
Serious Injuries	20
Slight Injuries	30

"Of the ninety-five motor vehicles involved in the accidents, forty-seven were written off for insurance purposes. Accidents of this magnitude highlight the splendid spirit of co-operation between the various ambulance, fire, hospital and voluntary services but the disaster should have been avoided. Drivers were travelling at speeds beyond their skill and the capability of their vehicles in the conditions that prevailed; in short – too fast, too close."

In his annual report for 1971 Mr Armstrong gave details of a sickening case of child abuse which showed the increasingly sophisticated techniques available to the constabulary in dealing with serious criminal offences. "During the year police officers were called to a house in Luton by the family doctor who had found a nineteen months old child already dead. The baby was covered in bruises and during the post mortem examination small wounds, believed to be bite marks, were found on the child's arm and shoulder. An odontologist was called to carry out tests and came to the opinion that the injuries were human bite marks caused by the child's mother.

"Both mother and father were prosecuted for manslaughter and ill-treatment of the baby, both were found guilty and sentenced to three years' imprisonment. An interesting feature was the evidence of the odontologist, as it was the first, in the manner presented, heard by any court."

1971 also saw the introduction of the constabulary's 'death benefit scheme'. Mr Armstrong reported: "The intention of the scheme is to provide immediate financial assistance to dependants in the event of the death of a member. All the members of the scheme contribute to a benefit fund organised by the local joint branch board of the police federation and administered by the trustees who are representatives of the federation and the superintendents' association."

Manpower Shortage & Building Programme.

The long-term concerns of the constabulary in the early 1970s remained the manpower shortage and the need to modernise the network of police stations in the county. Mr Armstrong reported: "It is interesting to note that since the formation of the Bedfordshire and Luton Constabulary, five years ago, the average annual increase in the strength of the force is under nine new officers. If future increases are restricted to this paltry figure it will be over a decade before we reach our authorised establishment which has not substantially changed for nearly six years and bears no resemblance to true needs. In view of the fact that the number of retirements will probably increase in the next few years, the general situation as regards the strength of the force must be viewed with some concern."

The constabulary responded to the manpower shortage through a major programme of civilianisation involving the introduction of traffic wardens to Dunstable, Kempston, Ampthill and Leighton Buzzard, and the employment of civilians as administrative and public relations officers, scenes of crime officers, driving instructors and vehicle examiners. Overall, the authorised establishment of civilians in the constabulary was increased to nearly three hundred employees.

With regard to the police building programme, Mr Armstrong reported on the development of plans which had been initially drawn up during Mr Pratt's term of office as chief constable. "There are three major building projects before the police authority at present.

1. New divisional headquarters at Luton.
2. New force headquarters.
3. New divisional headquarters at Dunstable.

"The plans for the new police station at Luton are practically complete and it is expected that building will commence in the summer of 1972. The force headquarters has been accommodated in a pleasant Victorian house since 1947 but it is quite inadequate in size and design for a modern police headquarters. The police authority has secured a site at Kempston for a new headquarters and it is hoped to commence building in two to three years time. No decision has yet been made regarding a suitable location for the new Dunstable police station but consultations are currently taking place with a view to acquiring a site in West Street."

Whilst the building programme progressed the constabulary coped with the shortage of space by occupying temporary accommodation. At Luton the road traffic department had already been moved to the old civil defence building in New Street and the regional crime squad office, which had transferred from Bedford, was housed in the Farley Hill sub-station. In Bedford, the training department moved out of 'The Pines' and into Putnoe sub-station whilst other headquarters departments were eventually transferred to five vacant rooms in the Shire Hall. Finally, at Dunstable, the police house adjacent to the police station was converted to provide extra office space.

The heavy expenditure on new police stations was partially offset by savings on other capital projects. By 1971 the demand for police housing had fallen as more and more police officers preferred to purchase their own homes. The house building programme was cancelled and surplus housing stock was gradually sold off. Unit beat policing had made the network of police sub-stations largely redundant and operations were scaled down at Sandy and Houghton Regis, whilst the sub-station at Stotfold was closed and the building leased to the county health authority.

In 1972 Mr Armstrong addressed the general need for long-term planning in the constabulary by establishing the planning and inspection department at force headquarters. "This is a new department consisting of a superintendent, inspector and constable. The work of the department relies to a great extent on liaison in many spheres; with the Home Office, local government authorities, other police forces and commercial organisations. For example, the department is working in conjunction with the Home Office and the police authority architect to draw up the specifications for the new force headquarters. It is also assessing the possible uses for computers in duty planning, maintaining firearms records and producing accident and crime statistics. This study is being carried out with the co-operation of the computer section at County Hall in Bedford.

"The activities of the department extend beyond long-term planning and also include studies on quick return innovations and projects. For example, new charge sheets are to be introduced during 1973 which streamline the charging procedure by combining the charge and bail notices to the accused. Earlier in the year an officer and a police dog were injured with an axe at Luton and some thought was given to obtaining protection from such attacks in the future. After a survey of the materials available six perspex riot shields were purchased. These will stand up to any blow with a blunt instrument but are not bullet proof."

Second Large Scale Accident on Motorway.

At 8.15 a.m. on 16th March 1972, less than six months after the first serious accident on the M1 in Bedfordshire, a second large scale multiple accident occurred on the southbound carriageway of the motorway, near Brogborough. Mr Armstrong reported: "The accident extended north from junction 13 of the motorway for a distance of approximately one mile with the major portion of the accident covering a distance of eight hundred yards and involving two hundred and eight motor vehicles.

"Some five minutes after the multiple accident occurred, a series of eleven small accidents took place nearby on the northbound carriageway. In a distance of just over one mile a further forty-six motor vehicles were involved. The northbound carriageway was blocked until 1.30 p.m. the same day and the southbound carriageway was fully re-opened to through traffic at 11.10 p.m., some fifteen hours after the original accident occurred. The following figures indicate the magnitude of the incident.

Persons:	Deaths	9
	Serious Injuries	26
	Slight Injuries	50
Vehicles Damaged:	Heavy Goods Vehicles	128
	Light Goods Vehicles	33
	Private Motor Cars	93

"Seventy-eight vehicles have been written off for insurance purposes.

"On the day of the incident one hundred and twenty-three officers were engaged at the scene, including fifty-two from neighbouring forces. A further twenty officers and civilian employees were involved in the running of a casualty enquiry bureau at force headquarters or were deployed at hospitals. For a period of six months after the accident a sergeant and two constables worked as investigators and set up a bureau to liaise with vehicle owners, insurance companies and other interested parties. Fifty-five drivers were prosecuted in relation to the accident."

Following this second major accident the constabulary stepped up its regular patrols on the motorway and also deployed unmarked vehicles during a campaign mounted to detect offences of speeding and dangerous driving. The long winter of 1971 – 1972 remains the worst on record for serious accidents on the M1 in Bedfordshire.

The scale of the motorway crashes and the more frequent occurrence of major criminal investigations led the constabulary to acquire a mobile control facility. Mr Armstrong reported: "A twenty-two foot caravan has been obtained and converted into a major incident mobile control post that can be used in connection with any large scale police activity. The caravan is equipped with a conference room, public enquiry office, a small kitchen and a comprehensive communications system which allows for connection to the telephone network and the reception and transmission of messages by police wireless."

In his annual report for 1973 Mr Armstrong gave details of a case of interest which again showed the advances being made in forensic science. "On 12th April 1973, an armed robbery occurred at Barclays Bank, Marsh Road, Luton, when a number of men attacked two security guards as they were leaving the bank with £13,322. One of the robbers fired a shotgun into the ceiling of the bank whilst another of the raiders attacked one of the guards with an iron bar.

"Extensive enquiries were made and within a few days four men were arrested in connection with this robbery. Two of the four men were committed for trial and a fifth man, who was subsequently arrested in London, was also indicted to appear at St. Albans Crown Court. All three were convicted and received sentences of ten years' imprisonment. An interesting feature of the case involved a vehicle used in the robbery which was found to have several pieces of rubber missing from one of the tyres. A thorough examination of a site where a change over of vehicles had occurred revealed several pieces of rubber and seven mechanical fits were made by the forensic laboratory, proving that the pieces of rubber came from the damaged tyre. This evidence was vital in proving the case against one of the convicted men."

Internal Re-organisation.

1973 also saw the installation of the first police national computer terminals at force headquarters in Bedford but the major event of the year concerned a further revision of the divisional structure of the constabulary. The chief constable reported: "The force was re-organised on 1st April 1973 in anticipation of the local authority district changes scheduled to occur on 1st April 1974. In effect, the eastern portion of 'B' division (Bedford), comprising Biggleswade urban and rural district council areas together with the Sandy urban district council area, was transferred to 'D' division (Dunstable). 'D' division itself was divided into two sub-divisions, the northern with headquarters at Biggleswade and the southern with headquarters at Dunstable. Luton, formerly 'F' division was renamed 'C' division but the village of Hyde, technically part of 'D' division, continued to be policed by officers from Luton because of the geography of the county."

The local authority district changes were implemented on 1st April 1974 by virtue of the Local Government Act of 1972. Under the terms of this Act, Luton lost its status as a county borough and the town became subject to the authority of the Bedfordshire County Council. The Bedfordshire and Luton Constabulary ceased to exist at midnight on 31st March 1974 when it was renamed the Bedfordshire Police. The new police authority consisted of eighteen county councillors and nine magistrates appointed by the magistrates' courts committee, the Court of Quarter Sessions having been abolished in 1971.

Rising Crime and Crime Prevention.

The administrative reforms of 1974 were overshadowed by the 18,121 criminal offences committed in Bedfordshire during the year, an increase of twenty-five per cent on the previous twelve month period. Mr Armstrong reported: "The impact of this very disappointing increase, which is in line with national crime figures for 1974, is heightened by the fact that with very few exceptions increases were experienced across the whole spectrum of offences. The figures represent a catalogue of dishonesty, violence, and destruction, at a level never before experienced in Bedfordshire.

"One welcome feature was the number of detected offences which rose by a little over 1,750 enabling the overall detection rate for 1974 to remain steady at just over forty-eight per cent. This was achieved by a force operating with a manpower deficiency of more than one hundred officers."

There was a growing recognition that many of the factors which contributed to the rising crime rate were beyond the control of the police and that crime prevention needed to be examined in the widest possible context. With a view to developing a comprehensive inter-agency approach to crime prevention Mr Armstrong reported: "Excellent contacts established with local authority architects have resulted in consultation at the drawing board stage and the incorporation of crime prevention features in the design of new buildings. Contact has also been made with the Bedfordshire branch of the Institute of British Architects and discussions have begun to examine the possibility of producing a crime prevention supplement to 'The Architects' Journal'. Although no research has been carried out, it is quite evident that new shop and office premises are not so frequently burgled as the older type of building. The dwelling house converted into a business premises is particularly vulnerable and fortunately these are disappearing. Demolition, rebuilding and new planning concepts may well be affecting the pattern of crime, particularly in Luton, where new shopping centres and office blocks are under construction."

One aspect of criminal behaviour which characterised the 1970s was the emergence of football hooliganism. One serious incident occurred at Kenilworth Road in Luton in April 1974 when rivalry between Luton Town and Millwall fans resulted in fighting, the collapse of barriers, and a crowd surge onto the pitch. In the following year the chief constable reported that the problem of hooliganism was becoming more prevalent. "During a number of games throughout the country crowds invaded the pitch and these incidents were reported extensively in the press and on television. It then became fashionable for some supporters to adopt this kind of behaviour and in the match against Chelsea at Kenilworth Road on 30th August 1975 there was a serious mass invasion of the pitch followed by disorder both at the ground and in the town. Later in the year, on 1st November, a number of youths ran onto the pitch before the game against Bristol City and on this occasion police dogs were used to assist the dispersal of the hooligan element.

"All police officers engaged on duty at football matches are regularly subjected to considerable abuse and the threat of physical violence and it is to their credit that they stand up so well to this extreme provocation."

In order to minimise the risk of disorder at football matches in Luton the police arranged for the sale of alcohol to be restricted inside the ground. The constabulary also segregated home and away supporters on the terraces and escorted visiting fans to and from the football ground. Mr Armstrong took additional steps to deal with football hooligans passing through Bedfordshire on their way to matches in other parts of the country. "Throughout the football season efforts are made to ensure that the service area on the M1 is adequately policed whenever the more notorious groups of supporters are believed to be travelling on the motorway. To date only minor incidents have occurred at Toddington but because outbreaks of hooliganism are so unpredictable many man hours are taken up on standby duty."

In his annual report for 1975 the chief constable reported: "The Sex Discrimination Act came into operation on 29th December resulting in the full integration of the male and female establishment of the force. The policewomen's department had already been disbanded in one division of the force, in September 1974, in anticipation of the new legislation. The changes have gone well, with the majority of policewomen preferring the new system, finding their work more interesting and wider in scope. There will, however, always be a need for policewomen to engage in specialist work such as dealing with some sexual offences, female prisoners and children."

By 1976 the country was facing an economic recession and the Government was forced to make drastic cuts in public expenditure. The chief constable reported: "1976 will be remembered as the beginning of a period of severe financial stringency. The cutback on police spending in Bedfordshire has necessitated reducing the mileage of police vehicles by ten per cent and extending the life of vehicles before disposal. Plans have also been drawn up for a phasing out of the cadet corps and a reduction in the amount of time spent in training. It is not possible to contemplate any further substantial cuts without there being a reduction in the degree of law enforcement and a down-grading of the service which the public expect from the police."

The building programme was unaffected by the financial restrictions and Mr Armstrong was able to report: "The new police station at Luton became operational on 29th March 1976 and it is undoubtedly one of the finest divisional headquarters anywhere in the country, providing an excellent environment for the officers based at 'C' division. The old police station has been sold to the General Post Office and the former regional crime squad offices at Farley Hill are being converted into flats. The former traffic division offices in New Street have also been vacated."

Royal Visit to Bedford.

On May 11th 1976 Her Majesty the Queen and His Royal Highness, the Duke of Edinburgh, visited Bedford – the first royal visit to the borough by a reigning monarch since 1918. The chief

The Tanker accident at Westoning

constable reported: "The visit involved not only the complete utilisation of Bedford divisional personnel but also large contingents of police officers from other divisions and the special constabulary. The itinerary for the royal party included a visit to the John Bunyan School and Sports Centre, lunch at the County Hall, a 'walk about' at St. Mary's Embankment, and visits to the Puttenhoe Old People's Home and Bedford Modern School."

The busy sequence of engagements began with the arrival of the royal couple at the Midland Road railway station at 10.45 a.m. where they were met by the Lord-Lieutenant of Bedfordshire, Major Simon Whitbread, and a number of local dignitaries including Mr Armstrong and his wife. The policing operation mounted in connection with the royal visit was designed to maintain tight but unobtrusive security. The upsurge of terrorist activity on the British mainland by the Irish Republican Army in the 1970s was an additional cause of concern to the police. Diversions were set up to keep the route taken by the royal couple free of all traffic and any vehicles left parked along the designated roads were towed away. Police officers were also stationed at regular intervals along the route to watch and control the crowds of spectators who gathered hoping to see the Queen and Prince Philip. The policing arrangements received favourable coverage in the local press and Mr Armstrong reported that he had received a letter of appreciation from the Lord-Lieutenant congratulating him on the professionalism of the security operation.

At 7.10 a.m. on Saturday, 11th September 1976 an articulated Texaco petrol tanker skidded on the road as it entered Westoning, in mid-Bedfordshire, and overturned. Mr Armstrong reported: "Petrol then escaped from the tanker and a serious fire ensued, completely destroying a bakery, a butcher's shop, the village post office and general store, and five houses. Fortunately, even the tanker driver scrambled clear and there was no loss of life although the total amount of damage sustained through the accident was in the region of £200,000."

The Bedfordshire Times gave a more graphic account of the disaster. "When the emergency services arrived they found a raging inferno and complete chaos. Houses and cottages were blazing on both sides of the street and in the middle of the horror was the overturned tanker engulfed in huge flames. Up to sixty fire fighters were quickly into action pouring high density foam on the burning tanker whilst the police sealed off the road and evacuated villagers from nearby houses. How was it no one was killed? Part of the reason may be the speed and efficiency of the emergency services – the villagers were full of praise for the fire brigade and the police and said they did a marvellous job."

Computer Technology.

In his annual report for 1977 the chief constable detailed the constabulary's increasingly successful use of the facilities provided by the Police National Computer. "The computer has become a great asset and has been especially effective in securing a large number of arrests. Over the course of 1977 a total of 313 people were arrested due to the direct assistance of the computer, an increase of 115 over the previous year. This was partly due to the introduction of the Criminal Names Wanted Index which became operational on 8th August 1977. Over 2,200 stolen vehicles were recovered in Bedfordshire after being identified through the use of the computer and the number of arrests made in connection with offences of vehicle theft remained high.

"One particular incident which took place in Bedfordshire during the year illustrated the value of the PNC. A rape victim reported that her assailant was in possession of a blue motor vehicle. A slightly incorrect index number was taken by the victim but it was possible to limit the vehicle registration to two series of combinations which reduced the number of suspect cars to fifty-two. Enquiries were made on the Police National Computer Vehicle Owner Index which revealed that there were only two blue saloon cars of the make stated with a likely registration number. Both owners were Londoners and with the co-operation of the Metropolitan Police the driver of one of the cars was arrested. He later admitted the rape and two other similar offences."

The potential for applying computer technology to police work significantly influenced the constabulary's plans for equipping the new force headquarters under construction at Kempston. The chief constable reported: "I have considered all the alternatives and concluded that centralisation of control will be the most efficient and, in the long term, cheapest method of organisation. A command and control system based on a mini-computer would enable staff in a central control room at headquarters to know the location and availability of every officer and vehicle through a resource display on a computer terminal. At the same time modernised and improved communication systems will allow central controllers to establish wireless contact with any of the officers on duty. All emergency calls for service will be routed to the force control room which will be responsible for directing the immediate operational response to the incident and deploying officers to the scene. Each incident and the resultant police action will be logged on the computer which will offer a number of other useful features including:

1. Message switching via a link to the teleprinter system or through the network of computer terminals to be installed on divisions.

2. Information regarding keyholders and access points for premises connected to the headquarters by direct line burglar alarms.

3. Production of daily duty reports by collating and printing all the incidents logged.

4. Management and operational analysis applications. The computer will collate and store information regarding different types of incident, deployment, response times and personnel.

"Whilst the provision of a command and control system represents a major advance in our use of computers, looking to the future I regard the scheme as only the first step to making all our operations and records computer based."

Three companies, Ferranti, Honeywell and Plessey, offered tenders to supply the command and control computer system to the Bedfordshire Police. Plessey had already installed a similar system in Dorset while Honeywell had provided a limited computer command facility to the City Police in Rome. Honeywell also offered the lowest tender, £148,550 and their bid was accepted.

During the 1970s it became fashionable to hold pop music festivals in the grounds of stately homes in Britain and Mr Armstrong reported: "On Saturday, 2nd July 1977 the American artist, Neil Diamond, held an open air concert at Woburn Abbey. Pop fans began arriving early in the morning and an estimated fifty-five thousand people attended in twenty thousand vehicles. Six entrances to the park were used and the provision of an overflow car park also proved necessary. A total of forty-eight officers policed the event and the mobile major incident post was used as a police station and control centre. The concert commenced at 8 p.m. and concluded at 10.45 p.m. Many of those attending camped in the park overnight but the police assisted in clearing the grounds during the following day. There were no untoward incidents in connection with the concert."

Towards the end of 1977 national strike action by the firemen's union led the Government to call upon the armed forces to assume the role of the fire brigade. Mr Armstrong reported: "Since the beginning of the strike on November 14th a pilot car has been provided by the police for each of the Army fire service units stationed in Bedfordshire. The Army fire engines are stationed at Bedford and Luton and the pilot cars are used to direct them with speed and safety to the scene of any fire." The dispute lasted for nine weeks and at its conclusion the Bedfordshire police committee resolved to "record their appreciation for the manner in which the police service undertook duties outside their normal responsibilities during the period of the industrial strike by the firemen."

Opening of Kempston Force Headquarters.

The most significant event of 1978 for the Bedfordshire Police was the opening of the new force headquarters at Kempston. Mr Armstrong informed the police committee, "This magnificent building with its excellent facilities was occupied in April with the exception of the control room and crime bureau which will remain at 'The Pines' until the introduction of the new communications system. The premises were officially opened on 17th October 1978 by Her Royal Highness, the Duchess of Kent."

The Bedfordshire Times reported that "with the cheers of hundreds of children to warm her, the Duchess of Kent flew in by helicopter, touching down on the sports field beside the new £2m police complex where she was met by Lieutenant-Colonel H. C. Hanbury, the Lord-Lieutenant of Bedfordshire. The Duchess was accompanied by the Chief Constable, Mr Anthony Armstrong, on a tour of the building before she was joined by invited guests for a special luncheon. In unveiling a plaque to mark the opening, the Duchess said: "May the courageous men and women whose work takes them inside and outside these walls find satisfaction and reward in their task and may we continue to show our pride in the police force."

Although the new centralised command and control system did not become operational until 1979 the opening of the new headquarters resulted in immediate benefits to the force in a number of other ways. "The rehousing of the several headquarters departments occupying offices at the Shire Hall, Greyfriars police station and Putnoe sub-station, has greatly increased efficiency and the splendid new twenty acre site will allow further scope for expansion when this proves to be necessary. The facilities for training at the new headquarters are particularly excellent and exceed anything that has been available in the past. Courses for probationer constables which were previously run for one day per month have been re-organised so that the constables attend four one-week courses during their first two years of service. The facility

The modern Police Headquarters at Kempston was opened on 17th October 1978 by HRH The Duchess of Kent

The force control room at the new Headquarters. Bedfordshire was one of the first forces to install a command and control computer

of a sports hall has meant that physical training has been introduced into the syllabus of most courses."

In his annual report for 1978 Mr Armstrong gave details of other important developments which had taken place during the year. "The force Fraud Squad was formed on 19th June and consists of a detective inspector, a detective sergeant and two detective constables. These officers are based at force headquarters and the object of the squad is to deal with any major fraud likely to require protracted enquiries or involving persons holding responsible offices. During recent years there have been several major frauds committed in the county which were investigated by divisional detective officers. This resulted in the local criminal investigation department strength being depleted for a long period of time as many of the fraud squad investigations continued for up to two years. The formation of a central fraud squad resolved this problem and allows divisional detective officers to devote their time to normal crime enquiries."

Mr Armstrong further reported: "The Edmund-Davies report published in the late summer of 1978 was a milestone in the history of police pay but there was not the immediate expected increase in the number of candidates applying to join the force, nor was there much improvement in the standard. In common with other forces I found it necessary to recruit from outside our own area and early in the year a recruitment campaign was mounted in the Tyneside district which has been hit by particularly high unemployment. A small team led by myself undertook an intensive exercise for a period of one week in conjunction with the Newcastle upon Tyne job centre. As a result of the campaign eighteen young men and women were recruited to the ranks of the Bedfordshire Police Force."

Lord Edmund-Davies had headed a Government enquiry into police pay and conditions in response to a groundswell of discontent in the ranks of the police service following the collapse of wage negotiations in 1976. The Edmund-Davies report recommended substantial pay increases for the police which were accepted by the Government but which were scheduled to be paid in two instalments. Following the General Election of May 1979 the newly elected Government decided to implement the pay award in full with immediate effect and there was a sustained improvement in recruitment to the police service as a result. In the 1980s the force was able to recruit up to establishment with relative ease and Mr Armstrong's recruitment campaign on Tyneside was the last mounted by the Bedfordshire Police in response to a large number of vacancies in the ranks.

In 1979 Mr Armstrong reported: "Since 29th May all '999' emergency calls have been directed to the control room at police headquarters, Kempston, and the force is now one of only seven to possess a computerised command and control system. A number of forces have visited the new headquarters to study the operation of the control room."

Later in the year the chief constable informed the police authority: "Bedfordshire Police support units were mobilised on 26th October and 1st November 1979 to provide mutual aid to the Norfolk Constabulary and the Northamptonshire Police respectively. In October two units comprising a total of sixty-nine officers performed duty on the occasion of the annual conference of the National Front at Great Yarmouth. In November two further units were deployed during a demonstration in connection with the closure of the Corby Steel works."

Retirement of Mr Armstrong.

Mr Armstrong retired from the Bedfordshire Police on 11th November 1979 after a long and distinguished police career spanning thirty-three years. He was awarded the Queen's Police Medal in the New Year's Honours List in 1974 and five years later he received the O.B.E. Following Mr Armstrong's retirement, his successor as the Chief Constable of Bedfordshire, Mr William Sutherland, who has since been knighted, wrote: "During his eight years as chief constable policing became more complex and there was a rapid expansion in the force's use of new technology and equipment both in the operational and administrative fields. His foresight is reflected in the development of a comprehensive building programme providing the force with new headquarters and a modern network of divisional headquarters stations, all of which contribute greatly to the high morale and efficiency of the staff. Such achievements reflect his energy, enthusiasm and sound management during the period of his command."

A married man with two children, Mr Armstrong was held in high esteem by the members of the police force for the personal interest he took in the welfare of the officers and their families – he secured the appointment of the first full-time welfare officer in 1976. Mr Armstrong remained in Bedfordshire after leaving the force, teaching English to foreign students, and he and his wife continue to enjoy an active retirement.

Modern police dogs are additionally trained to search for drugs or explosives

SIR WILLIAM G. M. SUTHERLAND, QPM

CHAPTER NINE

THE DEVELOPMENT OF MODERN POLICING

1979 – 1983
SIR WILLIAM SUTHERLAND

WILLIAM George MacKenzie Sutherland was born on 12th November 1933 at Inverness in the north of Scotland. He attended the Inverness Technical High School until the age of fifteen when he started work at the local post office, continuing with evening classes at the school. In March 1952 he was called up for National Service and joined the Royal Engineers, attaining the rank of corporal. After completing his two years in the Army Mr Sutherland decided on a career in the police force and in May 1954 he joined the Cheshire Constabulary, spending the first five years of his service on uniform foot patrol duties and a further two and a half years as a detective constable. Subsequently he was promoted to sergeant in 1962 and inspector in 1964. Between 1962 and 1965 he studied criminal law, and the sociology and psychology of crime at the extra-mural department of Manchester University.

In January 1969 Mr Sutherland was appointed chief inspector in charge of communications, and press and public relations in Cheshire. Eleven months later he was promoted to superintendent and in the summer of 1973 he transferred to the Surrey Constabulary on appointment as chief superintendent, taking charge of the force traffic division.

In 1975 Mr Sutherland was appointed an assistant chief constable in Hertfordshire and became the deputy chief constable there two years later. In 1979 he was one of eleven candidates to apply for the position of Chief Constable of Bedfordshire on Mr Armstrong's retirement. The Bedfordshire police authority interviewed three deputy chief constables from county forces for the post: Mr R. W. Cozens from Lincolnshire, Mr R. J. Palastanga from Gwent, and Mr Sutherland from Hertfordshire. The police authority selected Mr Sutherland as the eighth Chief Constable of Bedfordshire and he commenced his duties in the county on 12th November 1979, his forty-sixth birthday.

Mr Sutherland's appointment to the head of the county force was only one of a series of changes affecting the senior policing posts in Bedfordshire in late 1979 and early 1980. In his annual report for 1979 Mr Sutherland informed the police committee: "Mr Kenneth Mayer, QPM, the former deputy chief constable of Bedfordshire, seconded to central service as assistant to Her Majesty's Chief Inspector of Constabulary, was appointed Chief Constable of the Wiltshire Constabulary on 1st October 1979." Mr Sutherland further reported: "Mr George Charlton, the deputy chief constable, has been appointed Chief Constable of the Norfolk Constabulary with effect from 1st March 1980. Both appointments reflect great credit on the Bedfordshire Police Force and its standing within the police service."

One of Mr Sutherland's first duties as chief constable was to report the opening of the new police station at Dunstable. "The new divisional headquarters replaces an old building which has been in use since the early 1930s. Construction work commenced in March 1977, was completed in September 1979, and on the following 18th December the new police station became operational. Approximately one hundred police officers and civilian personnel work from the station which provides, for the first time at Dunstable, a canteen, recreational facilities, and a separate block containing fourteen bedrooms for single officers."

Return to Traditional Policing.

In 1980 Mr Sutherland began to implement a policy designed to increase the number of uniformed officers patrolling on foot in the county. "Of late years, due to insufficient strength, the force has become a reactive service, responding to incidents as they occur rather than in a preventive role maintaining a strong uniformed police presence on the streets. However, with the recent increase in manpower following the Edmund-Davies pay award, it has been possible to fill all the established resident beats. These neighbourhood constables will be given greater responsibility and their role as the best possible community relations officers for the force will be emphasised.

"The force must be able to provide a rapid response to priority incidents, but in the forthcoming years greater effort will be made to ensure that this service is coupled to more traditional methods of patrolling on cycle and on foot, with the objective of obtaining greater public support at grass roots level. Nevertheless, given the present authorised establishment, it will not be possible to proceed as far as I would wish in this direction."

With the improved prospects for recruitment the authorised establishment of the force became much more important in the 1980s. The chief constable reported: "During 1979/80 a detailed study was carried out to assess a realistic establishment for the Bedfordshire Police bearing in mind the increasing demands made upon the force in the modern day. The present authorised strength is 960 officers but while the ratio of police to population in Bedfordshire is much lower than the national average the density of crime per thousand population is exceptionally high. As a result of the establishment review I concluded that the force requires a strength of 1,158, an increase of 198 on the current manning level." Such a large increase in establishment was economically unviable in the short-term but modest gains in the authorised strength of the force over the ensuing years were of some use in augmenting the number of officers patrolling on foot.

Minor developments in 1980 included the introduction of a new type of personal radio. "The Stornophone UHF personal radio was issued to some officers during the year as part of field trials conducted by the Home Office and its performance proved to be of a high level. This style of radio will become standard issue in the force in the near future." Mr Sutherland further reported on an expansion in the duties of the dog section. "The strength of the section is now one sergeant and thirteen constables. As an extension of their more traditional role, four dogs have been trained for drug detection and two for the detection of explosives."

On the night of 14th August 1980 two inches of rain fell throughout Bedfordshire, the heaviest locally recorded rainfall for over twenty years. The chief constable reported: "Widespread flooding of roads and, to a lesser extent, flooding of houses and property occurred, thrusting a great burden on the police and other essential services. Many accidents, burglar alarm activations and road diversions necessitated police action, and assistance was afforded to residents and motorists.

"The most serious flooding occurred in the north of Bedfordshire, and Bromham in particular, was severely affected when a brook flowing through the village rose rapidly to a height of fourteen feet. Forty houses in Rosemary Drive were flooded and considerable damage was also occasioned at a nearby caravan site. Emergency and relief services were quickly on the scene and members of the force worked long hours in difficult conditions, assisting residents to move furniture to safety and preventing water from entering further homes.

"Later, general support was given to a number of villagers in the drying out of carpets, underlay and bedding. Many such items were transported to Bedford police station and dried in the garage by fan heaters before being returned." The Bedfordshire Police received many letters of appreciation for their ready efforts on the night of the flooding and the chief constable congratulated the officers involved on their excellent work.

Five officers from Bedfordshire performed duty in Rhodesia at the time of the elections in 1980 and the chief constable later reported: "Inspector Ralph Miller, Detective Constable Peter Thorn, and Constables Robert Dover, Simon Scott and Merris Cotterill were presented with the Rhodesia Medal in July 1981 at a ceremony held at police headquarters and attended by Councillor F. S. Lester, O.B.E., the chairman of the police authority. The medals were presented by Lieutenant-Colonel Hanbury, the Lord-Lieutenant of the county."

Urban Riots.

In the summer of 1981 there were outbreaks of serious public disorder in towns and cities across Britain and in Bedfordshire disturbances arose in Luton, Bedford, and Leighton Buzzard over the weekend of 10th to 12th July. The chief constable reported: "The most serious disorder of the weekend occurred in Luton when large numbers of business premises were attacked and damaged by groups of rampaging youths. Most of the damage consisted of broken shop windows but there were also a number of incidents of arson and looting from shops. In several instances police officers and their vehicles came under attack from missiles thrown at them including petrol bombs."

Trouble broke out on Friday evening in the town centre at Luton when a gang of youths streamed along George Street smashing

Althorp Road in Luton was the scene of serious rioting in the summer of 1981

shop windows. The disturbances later moved to the Bury Park area where further shops were damaged and petrol bombs were thrown at the police in Westbourne Road. Twenty-eight officers from Hertfordshire were called to Luton to assist the county force and the disorder was quickly brought under control.

More serious rioting occurred on Saturday night when a clothing shop and hat factory in the High Town area were set on fire and shops in Dunstable Road and Leagrave Road were looted. The Luton News reported: "The constabulary recovered a formidable array of weapons during the disturbances. Bricks, bottles, knives, motorcycle chains, and home made clubs spiked with nails were all used in street battles fought on the run in Luton. Saturday night's violence culminated in a pitched battle between police and a large crowd of youths in Althorp Road. The vandals broke pieces from garden walls and used them as extra ammunition against the officers trying to restore order. However, swift action by the police, who sealed off both ends of the road and moved in, meant that the crowd soon dispersed."

Mr Sutherland informed the police authority: "At the height of the disturbances on Saturday night over two hundred police officers were deployed in Luton and it was necessary for riot shields to be brought into use. A total of one hundred and seven persons were arrested in connection with the disorder at Luton, six for offences involving the possession, use or manufacture of petrol bombs. Other offences ranged from assault, damage, and burglary, to breaches of the peace. Despite the violent nature of the confrontations only ten officers were injured, none seriously."

The chief constable continued, "In Bedford the scale of the disorder was not as great. Twenty-four premises sustained damage, mainly as a result of broken windows and in some instances the vandalism was accompanied by theft of electrical goods and alcohol. Seventy-four officers were deployed in Bedford during the disturbances on Saturday night and sixteen offenders were arrested. On the night of Sunday, 12th July an incident involving damage to a number of commercial premises occurred in Leighton Buzzard. Fourteen youths were arrested in connection with this incident by the few officers normally on duty in the town. Fortunately no additional support proved necessary, for a total of fifty-four officers from 'D' division were on duty at Luton and Bedford.

"All the officers who were involved in containing the disturbances over the weekend of 10th to 12th July 1981 were placed under enormous pressure and displayed great courage and restraint, at times under extreme provocation. They were required to work long and tiring periods of continuous duty, in most cases in excess of twelve hours. The causes of the violent outbreaks of disorder within the county can only be the subject of speculation. The disturbances were not race-riots although there was undoubtedly a degree of racial tension running through many of the incidents. In the main the events seemed to follow a pattern of criminal hooliganism and imitation of events that had occurred elsewhere in the country."

The Bedfordshire police received widespread praise for their handling of the disorder and the police authority resolved "to place on record their whole hearted support for the way in which the disturbances in Bedfordshire were dealt with and to convey to all the police officers involved, the thanks of the committee for their efforts in dealing with the situations that arose."

The constabulary maintained a strong presence on the streets following the disturbances whilst working with social agencies and other local organisations to prevent any recurrence of the disorder. "Efforts have been made to mobilise the fullest community support through our continuing policy of developing closer relationships between the police and the local community. In order to dispel the atmosphere of tension that existed immediately after the disturbances meetings were held with local youth officers and youth leaders, the leaders of local ethnic groups, and community relations council officers."

Steps were also taken to improve the equipment available to the county force in the event of public disorder. A Home Office circular explained that "the traditional police helmet, even when reinforced, does not afford sufficient protection against the degree of violence experienced in the recent disturbances, nor does the ordinary police uniform provide sufficient body protection against petrol bombs. It is recommended that a form of crash helmet with visor, fire resistant clothing and other equipment be provided to afford better protection for police officers deployed during incidents of disorder." The police committee "approved the expenditure of £7,500 as a matter of urgency to purchase new protective helmets, clothing and equipment for the Bedfordshire Police following the experience of the disturbances and riots in certain parts of the county."

The Bedfordshire Police benefited from the arrangements for mutual aid during the disorder at Luton and later in the summer of 1981 the county force furnished assistance to the police in Liverpool and London. In his annual report for the year Mr

Sutherland informed the police authority: "A support unit from 'B' division assisted the Merseyside Police during the weekend of 13th to 15th August on the event of a large demonstration following the Toxteth riots. Two and a half weeks earlier the force supplied aid to the Metropolitan Police on a happier occasion. Thirty-four officers performed duty at the Royal Wedding of His Royal Highness, the Prince of Wales, and the Lady Diana Spencer on 29th July 1981. They were deployed to line the route in the area of St Paul's Cathedral and although the duty was long and tiring, all the officers thoroughly enjoyed the experience and were pleased to be included on such an historic occasion."

Implementation of the Scarman Report.

In November 1981 Lord Scarman published his report into the Brixton riots and Mr Sutherland informed the police authority: "The report contains a number of proposals for change within the police service, concerning in particular, training, methods of policing, accountability and the police handling of public order situations. This force can take some pride in the fact that much of what has been recommended has already been implemented in Bedfordshire and that policing in this county has moved steadily in the direction advocated by Lord Scarman for some time. However, there is no room for complacency, and careful consideration will be given to full implementation of the Scarman report in co-operation with the police authority and other organisations."

The Scarman report gave fresh impetus to the change to the more traditional methods of policing adopted by the chief constable. "Lord Scarman concluded that policing methods should be based on consent. In Bedfordshire a move towards a locally based patrol system had already been introduced, allowing a much wider degree of public contact, and together with a greater commitment to community involvement, this system is already achieving increased public support.

"The effectiveness of these methods depends very much upon the qualities of individual officers, particularly resident beat constables. This is a fact that Lord Scarman saw as being crucial and steps have been taken to enhance the role and stature of resident beat officers within the force with a view to attracting some of the more experienced and able personnel to this important duty.

"The deployment of officers to foot patrol duties has continued to increase whilst there has been a reduction in the number of mobile 'Panda' patrols. The figures below relate to the average number of patrol officers on duty in the county by function:

	Nov 1980	*Nov 1981*	*Nov 1982*
Mobile Patrols	31.7	28.3	25.5
Resident Beat Officers	6.0	17.4	19.8
Foot Patrol Officers	11.0	14.6	19.5
Total	48.7	60.3	64.8"

The chief constable further reported: "Lord Scarman recommended that training programmes should be revised to take into account the contemporary demands made on the police service. Probationer training has been redesigned and constables returning from district training centres now spend their first eight weeks of duty in company with a tutor constable performing resident beat duties. Constables are not trained to become car drivers until they have spent two years on foot patrol duties and this assists them in developing their skills in communicating and dealing with people."

The Scarman report also encouraged police forces to foster a better relationship with the public by becoming more involved with the community at large. Mr Sutherland reported that five new crime prevention panels had been established in Bedfordshire in 1981 to involve the wider community in the fight against crime. "New panels came into existence at Dunstable, Leighton Buzzard, Biggleswade, Ampthill and Bedford. They meet bi-monthly to discuss and implement crime prevention measures aimed specifically at the problems of the locality and a determined effort has been made to ensure that the panel members are drawn from all walks of life. Luton has had a crime prevention panel for many years and also possesses a junior panel with representatives from schools and youth organisations. It is hoped that the operation of the panels will bring the police far closer to the public and help combat the growth of crime."

In 1982 the chief constable further reported: "In September this year, following an increase in the authorised establishment, I was able to form a Community Involvement Unit based at police headquarters to co-ordinate the work of the force in relation to community liaison, crime prevention, road safety and juvenile liaison." 1982 also saw the introduction of a police/schools liaison scheme "to generate among school children a better understanding of the role of the police in society. The scheme involved the appointment of a constable, usually a resident beat officer, to each school in the county to give talks on police work and assist with extra curricular activities. The scheme was introduced with the full support of the county education officer and school head teachers."

Further initiatives aimed at promoting a proper understanding of the police service in young people included a police/scout liaison scheme and a volunteer cadet scheme.

The special constabulary was seen as a valuable additional link between the police and the community although by 1982 there were only 178 special constables serving in the county. A concerted recruitment campaign failed to attract more members to the special constabulary which, nevertheless, continued to render assistance to the regular force by carrying out routine duties and providing support at major public events including Luton Town football matches.

Disaster Planning.

In 1982 Mr Sutherland reviewed the arrangements for dealing with major emergencies in the county. "In an increasingly complex industrial society major accidents or catastrophes are an ever present possibility and the scale of loss of life, injury or damage, may depend in no small way on an efficient and co-ordinated response by the emergency services. In order to improve co-operation and co-ordination in this regard a major incident steering committee was formed, comprising the chief officers of the police, fire, and ambulance services, together with senior officials from the district health authority.

"A feature of the new arrangements is that an exercise based on a simulated major incident will be organised annually by the committee to permit a review of the procedures and training. The first of the annual exercises was held at Luton Airport on February 24th 1982 and was designed to test the response of the emergency services to an aircraft crash."

At 2.14 a.m. on 9th December 1982 an express passenger train, travelling from Euston to Glasgow, was derailed as it emerged from Linslade tunnel and collided with a bridge parapet before coming to rest. There were 107 passengers on board, many of whom were travelling in sleeping cars. The chief constable reported: "The emergency services were at the scene very quickly and members of the force assisted with the rescue of injured persons and the transfer of uninjured passengers to another train. Officers were also deployed to liaise with the media, co-ordinate the activities of the emergency services, and protect the scene of the crash until British Transport Police officers arrived to assume responsibility. Sadly the senior driver on board the train was killed but in the circumstances it was remarkable that there were not more fatalities. The co-operation between the emergency services was first class and these factors were considerably enhanced by the joint major incident planning initiatives."

In his annual report for 1982 Mr Sutherland informed the police authority: "One notable event during the year was the appointment of Mr Brian H. Weight as the Chief Constable of the Dorset Police. Mr Weight is the third deputy chief constable from this county to be appointed as a chief constable in the last four years, a remarkable achievement for one of the smaller police forces of England and Wales. Mr Alan Dyer has been appointed as the new Deputy Chief Constable of Bedfordshire."

Mr Sutherland further reported: "Canon Kenneth Habermehl, the incumbent of All Saints' Church, Kempston, was appointed as force chaplain during 1982. The purpose of the chaplaincy is to create a further link between the church and the police and to provide a non-denominational pastoral ministry to members of the force."

There was no repetition of the widespread disorder experienced in 1981 and Bedfordshire Police support units were only mobilised on one occasion during the year. "A contingent of seventy officers assisted in Warwickshire with the policing arrangements for the open air Mass at Baginton Airfield, Coventry, on May 30th 1982 during the visit of His Holiness, Pope John-Paul II. Although the crowd control and security duties performed by the officers were arduous, the prevailing goodwill made the occasion a memorable and enjoyable one."

Early in 1983 Mr Sutherland reported to the police authority on the night-time closure of Ampthill police station. "Research has shown that very few members of the public telephone or visit Ampthill police station at night. Accordingly I have decided that the premises should be closed between the hours of midnight and 7 a.m. as from 10th January 1983. This will relieve an officer of duty in the reception area and provides instead an additional patrol officer, making better use of the available manpower. This decision was taken after consultations with the local community and has been endorsed at a previous meeting of the police authority. A direct line telephone connected to police headquarters will be available to any member of the public who calls at the police station at night."

Other minor developments in the early months of 1983 concerned the introduction of new legislation. "During the first three months of the year all police officers within the force received one day's instruction in the new drink/drive law brought into effect by the implementation of section 25 of the Road Transport Act

Mr Sutherland implemented a policy designed to increase the number of uniformed officers patrolling on foot in the community

1981. The new law considerably strengthens the powers of the police to deal with this growing social problem. Ninety officers attended a further two days course on the operation of the Lion intoximeter substantive breath-testing machine. The force also received instruction on the new legislation regarding the wearing of seat-belts which came into effect on 1st February 1983."

New Appointment in Lothian & Borders.

In March 1983 Mr Sutherland announced that he was returning to his native Scotland to take up an appointment as the Chief Constable of Lothian and Borders, a force more than double the size of the Bedfordshire Police and based in Edinburgh, the capital city. Generous tribute was paid to his service in Bedfordshire at a meeting of the police authority on 12th March 1983 when the chairman, Councillor Lester, expressed his appreciation of the exemplary manner in which Mr Sutherland had carried out his duties and praised the chief constable's professionalism and humanity.

Settling in Scotland with his wife Jennie and their two daughters, Mr Sutherland commenced his new duties on 13th June 1983. He was awarded the Queen's Police Medal in 1981 and seven years later he received a Knighthood in the Queen's Birthday Honours List of 1988. Sir William George MacKenzie Sutherland continues to serve in his prestigious office as the Chief Constable of Lothian and Borders.

MR ANDREW K. SLOAN, QPM, BA

1983 – 1985
ANDREW KIRKPATRICK SLOAN

ANDREW Kirkpatrick Sloan was born on 27th February 1931 at Dumfries in the south-west of Scotland. At the age of eleven he won a scholarship which allowed him to study at the Kirkcudbright and Dumfries Academies but at the age of fourteen he left school for economic reasons and worked for his father on a dairy farm.

In January 1947 Mr Sloan joined the Royal Navy as a boy seaman and underwent training at HMS Ganges at Shotley Gate, near Harwich. During his naval career he served on board the light cruiser HMS Euryalus and the submarines 'Tireless' and 'Alderney'. In 1953 he married a Norwegian, Agnes Sofie Storvik, and in March 1955 when he left the Navy in the rank of petty officer, he took up employment in Norway, in a paper mill at Trondheim. Six months later he returned to England with his wife and on 5th December 1955 he joined the West Riding Constabulary which later became part of the West Yorkshire Metropolitan Police Force.

Mr Sloan spent the first seven years of his service on uniform patrol duties before joining the CID at Shipley in 1963. He was promoted to detective sergeant in the following year and between 1966 and 1968 he worked as a detective inspector on attachment to the No. 3 regional crime squad at Leeds. In the summer of 1968 he was appointed as a detective chief inspector on division at Goole before returning to the regional crime squad in 1970 in the rank of detective superintendent.

From 1973 Mr Sloan gained experience as a uniformed superintendent at Otley and Wakefield, and in August 1975 he was promoted to chief superintendent, taking charge of the Bradford division of the West Yorkshire force. Twelve months later he was appointed as an assistant chief constable in Lincolnshire and in 1979 he took up a central service appointment at the Home Office as the national co-ordinator of the regional crime squads. In November 1980 Mr Sloan was part of a team of experts called in to assist the West Yorkshire Police during the later stages of the 'Ripper' enquiry. He returned to Lincolnshire in the following year to take up an appointment as the deputy chief constable of the county.

In 1983 Mr Sloan was one of three candidates shortlisted for the post of Chief Constable of Bedfordshire together with Mr E. R. James, the Deputy Chief Constable of North Yorkshire, and Mr S. W. Crump, the Deputy Chief Constable of Cambridgeshire. After formal interviews with the candidates on 11th May 1983 the police authority offered Mr Sloan the appointment and he commenced his new duties on 12th July.

On 30th July 1983 the deputy chief constable, Mr Alan Dyer, suffered a severe heart attack and was unable to return to work until the New Year. At the same time Mr Norman Green, the assistant chief constable, retired from the force. Consequently Mr Sloan served as the Chief Constable of Bedfordshire without the assistance of these key members of his staff from the end of July until the appointment of Mr William Gray as the new assistant chief constable in November 1983.

Local Liaison Committees.

One of Mr Sloan's first duties concerned the operation of a series of consultative committees created in Bedfordshire during the final months of Mr Sutherland's tenure of office as chief constable. Mr Sloan reported: "In accordance with the recommendations of the Scarman report, four local liaison committees were established in the county during 1983, covering the areas of Bedford and north Bedfordshire, Luton, south Bedfordshire, and mid Bedfordshire. The committees were formed by the police authority which also determines the constitution and membership of each committee.

Their purpose is to provide a forum for discussion and consultation whereby the police can ascertain and respond to the needs and views of the local community and explain policies and areas of difficulty. Specifically excluded from discussion are matters relating to the deployment of officers, the method and timing of police operations, and cases of complaint against individual police officers."

Mr Sloan further reported: "The members of each police liaison committee are selected from agencies and organisations which are representative of the whole community. Meetings are generally held in private but each committee arranges an open forum for public consultation at least every six months. The inaugural meetings of each committee were held in June 1983 and the first open forums were held in the following November and December." All the local liaison committees continue to hold regular meetings in the county and the majority are now open to the public.

In his annual report for 1984 the chief constable informed the police authority: "The force was stretched, as never before, with the demands placed upon it by a protracted major investigation into a series of crimes of a sexual nature and by the need to deploy officers to other force areas under the mutual aid scheme as a consequence of the miners' strike. Even without these extra commitments, 1984, was a very busy year."

The first major operation mounted by the county police in 1984 concerned the theft of a priceless collection of silverware from Woburn Abbey. The offence occurred during the early hours of Thursday, 15th March and The Times newspaper reported: "The burglars managed to breach a highly sophisticated security system, breaking in through a first floor window located in the north wing of the Abbey. Once inside they entered the state dining room and Queen Victoria's state bedroom, seizing forty-seven pieces of silver and gilt including the Reform Cup – a silver trophy presented to Lord Russell during the last century in recognition of his valuable work in drafting the Reform Act of 1832. The stolen items of silver, which attracted many visitors to the Abbey, are nominally valued at £5m."

The investigation into the burglary continued over a period of four months and detectives from the No. 5 regional crime squad were called in to assist with the enquiries. The police operation led to the recovery of all the stolen silverware at a water pumping station in Eaton Socon but unfortunately the offenders escaped detection. The silver was returned to Woburn Abbey but it is no longer kept on permanent public display.

Operation Peanut.

A second major criminal investigation was mounted in the south of Bedfordshire during the summer of 1984. Mr Sloan reported: "This enquiry, code-named 'Operation Peanut', involved five police forces and was the largest ever undertaken within the force area. The investigation eventually encompassed some eighty offences including three rapes, and a series of aggravated burglaries, indecent assaults, and firearms offences."

The activities of a man, nicknamed 'The Fox' by the media, terrified the local community living in the area between Leighton Buzzard, Tring, and Eddlesborough, which became known as 'the triangle of fear'. The horrific crimes perpetrated by the masked rapist, who armed himself with a sawn-off shotgun, attracted enormous media coverage and the police investigation of the case was the subject of daily reports in the national press and on television.

The chief constable outlined the development of the case in a report presented to the police authority in the autumn of 1984. "The enquiry began when a number of offences in Leighton Buzzard and the surrounding districts were linked together. The nature of the crimes committed became progressively more serious and on 3rd July the Bedfordshire, Hertfordshire, and Thames Valley police forces mounted a joint operation led by Bedfordshire's Detective Chief Superintendent Brian Prickett, and run from an incident room at Dunstable police station.

"Following the commission of two offences of rape in the middle of July, the incident room was expanded and the investigation was pursued on two fronts. A force of one hundred and fifty detectives made extensive enquiries into the crimes by day whilst observation teams and armed response units were deployed to protect the public and keep watch for the offender by night. Up to two hundred and fifty officers, under the supervision of a superintendent, were routinely engaged in the night-time operation."

At this stage of the enquiry a microdata computer was used to assist the investigation and the equipment was installed at Dunstable police station. "The use of the computer played a crucial role in the storage and retrieval of the information gathered during the enquiry. At the height of the investigation the incident room at Dunstable was receiving two hundred and fifty telephone calls an hour.

"Over three thousand persons were suggested by the public as possible suspects in the case and our enquiries resulted in the arrest of seventy-three persons and the submission of nearly eight hundred items to Home Office laboratories for forensic examination. A senior scientist from the Home Office laboratory at Huntingdon was seconded to the investigation to help co-ordinate the work of the various laboratories and to assist in the interpretation of the forensic results.

"The investigation was concentrated on an area within a twenty mile radius of Leighton Buzzard until the night of 12th August when an offence of burglary and rape occurred at Brampton, in South Yorkshire, and three further offences of burglary occurred at Peterlee in County Durham. All the crimes were linked with the major enquiry in Bedfordshire and this new facet of the investigation enabled the detectives at Dunstable to direct their efforts towards suspects who were, or had been, resident in the Leighton Buzzard area and who were also known to have connections with South Yorkshire or the north east of England."

On 11th September 1984 a man named Malcolm Fairley was questioned at his flat in Kentish Town by Detective Constables Richard Henkes and Nigel Tompkins during a routine trace and interview assignment. Fairley had recently left the Leighton Buzzard area and was believed to have originally come from Sunderland. A search of the flat and Fairley's car revealed two sets of green overalls of a material identical to that of a mask cut out of a trouser leg and discarded by the rapist after an earlier assault. The rapist was known to wear a distinctive chrome watch on the right wrist and when Fairley was found to do the same he was arrested by Detective Constable Henkes. Further police enquiries provided conclusive evidence of his guilt.

Fairley pleaded guilty to a series of rapes and burglaries at St. Albans Crown Court in 1985 when he was sentenced to six terms of life imprisonment. At the conclusion of the trial Mr Justice Caulfield made the following remarks: "I am sure the public are relieved to know of the intense efforts made by the police. This was a first-class investigation and it amazes me that the police caught their man so quickly. The public should be proud of their police force."

The Miners' Strike.

The third major commitment for the county police force in 1984 concerned the provision of mutual aid to the coalfields during the miners' strike. The chief constable reported: "Between 15th March and 16th December 1984 Bedfordshire Police support units were deployed to Humberside, Kent, Leicestershire, Nottinghamshire, South Yorkshire, Staffordshire, and Warwickshire, representing a

Bedfordshire Police support units preparing to travel north on mutual aid during the miners' strike

On 15th March 1985 Millwall football supporters rioted after their team lost to Luton Town

total of 15,649 working days. The provision of mutual aid was temporarily suspended for a short period during the major criminal investigation in the Leighton Buzzard area."

More than ten per cent of the force was regularly deployed under the mutual aid scheme: "On average, the weekly number of officers deployed to other force areas was one hundred and thirteen, with a maximum of one hundred and sixty-three officers on one occasion. In consequence there was a lowering of the level of manpower on divisions but although patrol strengths were reduced, the redeployment of resources and the working of extended tours of duty allowed adequate levels of cover to be maintained.

"Members of the special constabulary made a valuable contribution to the policing of the county throughout this period by increasing their availability for duty by as much as forty per cent. Regrettably all training commitments had to be discontinued except for those relating to probationer constables and emergency procedures."

The chief constable played an important role at New Scotland Yard during the strike, assisting in the running of the National Reporting Centre which received requests for mutual aid from the areas involved in the dispute and co-ordinated the supply of police support units from forces throughout England and Wales. Mr Sloan reported: "I commenced my duties at the centre in March and Mr Dyer assumed command of the county force during my absence. The operating procedures at the centre were quickly established and my duties have since become part-time, requiring my absence from the force for an average of two and a half days a week."

One of the most widely publicised incidents of disorder during the miners' strike occurred at the British Steel coking plant at Orgreave, near Sheffield, on Monday, 18th June 1984. The Times newspaper reported that the National Union of Mineworkers had made the plant a target in an attempt to stop the daily convoys of lorries taking coal to the nearby steelworks at Scunthorpe. "Eighty people were hurt and more than a hundred arrested during hours of running battles between some 6,500 pickets and 3,300 police. It was the worst violence in a British industrial dispute since the war. The police were at first overwhelmed by the pickets but then regrouped to advance under a hail of stones, bottles, and bricks, until the demonstrators were forced to retreat behind a barricade of burning cars, lamp-posts, and stones from a wall which they had demolished."

Bedfordshire Police support units were in the thick of the action at Orgreave and Mr Sloan reported: "At one stage officers from the county force came under a heavy barrage of large stones taken from a dry stone wall, resulting in severe damage to six Bedfordshire personnel carriers. Fortunately none of the officers were injured before order was finally restored – a fact due in large part to the high standard of protective equipment issued to the men and fitted to the vehicles."

In general the duties performed by Bedfordshire Police support units during the miners' strike were more routine. In his annual report for 1984 Mr Sloan informed the police authority: "The normal tasks undertaken by officers from this county, under the direction of the senior command of the receiving force, included attendance at mines and patrol work to reassure the inhabitants of local communities. I am pleased to report that no complaints were made against any member of the force by persons taking part in the industrial dispute or by any member of the public. The senior officers of certain receiving forces have written to me complimenting my officers for their exemplary conduct whilst deployed under their command."

The annual report for 1984 also included details of the establishment of a computer development section at force headquarters: "This new section was formed at the beginning of the year and comprises a chief inspector, the force systems analyst, and one constable. The work of the section is to determine the long term computer needs of the force and produce a five year computerisation strategy."

A further development during the year concerned the introduction of Home Watch schemes throughout the county in an attempt to involve the wider community in crime prevention initiatives. Similar schemes had already been successful in other parts of the country and by the end of 1984 forty-eight home watch groups had been established in Bedfordshire.

In 1985 the county force continued to respond to requests from the National Reporting Centre for the provision of mutual aid to police forces involved in policing the coalfields. This commitment continued until 2nd March when the miners' strike action ceased. Mutual aid was also supplied to the Cambridgeshire Police on nine occasions between February and May 1985 in connection with a series of 'peace' protests against the siting of nuclear weapons at RAF Molesworth.

Football Riot.

On the evening of 15th March 1985 events in Bedfordshire again became the subject of national media coverage when Millwall football supporters rioted after their team lost to Luton Town in a sixth round F.A. cup tie at Kenilworth Road. There had been disturbances at the ground before and during the match but the worst scenes of violence occurred after the final whistle. The Millwall supporters made no attempt to leave the ground at the end of the game and the chief constable reported: "Hostility was then directed at the police with a venom not previously witnessed. Seats and other missiles were thrown from the stand and the crowd were pointing at the police officers on the pitch, chanting repeatedly, 'Kill the Bill'. A metal gate at the foot of some of the terracing was forced open by bodily pressure and supporters began pouring through onto the pitch, despite the presence of some fifty officers posted with a view to preventing this.

"The immediate deployment of dog handlers stemmed the movement of the crowd through the gate and coins and other missiles were thrown at the police, including a ladder normally used to gain access to a television gantry. A baton charge by the police from the half-way line cleared the pitch and many of the supporters forced back subsequently left the ground, promoting a more general departure from the stands. Officers had been deployed in the roads leading from the ground but damage was caused to cars, shops, and houses in the vicinity, and some members of the general public were assaulted in Ivy Road."

Sixty persons were injured during the disturbances, forty of whom were police officers. The damage caused inside the ground amounted to £15,000 and further damage totalling £5,000 occurred outside. At the height of the disturbances three hundred and sixty police officers were on duty at Luton, including a contingent of Hertfordshire officers on mutual aid. However, the chief constable later informed the police authority: "Greater deployment of manpower on 13th March 1985 may not have significantly improved the police capability to handle this hostile and aggressive crowd. Events since that date, in other parts of the country, have shown that even where numbers of officers reached nine hundred, the ability to control a hostile crowd, intent on causing the maximum disorder, was severely limited."

Thirty-three arrests were made during the disturbances and there were a further ten arrests following an examination of video recordings of the disorder. In the short-term the disturbances resulted in modifications to the ground to improve arrangements

A modern WPC and her counterpart, circa 1950

for the secure segregation of fans, improved police surveillance and communications systems and the deployment of police horses from the City of London on match days. In the longer term the disorder contributed to the introduction of a highly successful local initiative designed to combat soccer hooliganism during the 1986/87 season.

The county constabulary mounted a major security operation on 11th July 1985 when His Royal Highness the Prince of Wales visited the borough of Luton, flying to the town in a Wessex helicopter and landing at Stockwood Park at 10 a.m. Prince Charles' first engagement was at the Stockwood Park Museum where he was invited to inspect a display of craftwork and millinery.

The Prince subsequently visited the Youth House in St Mary's Road before travelling on to Vauxhall Motors where management and staff explained the operation of the production line. The Luton News reported: "The final venue on the royal tour was the international airport. After light-heartedly apologising for the long gap since the last official royal visit to Luton, in 1962, when the Queen opened the central library, the Prince unveiled an inscription on a plinth, to officially open the new extension to the terminal building.

"Tight security was maintained throughout the visit and there was one arrest during a small demonstration against the Prince outside the Youth House. Over three hundred police officers were deployed along the route taken by the royal car and at the various locations included in the royal itinerary. The security operation, which also involved the use of 'sniffer' dogs, was controlled from Luton police station."

New Appointment in Strathclyde.

In the summer of 1985 Mr Sloan was appointed as the Chief Constable of Strathclyde Police and he commenced his new duties in Glasgow on 1st September that year. The chairman and members of the Bedfordshire police authority "congratulated the chief constable on his new appointment and expressed their sincere appreciation of his services to the county." Her Majesty's Inspector of Constabulary, Mr R. S. Barratt, C.B.E., QPM, reported: "Mr Sloan's appointment to the important and demanding post at Strathclyde reflects well, both on him and on the Bedfordshire police force as a whole."

Mr Sloan obtained a Bachelor of Arts degree from the Open University in 1980 and was awarded the Queen's Police Medal in

Modern road traffic patrol cars. A Land Rover and a Vauxhall Opel Senator

the New Year's Honours List of 1983. He and his wife have a family of three grown up daughters, two of whom followed in their father's footsteps and joined the police service. Mr Sloan continues to serve in his native Scotland as the Chief Constable of Strathclyde.

MR ALAN DYER, O ST. J., QPM

ALAN DYER
APPOINTED TENTH CHIEF CONSTABLE OF BEDFORDSHIRE 1st SEPTEMBER 1985

ALAN Dyer was born on 4th January 1934 at Bircotes in Nottinghamshire. Originally named Alan Butt, he was placed into care with the local authority in September 1939 and was raised by foster parents. During this period of his life he was known as Alan Bond. He was educated at the Henry Mellish Grammar School in Nottingham, obtaining the London Schools' Certificate before leaving school at the age of fifteen.

He subsequently left his foster parents and lived with Nick and Doris Dyer who became his adoptive father and mother and he officially changed his name by Deed Poll in 1955. His adoptive parents had lived in Bedford before moving to Nottingham in the 1930s and Mr Dyer became familiar with Bedfordshire when he accompanied his parents on their regular visits to friends and relatives in the county.

He obtained his first employment in 1949 working in the office of the Clerk of the Peace at Nottingham, and in 1952 he joined the Royal Navy, serving as an able seaman on board the minesweeper, HMS Pincher, and spending some time on fishery protection duties in Arctic waters. On 2nd April 1954 Mr Dyer joined the Nottinghamshire Constabulary, serving on uniform patrol duties at West Bridgford and Beeston before transferring to the criminal investigation department in 1957. He was promoted to detective sergeant in 1963 and detective inspector in 1966, working in Nottingham and Retford prior to his appointment as a detective chief inspector in 1968. Between 1969 and 1971 Mr Dyer gained experience as a uniformed chief inspector, taking charge of a sub-division in Mansfield. In 1971 he was promoted to superintendent and seconded to the Home Office police research branch where he was involved in the development of the photo-fit system and the implementation of the country's first computerised command and control facility at Birmingham.

Mr Dyer returned to Nottinghamshire in 1973 working as a sub-divisional commander in Nottingham before gaining promotion to chief superintendent in 1977 and accepting an appointment as an assistant director of command courses at the police staff college at Bramshill. In March 1980 Mr Dyer was appointed as an assistant chief constable in the Durham Constabulary and he joined the Bedfordshire Police as deputy chief constable on 12th July, 1982.

In 1985 Mr Dyer was one of twelve candidates to apply for the position of Chief Constable of Bedfordshire. He was shortlisted for the appointment and appeared before the police authority for interview on 25th July together with Mr J. H. Burrow, the Deputy Chief Constable of the Merseyside Police, and Mr M. J. Hirst, the Deputy Chief Constable of Lincolnshire. At the conclusion of the interviews the police authority resolved: "That subject to the approval of the Secretary of State, Mr A. Dyer be appointed chief constable of the county with effect from 1st September 1985."

The decision to appoint Mr Dyer as the tenth Chief Constable of Bedfordshire was a popular one with the force bringing a measure of continuity and stability following the numerous changes which had affected the senior policing posts in the county during the early 1980s. Mr M. Taylor was appointed as the new deputy chief constable on 1st January 1986.

Nine days after assuming command of the force Mr Dyer responded to a request for mutual aid from the West Midlands Police Force. The chief constable reported: "Three Bedfordshire Police support units comprising seventy-seven officers were sent to the Birmingham area on 10th – 11th September 1985 in connection with the riots at Handsworth. The officers performed exceptionally long hours of duty – twenty-one hours in one case – and were deployed to prevent any recurrence of the disturbances."

In-Force Training.

The county constabulary commenced an extensive programme of in-force training in 1985 to prepare for the implementation of three major pieces of legislation during the following year. In his annual report for 1985 the chief constable informed the police authority: "Taken collectively, the Police and Criminal Evidence Act 1984, the Prosecution of Offences Act 1985, and Part III of the Transport Act 1982, represent the most complex and far reaching changes in basic duties and powers ever experienced by serving police officers. Training with regard to the Police and Criminal Evidence Act commenced at the beginning of August and finished in mid-December. Eight hundred and thirteen officers each received a three days' course, with one hundred and eighty others, mainly sergeants and inspectors, who will have special responsibility for persons held in custody, receiving a five days' course. The training was carried out at three locations – headquarters, Luton, and Dunstable, with up to forty-five officers receiving instruction each day." The Police and Criminal Evidence Act came into operation on 1st January 1986 and effected important changes in relation to police powers of stop, search and arrest, and the interview and treatment of persons detained in police custody.

Further in-force training was provided in 1986 regarding the Prosecution of Offenders Act 1985 which established the Crown Prosecution Service "to take over the conduct of all criminal proceedings instituted on behalf of the police," thereby separating the responsibilities for the investigation of crime and the prosecution of offenders under the judicial system. The branch of the Crown Prosecution Service for the Bedfordshire and Hertfordshire area became fully operational in October 1986.

Earlier in the year, in February and March, all uniformed officers up to the rank of inspector underwent training with regard to the legislation contained in Part III of the Transport Act 1982. The chief constable reported: "This legislation provides for the extension of the fixed penalty ticket system which has previously been used to enforce parking restrictions. From 1st October 1986 the number of offences falling within the bounds of the fixed penalty scheme will be increased from fourteen to two hundred, with the intention of reducing the number of minor traffic offences dealt with by the Magistrates Courts."

A vehicle defect rectification scheme was also launched on 1st October 1986 to provide the police with yet a further option in dealing with offending motorists. "The scheme, which has been introduced on a national basis, enables a driver to have a defect on his vehicle put right by a recognised repairer within fourteen days of the date of the offence and so avoid the need for prosecution. Between 1st October and 31st December 1986, 467 notices were issued under the scheme in Bedfordshire, covering 819 vehicle defects. 76 per cent of the drivers complied with the requirements of the scheme and rectified the faults on their vehicles."

Major Incident Computer.

Both the extended fixed penalty and vehicle defect rectification schemes were administered through the use of new computers but a more important development with regard to the force computerisation strategy during 1986 concerned the provision of a major enquiry system similar to that loaned to the force in connection with 'Operation Peanut'. Mr Dyer reported: "A Honeywell computer was installed at force headquarters in January to run the Home Office large major enquiry system (HOLMES), and incident rooms were equipped to house terminals at Bedford, Luton, and Dunstable. The system is the result of a research project undertaken by the Home Office scientific research and development branch and allows the total integration of incidents between forces during multi-force investigations.

"Four members of the county force successfully completed a Home Office instructors' course in February and during the remainder of the year they, in turn, trained thirty-nine other officers in the use of the computer. This force was one of the first in the country to be fully operational in the use of the system and a computerised incident room was opened at Luton on 29th May 1986 to investigate petrol bombings in the town.

"On 2nd September 1986 the force responded to a request from the Hampshire Constabulary for assistance in establishing a computerised incident room to investigate the murder of five people in the New Forest area. Five Bedfordshire officers worked alongside Hampshire officers for sixteen days providing a valuable source of expertise in the operation of the major enquiry system. Three persons have been arrested and charged in connection with the murders."

The cost of implementing the HOLMES package in Bedfordshire was offset against a temporary reduction in establishment. Mr Dyer reported: "Budget provision for computer development in 1986 was achieved through a reduction in the strength of the regular force of ten officers during the financial year 1985/86. It is unfortunate that major capital projects should have to be funded in this manner but the 'lost' officers will be regained in 1986/87."

Economic constraints on the police budget also led to the disbandment of the underwater search and recovery section. The chief constable reported: "The section was disbanded in August

1986 and arrangements were made with the Cambridgeshire and Thames Valley police forces to provide emergency cover. There was no requirement for the services of the diving teams from these forces during the remainder of the year."

The Home Office provided some extra funding for police forces in 1986 by increasing the proportion of expenditure on the police service, met by central Government, from fifty to fifty-one per cent. The Home Secretary, Mr Douglas Hurd, explained that the increase in expenditure was intended "to help police authorities ensure that their forces have the resources to meet the increasing demands made upon them." Part of the additional funding was earmarked for the establishment of drugs wings attached to the regional crime squads.

Developments at Luton.

There were a number of developments in 1986 affecting the Luton division of the county force. The first of these concerned the opening of a small sub-station at Leagrave in September. The chief constable reported: "The new building provides accommodation for a team of eleven resident beat officers who operate in six ward areas in the vicinity of the sub-station. The facilities include an office for a sergeant who will supervise the activities of the team, a report writing and general office area, and an enquiry office with adjacent interview room. The site was chosen to allow for expansion should further development of the sub-station prove desirable in the future."

The chief constable further reported: "For some years, street prostitution has been the cause of regular complaint in Luton, and during the year the divisional commander appointed a small team of officers to concentrate on this problem. The officers were successful in drastically reducing the scale of the problem on the streets and our efforts in this direction will continue, with a view to preventing any deterioration in this improved position."

In his annual report for 1986 Mr Dyer gave details of an incident of violent disorder at Luton arising from the widely publicised industrial dispute between the print workers unions and News International. "This dispute became a local issue when demonstrators gathered at the TNT transport depot at Cosgrove Way in Luton. During the night of 17th April approximately one hundred and fifty print workers arrived without warning and a determined but orderly demonstration took place. The same was not true on the night of 24th June when approximately two hundred pickets arrived without warning. The initial contingent of forty caused considerable damage by forcing the fence of a compound and breaking windows in offices, delivery vehicles and company drivers' private cars. Divisional officers were deployed to the scene and a number of arrests were made in restoring order." TNT was one of the companies contracted to distribute newspapers from the News International premises at Wapping.

The annual report for 1986 also contained details of important changes in relation to firearms training in the force. "Following the submission of the final report of the force working party on firearms training it was decided to reduce the number of authorised firearms officers in the county but increase the level of training for the remaining officers. Accordingly the operational support unit, comprising one inspector, two sergeants and twenty constables was formed early in 1986 to ensure a highly professional response to all firearms incidents in the county. While the operational support unit is available to assist with other areas of policing, the high level of firearms training involved necessarily limits the unit's availability for alternative duties."

Purchase of Plastic Baton Rounds.

In September 1986 Mr Dyer approached the police authority with reference to the acquisition of plastic baton rounds for use in the event of serious public disorder. The chief constable reported: "Since 1981 disorder on a major scale, whilst not commonplace, has increased. In recent months serious rioting has occurred, not only in London but also at Handsworth, in Birmingham. The scale and ferocity of these last bouts of disorder may even have surpassed those of 1981.

"These events have persuaded me that a chief officer of police faced with a situation where there is the risk of the loss of any life, serious bodily injury or widespread damage should, when circumstances demand, be in a position to authorise the use of plastic baton rounds. They would only be used when conventional tactics had failed and only as a last resort during instances of serious rioting. The object of their use would be to distance a rioting crowd to prevent injuries to innocent people or police personnel, to incapacitate and arrest identified ringleaders or to achieve complete dispersal of the rioters."

Mr Dyer's report also contained full details of the stringent guidelines laid down by the Home Office to govern the use of plastic baton rounds and the warnings which must be given before they can be fired. The Home Office had already sanctioned the acquisition of plastic baton rounds in Bedfordshire as a

Specialist police roles. A member of a Police Support Unit in full protective riot equipment and a Firearms Officer from the Operational Support Unit

precautionary measure and a majority of the members of the police authority resolved "that the purchase of baton rounds, dischargers and storage equipment be approved at a cost of £5,200."

The acquisition of plastic baton rounds proved to be a controversial issue which raised questions concerning the respective duties and powers of the police authority and the county council. The council tabled a motion asking the police authority to reconsider their decision. The motion indicated that the council did not approve of the purchase of baton rounds and that the required funds would be withheld.

The police authority questioned the legality of the action proposed by the county council. The council then took legal advice and found that it could only withhold funds from the police authority on financial grounds and not on matters of policy. The original motion was subsequently amended to include an objection concerning the cost effectiveness of baton rounds before it was carried by a vote of thirty-four councillors to thirty-two.

Although the county council succeeded in withholding the required funds from the police authority, Mr Dyer found it was possible to purchase baton rounds and dischargers from savings within the existing police budget. The county council passed a motion of censure against both the chief constable and the police authority for their bi-lateral action in making the purchase but the issue was not allowed to sour an otherwise sound working relationship.

Luton Football Membership Scheme.

In 1987 the chief constable reported to the police authority on the success of an initiative at Luton designed to reduce the level of football hooliganism in the town. "Following serious incidents of disorder, especially after the match against Millwall in March 1985, Luton Town Football Club recognised the need to combat violent behaviour on the terraces. After a series of consultations between the club and the police a Home Supporters Only scheme was devised which involved the issue of personal identity cards to supporters who registered as members with the club. Computerised turnstiles, operated by the identity cards, were installed at the ground and admittance was restricted to registered members, their guests and bona fide guests of the visiting team. Each member was allowed a maximum of three guests provided that their tickets were applied for at least twenty-four hours before kick off.

"The scheme was introduced at the start of the football season in 1986 and the results have been spectacular. In the 1984/85 season there were one hundred and ninety football related arrests and in 1985/86 there were one hundred and two. During the 1986/87 season there were no arrests and, unlike previous years, there were no complaints of assault, damage, rowdyism, or theft in the immediate area of the football ground or in the town centre. The groups of youths who had previously gathered on match days, with the apparent intention of attacking visiting supporters, ceased to congregate in the town. The whole community benefited from the improved atmosphere when Luton played at home and it is puzzling as to why this innovation has not received greater acclaim from the football authorities, the public, and police staff associations."

The home supporters scheme produced equally impressive results in the following seasons. The club has been forced to admit the supporters of visiting teams during cup competitions and the increased level of crime and disorder experienced on these occasions has only served to highlight the benefits of the scheme which remains one of the most successful exercises in crime prevention ever undertaken in the county.

A further development in 1987 concerned the introduction of a Lay Visitors Scheme in Bedfordshire. The chief constable reported: "Such schemes provide for the carrying out of random checks by independent observers on the detention and treatment of persons held in custody at police stations. The object is to secure greater understanding of, and confidence in, the legal provisions concerning the welfare of suspects detained by the police." The Bedfordshire police authority appointed lay visitors from among its own councillor members in May 1987 to cover all six of the county's police stations which may be visited at any time.

In his annual report for 1987 the chief constable informed the police authority: "For some years now the Home Office has required each police force to state its annual objectives. This force has previously set itself various wide ranging goals and priorities but in 1987 it was unusually decided to set a single objective: to reduce the number of domestic burglaries – that is, those committed against private residences. This type of crime rose steeply in 1986 and often has a traumatic effect on the victim." As a result of a concerted campaign mounted throughout the year there was a reduction of nearly thirteen per cent in the number of house burglaries in the county, from 4,326 in the previous twelve months to 3,831 in 1987.

Mr Dyer further reported on the decision to extend the experiment regarding the night-time closure of police stations in the county to include those at Leighton Buzzard and Biggleswade. "This decision was taken in the light of the successful experience at Ampthill and after full consultation with the local councils involved. Night-time telephone enquiries to Biggleswade and Leighton Buzzard were re-routed whilst personal callers at the two stations were provided with a direct line telephone connected to Dunstable police station. A survey of calls and visitors to the stations during the first months of the closure period revealed that on average only two telephone calls were re-routed each night. The closures released one additional officer for patrol duties on the beats served by each police station and this represents a more effective and efficient use of resources."

One incident which received national media coverage in 1987 concerned the fire bombing of a department store at the Arndale Centre in Luton. Mr Dyer reported: "On 12th July an incendiary device exploded at the Luton branch of Debenhams causing a fire and damage to the value of £5m. The device was concealed in the basement area of the store which had been closed since the previous day. Similar devices exploded at Debenhams' branches in Harrow and Romford on the same morning and an anonymous caller telephoned the Press Association saying that the fire bombs had been planted as a form of economic sabotage against stores selling fur coats. Prolonged enquiries involving Scotland Yard's anti-terrorist branch eventually led to the arrest and conviction of a man from the London area in connection with the arson attack at Luton."

National Developments.

In 1988 the chief constable reported on three national developments which affected the policing of Bedfordshire. The first concerned new procedures regarding the interview of suspected offenders. "Following successful field trials in several force areas, the Home Office recently drew up plans to introduce the tape recording of interviews at police stations as a standard national practice by 1991. I am pleased to report that the provision of facilities for the tape recording of interviews with suspects, in this force, is already at an advanced stage. During 1988 six interview rooms – three at Luton, two at Bedford, and one at Dunstable – were adapted and fitted with the necessary sound proofing materials and technical equipment."

A second development concerned the implementation of new Home Office guidelines on the treatment of the victims of sexual offences and child abuse. "A victim examination suite, comprising an interview lounge, bathroom, kitchen area, and examination room, was opened at Greyfriars police station in October 1988 with local businesses donating the fixtures, fittings, and furnishings. Similar facilities will be provided at Luton and Dunstable police stations in the course of 1989. The object of these suites is to permit the medical examination and interview of the victims of sexual crimes in the most supportive, private and comfortable environment possible."

The third important development was the introduction of a revised training course for probationer constables from July 1989. "The new course is the most extensive programme of initial recruit training ever undertaken by the police service, providing both formal instruction and the opportunity to gain practical experience over a total period of thirty-one weeks."

During 1988 the Bedfordshire Police were required to perform crowd control duties at two major events. On Monday, 25th April there were celebrations when the Littlewoods Cup won by Luton Town at Wembley was paraded through the town centre. On 11th October, Her Royal Highness, the Princess of Wales visited Luton to open the new indoor bowls stadium. The crowds were well behaved and there were no untoward incidents on either occasion.

In his annual report for 1988 the chief constable informed the police committee that Bedfordshire Police support units had been mobilised on one occasion during the year following a request from the Wiltshire Constabulary. "On 20th and 21st June ninety-five members of the force provided mutual aid to assist with problems of disorderly behaviour during the summer solstice at Stonehenge."

Mr Dyer further reported on the introduction of crime screening on an experimental basis at Luton. "This is an administrative process applied to all but the most serious crimes after the investigating officer has attended the scene and carried out initial enquiries into the case. A set formula is used to assess whether it is probable that further enquiries into the crime will lead to its detection. Crimes which offer little or no prospect of detection are screened out, allowing officers to concentrate on those which stand a better chance of being solved. Offences which have been screened out may still be detected when offenders who have been arrested for one crime admit to committing a number of other crimes. The screening process will be extended to the other divisions of the force in 1989."

The chief constable also reported on important discussions which took place during the year concerning the policing of Luton Airport. "The passenger traffic passing through the airport has grown to nearly three million this year and is forecast to reach five million in the 1990s. I am now firmly of the view that the level of traffic at the airport and the potential risk to public safety are such that there should be a permanent police presence there – Luton International Airport is by far the busiest airport in the country without such a presence. The airport authority recognise the benefits of establishing a dedicated police unit at the complex but as they are obliged to pay for the policing operation there is some concern over the scale and cost of the proposed police presence. Negotiations are proceeding to determine a mutually acceptable level of policing. It is estimated that a force of between thirty and fifty officers would be required to provide an adequate presence at the airport. In the meantime it has been agreed that from August 1988 six police officers should be deployed to perform duties at the airport concentrating on the terminal building."

As the force approaches its 150th anniversary the county constabulary has been called on to provide emergency cover during national industrial action by the ambulance drivers. From 28th November 1989 the Bedfordshire Police deployed seven ambulances throughout the county and supplied pilot cars to escort six Army ambulances. All the ambulances are controlled from the major incident room at force headquarters and forty-nine police officers are routinely engaged in providing ambulance cover.

In Conclusion.

Mr Dyer was awarded the Queen's Police Medal in June 1986 in the Queen's Birthday Honours List and received the Order of St. John in 1989. He obtained a Diploma in English Criminal Law in 1962 and a Diploma in Political, Economic and Social Studies in 1971, studying at Nottingham University. He married in 1955 and his wife, Penelope, is distantly related, through her late father, to Sir Robert Peel, the founder of the Metropolitan Police Force. Mr Dyer is a long standing member of Rotary International which promotes charitable causes and his wife is a member of the Inner Wheel. They have a grown up family of one daughter, living in Amsterdam, and one son, who served in the Nottinghamshire Police for several years. The chief constable is the chairman of two ACPO standing sub-committees, one on emergency procedures and one on self-defence training and equipment. Mr Dyer is also the chairman of the chief constables' management committee at Ashford district police training centre which trains nearly one quarter of all provincial police officers.

Mr Dyer continues his able leadership with the assistance of Mr W. Gray, who was appointed deputy chief constable in October 1989, and Mr G. Spalding who became the assistant chief constable in the following December. Mr M. Taylor, the former deputy chief constable, left Bedfordshire in the summer of 1989 to take up an appointment as a deputy assistant commissioner in the Metropolitan Police.

The original constabulary of forty-seven men has progressively expanded to meet the changing demands of a vastly increased population and the Bedfordshire Police Force now has an establishment of one thousand and forty-six, including one hundred and thirty-five women officers. The modern force is also supported by one hundred and thirty-nine special constables and four hundred and thirty-six civilian employees. The constabulary has successfully responded to the many advances in communications, transport and technology.

Despite increased prosperity and better social conditions crime has continued to rise steeply. Nearly forty-one thousand crimes were committed in Bedfordshire during 1989. The vast majority of crimes are committed against property: crimes which are characteristic of a modern, industrialised society. Supermarkets, unattended motor vehicles and houses left unoccupied offer easy opportunities for theft and burglary. The Royal Commission of 1839, whose findings led to the formation of the first county police forces, had examined the causes of crime in the Victorian era and concluded that there was a connection between the incidence of crime and the opportunity to commit offences. "Having investigated the causes of depredation we find that in scarcely any cases is it ascribable to pressure of unavoidable want or destitution and that in the great mass of cases it arises from the temptation of obtaining property with a less degree of labour than by regular industry."

The fundamental principles of policing have remained constant over a period of a century and a half. The earliest surviving orders of the Bedfordshire Constabulary instructed the constables: "It should be understood at the outset that the principal object to be attained is the prevention of crime. It is imperative to protect the property and liberty of Her Majesty's subjects, not to infringe upon them." In the current policy statement of the force the chief constable reiterates these principles. "The primary aims of the force are the maintenance of a peaceful society and the prevention and detection of crime with a duty to keep strictly within the prescribed powers, refrain from arbitrary action and preserve the rights and freedoms of the individual."

In the 1990s the County Force continues to uphold the fine tradition of public service established by the Victorian constables, protecting the lives and property of the people of Bedfordshire.

THE FUTURE OF THE FORCE

LEAVING aside the impact of two World Wars, policing this century remained relatively peaceful until the early 1970s, since when urban disorders and violent industrial action have occurred all too frequently. This has stretched scarce resources, particularly in Bedfordshire, which is now considered to be a small force. In an attempt to achieve greater economy, effectiveness and efficiency, there are those who now increasingly advocate the formation of larger police forces, regional or even national, but in my view this would destroy local identity and would be harmful to the well established notion of policing by consent.

Steps are being taken to meet fresh demands which will have important implications for the policing of Bedfordshire in the 1990s, particularly developments at Luton International Airport. The programme for the future also includes the construction of a new police station at Leighton Buzzard and additional accommodation for the training department at Force Headquarters. Greater emphasis is being placed on the development of existing technology and plans are well in hand for the replacement of the computerised command and control system with a new operational information system. It is proposed that this will incorporate a facility for the automatic recording of the availability and location of police patrol vehicles. Recently the force has also started to computerise its crime recording and reporting systems and the indexing and searching of fingerprint records (Digitscan).

There has been a steady increase in the use of firearms by criminals in the commission of crime, which has led to extensive training of police officers in the use of weapons. Serious consideration has been given to permanent mobile armed response units in the county and whilst the idea has not yet been adopted, there is a certain degree of inevitability that such units will be deployed.

These are but some of the considerations which will take us into the next century, but above all the principle of prevention of crime will be maintained.

Alan Dyer,
Chief Constable of Bedfordshire,
Police Headquarters, Kempston.
21st March, 1990.